ADOLESCENT MALES

HOMOSEXUALITY

The Search for Self

BRODERICK S. CHABIN, PH.D.

brave dog
press · los angeles

bravedog
press · los angeles

DEDICATION

To Dorothy Boswell and Martha Chabin

CONTENTS

AUTHOR'S NOTE

This work contains case studies and vignettes that portray the psychological lives of teenagers who are attempting to understand their sexuality. These stories are integral to the discussion of the psychological challenges faced by these teens. At the same time, it has been essential that the lives of actual clients I have seen or people I have known not be shared, that my responsibility to maintain confidentiality be maintained faithfully and that the identities of my clients be protected. For that reason, all stories included in this work have been created as composites of many young people I have worked with. The stories here do not depict the actual experience of any one person and they are, in fact, fictional.

Beyond that, some clarification is needed about why this book is limited to a discussion of male homosexuality alone. The need for research into the experience of all LGBT teens, including lesbians, those who are bisexual, and those who are transgendered, is very strong. This book is restricted to male homosexuality only for reasons of scope. Because it considers many topics including history, culture, religion, society and psychology, it has not been feasible to consider those wide ranging areas in relation to all of the LGBT adolescent community. It leaves that essential work to other authors. With that in mind, and for the sake of clarity, the term homosexual and male homosexuality are used interchangeably throughout this document.

FORWARD

Recently, I was showing my beloved a box of memorabilia from my childhood, when I came across a letter I had scrawled to my parents from summer camp when I was twelve years old. "Nancy found a dead squirrel," it said. "She wouldn't let me and Lisa Barker look at it. I don't know why not. It wasn't that big of a deal."

Lisa Barker. I was arrested for a moment, unable to read the rest of the letter (later, I read it: "scratch Rascal's belly for me, tomorrow night is taco night, we lost the scavenger hunt because we could not find an old brown boot with a missing 'heal'"). "Who was Lisa Barker?" my girlfriend asked. Though I couldn't remember the slightest detail about who she was or what she looked like, I did remember the feelings I had for her, the amorphous, ambiguous feelings I had that I was later able to identify as a crush. It was not yet sexual because I was not yet sexual, but it was something more than friendship and something I had absolutely no words for.

Not yet.

I don't know what happened to Lisa. I do know that something happened later that year inside of a maze on Halloween, something to do with me wanting to get closer to her in some sort of way that was not okay for pre-pubescent girls.

The idea of experiencing sexual confusion inside of a maze would be symbolism of the heavy-handed kind, in the hands of a fiction writer, but it really happened to me. What did not happen was me coming out of the maze able to talk about this with someone, anyone. Even if I could have articulated what I felt in the moment, I inherently knew I had no one to articulate it to, no one who could help me understand what it might have meant or to stand with me while I wrestled through its meaning or to stand by me if it came to mean I was a lesbian.

Not yet.

This was two decades before the advent of the Internet, and four decades before the "It Gets Better" Project™ was conceived to assure LGBT (lesbian, gay, bisexual, and transgender) youth that if they could just hang in there through the often brutal days of junior high and high school, it would in fact get better. Even if this technological support system was available, I was not yet ready for the message that it would get better because I did not yet entirely know what "it" was.

Not yet.

When I was sixteen, four years later, I had my first girlfriend. In those four years between the ambiguity of Lisa Barker and the surety of my first love, I went through years of an internal struggle to come out of the fog of undifferentiated feeling into the clarity of young sexual love. It would take another four years until I could tell anyone about my love, until I was sure it was normal for me and not just an anomaly (for many queer youth, it is common to wonder if it's *just this one girl* or *just this one boy*, rather than face the fear that it's *just girls* or *just boys*). All said, these were the worst eight years of my life. Without family, friends, teachers, a religious mentor, or a therapist whom I felt I could trust, and without any sense of gay and lesbian history, I felt so very alone.

I share all this personal history as a way of highlighting the importance of Dr. Broderick S. Chabin's (to me, Brad) seminal work in the pages that follow. Brad understands this anguish.

Years before most of them will "come out," these teens must hide the truth of their inner world, quietly walking among our midst, often in an anguish misunderstood by even the most caring around them. They are hidden from hate, but, also, hidden from those around them who might be of service or aid. They are hidden from the view of parents, therapists, teachers and educators who do not know, cannot know, what their lives are like and cannot know clearly how to help these young men [and women] along on their paths.

His book is the book my older self wishes I could have handed to my younger self's family, friends, teachers, and others. The first chapters of his book would have contextualized my struggle inside of a larger struggle, and assured me and those around me that I was indeed not alone in my moment in history nor *any* moment in history. The final chapters of his book would have given me friends in the journey—Gabriel, Murphy, and Logan— fellow travelers along the difficult path of coming to understand, know, and ultimately accept both *who we are* and *how we are*. Though these are perspectives of young gay (perhaps) men, and not everything applies to a young lesbian (perhaps) woman or bisexual or queer or transgender (perhaps) youth, still there is something resonant and powerful in the stories.

And, there is something powerful in the heart of the storyteller. That's what Brad is to me, a storyteller whose stories are arrows aimed right at the heart of healing. Though I didn't meet Brad until I was a middle-aged woman, well settled in my own sexuality, still now I experience vicarious healing in his storytelling, in his solicitude for the souls of these young gay (perhaps) boys who seek his counsel and thrive under his care.

Ultimately, Brad is not invested in whether these boys identify as gay, straight, bisexual, transsexual, or asexual. Helping them land at the destination of identity, whether fixed or fluid, is not what his therapeutic work nor this book is about. Rather, this book is a companion for the journey all of us take when we companion our youth toward an understanding and acceptance of their unique identities, which include their sexual identities but so much more.

It's true that knowledge is power, and this book provides knowledge: knowledge of homosexuality and its relationship to science and psychology, to culture and history, to Christianity and mythology, to adolescent development, and to environmental, societal, and psychosocial considerations. It's also true that love is power, and with a little knowledge and a lots of love, not only can we keep these boys alive but we can help them thrive through the already tumultuous time that is adolescence.

As a former junior high and high school teacher for sixteen years, I have taught boys like Gabriel, Murphy, and Logan, and I have taught their female equivalents, girls like Brooke, Joey, and Mariana, and I have taught youth of all names on all places on the sexuality spectrum. Because I myself was once one of those youth, I bring with me a particular understanding of their questions and concerns, their wanderings and wonderings. This book you hold in your hands will offer you such an understanding, and for that, we all owe Dr. Chabin a debt of gratitude.

Jennifer Leigh Selig, Ph.D.
Professor of Depth Psychology
Pacifica Graduate Institute
Author of *What Now? Wise and Witty Advice for Life After Graduation* and *Reimagining Education: Essays on Reviving the Soul of Learning*

INTRODUCTION

The Lens Through Which We See

A young man named Danny came to see me in therapy just before his 16th birthday and he seemed miserable. Early in our work, I became well aware of the many aspects of his life that troubled him or excited him but only suspected the issue that seemed to take all his psychological energy. The cause of his apparent despair, the deeply hidden problem that he had thus far not shared, one day bubbled up, uncontrollably. I sat quietly as he struggled to finish the sentence that began with "I think…". He tried to speak but words simply would not come out. He turned his eyes up and down, closing them for a while, and then tried to speak again. His body shifted, nearly contorted, seeming to express the anguish he felt but could not say. "It's just that, you know…." he said, and the words trailed off again. He was in agony and as his therapist, I could sense, even feel, his agony. It seemed there was a powerful demand by Danny's psyche to be known, to be put into words, even as he seemed to encounter a horrible realization that once said the words could not be taken back.

After some time, sensing that he would retreat from the overpowering experience, withdraw again and put his secret back in some hidden compartment, I handed him my legal pad and asked if he thought he could write down what he wanted to say. He took it and slowly scribbled a note. "I am ashamed to say this—and I don't know if it's true—that I think I might be gay." He handed me his note and began to let tears build and then flow. I nodded to him and told him quietly it was ok and that I was glad he had shared.

I wanted to say more, wanted to reassure him and wanted to take away his suffering but knew that all such comments were, in that moment, beside the point. What mattered most was that Danny had encountered himself and had done so in the presence of another human being. He no doubt had said the words to himself privately on many occasions before but when he wrote them out and shared them with another, something powerful, irrevocable, and unexpected had happened. His words became a reality as if they could never fully retreat again. A new version of Danny's potential for life had been revealed. His feelings and his anguish were known now and all the consequences, with the potential for both exhilaration and terror, were now in existence as well. A new chapter in Danny's discovery of himself had begun. The hidden self had been revealed and the need for the safe discovery of what was now present had begun.

How long had he struggled to say "I think I might be gay" and why did he say it that day? What had changed? What compelled him to break through his powerful resistance, finally with no retreat possible, and to disclose something so important, confusing, and frightening to him? What changed in him after he shared what had been so secret just moments before? To know that, one would have to ask many questions about his nature, how he had imagined himself before, and how he thought of himself now. One might ask how his disclosure altered his hopes and dreams for the future or how it altered his expectations for the remainder of just that day. In the moment Danny declared himself gay, he became a person he did not know anymore because he did not know what it means to be gay. It was not the same Danny that he had come to know as a child, not the same person who had been treasured by so many people in his family or surroundings. Danny became another version of himself that day. He began a new chapter of the discovery of his life and it was a leap into the unknown. He was a mystery unfolding within the body and mind of a boy not yet 16 years old.

It would be one thing if by saying "I am gay" Danny could anticipate being embraced, cherished, prized and loved by his parents, by his friends, or by the broader society to which he belongs. If he was celebrated by saying "I am gay," we might anticipate that he would run to his identity, bond with his feelings, race to shout it out in the world and look forward to a life well loved. Yet, he did not. Chief among the questions to be asked about the moment Danny handed over his scribbled note is "Why, at the discovery of himself, did Danny cry?" Embedded in Danny's tears are his feelings about his nature, feelings that will serve as his psychological foundation for answering many other questions. In many ways, Danny's feelings about his nature will affect how he sees himself in the world.

Therapists working with these teens, young men like Danny, are faced with the simple question, "What next?" Is the process of the discovery of Danny complete when Danny says "I think I might be gay" so that the therapeutic approach is to help a young man struggling to overcome internalized homophobia, to come out to parents and friends, and to embrace an identity of being gay? Is the clinical picture of Danny largely to be explained as an issue of homosexuality and an individual's adjustment to it? Or, on the other hand, is Danny's scribbled note just the beginning of the process of discovering what is unknown in him? The attitude taken in this work is the latter. The perspective taken by this work is that an expansion of the therapeutic understanding beyond issues of "coming out" is required. From this perspective, for instance, Danny's dreams of himself beyond homosexuality are relevant, both those occurring in his night-time sleep and the dreams he imagines in waking moments of what he is to become or achieve in the future.

Danny's academic record can be explored as well as his manner of dress, the outward expression of who he is in his presentation to the world. Danny's friends, past and present, are relevant. They are his mirror. The contents of his life in his private moments alone, in isolation, and the depression he feels are important to consider just as are the moments when his eyes shine in joy. Active curiosity, guided by many questions, is needed to explore what is "becoming" in Danny's consciousness, both including and beyond homosexuality, even if that approach inhibits any tendency to fully explain him or his clinical problems.

How therapists understand Danny or others with same-sex feelings will, in many ways, determine the therapeutic approach taken. In turn, that therapeutic approach will deeply impact these young, vulnerable clients. As Coppin and Nelson explain, "How one see affects what one sees" (2009, p. 47). New information that broadens and deepens perspectives about adolescent homosexuality is necessary and important because the work of helping these young people is important, even urgent, and because there is a relative paucity of useful information about them.

During a presentation I made to other therapists several years ago about gay teens, many of the therapists asked questions that seemed based, at least to some degree, on what had been heard from our national dialogue about homosexuality. "Isn't it a choice?" "What do you mean when you say that Christianity doesn't condemn it?" Others seemed to have been sourced in Freudian or other psychological theory. "Does homosexuality form as a result of the boy's relationship to his mother?" The questions were all valid and all were asked in order to deepen the therapists' ability to help their young clients. At the same time, it seemed clear that the therapists were asking these fundamental questions precisely because there was insufficient, reliable information available to them about homosexuality, much less adolescent homosexuality. The void of reliable psychological literature about homosexuality had been filled, it seemed to me, by the material of our society's debate which frequently focused on the issues of psychological causation, choice and morality. When it is the basis for the therapeutic encounter, that often ungrounded and emotionally charged material has the potential to negatively affect the relationship between therapists and their clients, or worse, potentially injure a vulnerable client.

While there are useful resources emerging for therapists, such as the work of Savin-Williams (2005) and Peel, Clarke, and Drescher (2007) among others, much of the literature explores the experience of teenagers who have largely established an identity of being gay or have completed the process of "coming out." It should be noted that many young people who are gay are living open, successful and happy lives and by no means should there be an assumption that all gay teens have serious emotional or psychological issues. They do not. Teens who are "out", and discussions about their needs, while extremely important to consider, are not necessarily representative of the population of teenagers who have homosexual feelings. Many struggle more privately and this book is largely dedicated to them.

The broad population of teenage boys who have same-sex attractions is one that, in many ways, is hidden from view precisely because many of these teens cannot yet discuss their feelings or identify themselves to others as bisexual or gay. Their struggles are done secretly. Deep uncertainty, loneliness, a sense of ostracism or doom, suicidal feelings, unreported harassment, difficulties at home, poor academic performance or any number of other issues may be present in their struggle with their sexuality.

As will be discussed later in this work, many young men who must reconcile their sexual natures with other aspects of their lives, like Danny, suffer depression or other psychological problems. Some commit suicide, and many others try, because of the enormously difficult psychological challenges of having same-sex feelings when the environment around them condemns them for their feelings and any allegiance to them.

Gay teens represent a segment of the population that requires increased and sustained attention by the psychological community. As just one example of that need, researchers Haas et al. (2011) reviewed multiple surveys conducted throughout the last two decades assessing suicide rates among adolescents. They concluded that the rates of reported suicide attempts among gay, lesbian, and bisexual teenagers are two to seven times higher than the rates seen in the population of heterosexual teens (p. 8).

As mentioned previously, as part of the presentation to other therapists about the clinical issues faced by these teens, I discussed the dynamics of one group I had run. The group in question was conducted over a two year period and consisted of a small group of teens who struggled with homosexuality but were not fully identified as "gay." Of the nine boys who comprised that group, all nine had experienced depression, eight suffered significant anxiety or panic attacks, seven had experienced suicidal thoughts, and one had attempted suicide. All described long periods of feeling isolated and lonely and all described problems with their peers. Most (eight) had academic problems, five had been truant regularly, one cut himself, and six described serious problems at home (Chabin, 2008).

Yet none of those teens had yet told the world they were gay and most had no immediate plans to do so. Like Danny, they were hidden from view. Their sexual orientation was disguised, denied, or avoided as a matter of public conversation and as such, was hidden. They presented themselves publicly as heterosexual teenagers with problems of an unknown origin, problems that seemed almost inexplicable because the context of their origins was obscured. Years before most of them will "come out," these teens must hide the truth of their inner world, quietly walking among our midst, often in an anguish misunderstood by even the most caring around them. They are hidden from hate, but, also, hidden from those around them who might be of service or aid. They are hidden from the view of parents, therapists, teachers and educators who do not know, cannot know, what their lives are like and cannot know clearly how to help these young men along on their paths.

Therapists working with these teens must be armed with the most recent and most reliable information about homosexuality because it is, after all, the essential underpinning of the topic of adolescents who experience homosexual feelings. Yet, the issue of homosexuality is complex. What is meant, in a broad sense, by the term homosexual is defined in many ways by how cultures, religions and history have seen it. While it might be agreed that homosexuality is, as the American Psychological Association (2009) defines it, an "enduring pattern of emotional, romantic, and/or sexual attractions to" others of the same sex ("Sexual Orientation"), it is also true that homosexuality is defined as "an intrinsic moral evil" by Catholicism (John Paul II, 1986, pp. 1-2). Until the late 1960s, the psychological community, in *The Diagnostic and Statistical Manual I*, called it a mental disorder under the classification of "sociopathic personality disturbance" (Isay, 1989) while Socrates, the wise man of ancient Greece, called homosexuality a "necessary stepping stone" toward the experience of transcendent love (Downing, 1989, p. 239). Homosexuality has many meanings beyond the physical sexual act because it is defined through its association with many other qualities that range from the very beautiful to the very dark. In many ways, homosexuality is defined by the lens through which it is seen.

Understanding homosexuality's rich and diverse history, along with an awareness of how homosexuality is understood psychologically today, can dramatically improve the therapist's ability to help young people with these questions. The chapters in this book explore the topic of homosexuality by considering scientific research, biological and genetic evidence, prevalence studies, psychological attitudes from

Freud until now, religious and mythological views throughout history and finally, current social dialogues. Biases developed by our young clients or their families, developed by hearing the content of our often ill-informed national dialogues about sexuality, can be more easily set aside with new information, and with that, the sometimes tragic misunderstandings our young clients hold about their own homosexual feelings can be corrected.

Of course, it is also important to recognize that these young men have much broader and richer psychological lives than can be described in a discussion of their sexual orientation. They are more than "gay." In order to help therapists understand that broader experience, this work also considers how homosexuality in teenagers is understood psychologically, how it is affected by their social lives, and how it may affect relationships to others, especially parents and peers. It examines how young men struggle with the impact of homosexuality on their self-esteem, their confidence, and their willingness to interact openly and authentically with the outer world.

Psychologically, in fact, and as is the case with Danny, it is important to consider that two psychological relationships are being developed. For Danny, there is a relationship to his internal world, to his own nature and his consciousness of himself. There is a relationship Danny has and will develop between himself and the external world. If these two collide in direct opposition, as they surely will in the matter of Danny's homosexuality, Danny must choose which relationship he will rely upon emotionally. Because Danny has so many questions to consider and because he is in the midst of an unpredictable process of discovery, the question of whether he chooses to honor a relationship to his inner world or to deny its existence in deference to others is critical. It is a question that often arises in therapy and one that has been addressed, in one way or another, by many prominent writers in the field of psychology including Carl Jung.

Carl Jung described the process of individuation as the process of developing a personality that is fully conscious and whole. Such wholeness in a personality guides the individual in life despite an awareness of the many ways in which psychological separation from others has been needed. To Jung, the process is life-long and only a relatively few humans fully individuate in their lifetimes. The process, in fact, may be unwanted (Jung, 1939/1983, pp. 212-226).

> Clearly, no one develops his personality because someone tells him that it would be advisable to do so. The only thing that moves nature is causal necessity. Without necessity nothing budges, the human personality least of all. It is tremendously conservative, not to say torpid. Only acute necessity is able to rouse it. (p. 197)

Danny and young people like him may, at least to some extent, choose between an authentic relationship to their inner feelings or to a relationship to the world that may cause them to hide or abandon their inner homosexual feelings. If they choose to ground themselves to their authentic selves, in Jungian terms, they face an unwanted call to the development of personality, one undertaken not so much by choice but, rather, by causal necessity. Yet, according to Jung, to develop a deep and abiding relationship to one's inner world is a path toward the discovery of meaning in life. It is meaning earned at a heavy cost (Jung, 1939/1983, pp. 212-226).

> The words "many are called but few are chosen" are singularly important here, for the development of personality from the germ state to full consciousness is at once charisma and curse...its first fruit is the conscious and unavoidable segregation of the single

individual from the undifferentiated and unconscious herd. This means isolation and there is no more comforting word for it . . . . Yet the development of personality means more than just the fear of hatching forth monsters, or of isolation. It also means fidelity to one's own being . . . . To the extent that a man is untrue to the law of his being and does not rise to personality, he has failed to realize his life's meaning. (Jung, 1939/1983, p. 197)

Danny is young, at the beginning of a life and a life-long process of discovery. Because individuation is a process that occurs over a life time (Jung, 1939/1983, pp. 212-226), Danny cannot achieve the complete development of an "individuated" personality at his young age. Yet, he can decide, and in fact will decide, a central question of the individuation process which is whether or not to be loyal to himself psychologically. This question is central for the development of personality, according to Jung.

It also means fidelity to one's own being. For the word "fidelity" I should prefer, in this context, the Greek word . . . which is erroneously translated as "faith". It really means "trust", trustful loyalty, a loyal perseverance and confident hope . . . personality can never develop unless the individual chooses his own way, consciously and with moral deliberation. Not only the causal motive—necessity—but conscious moral decision must lend its strength to the process of building the personality. (Jung, 1939/1983, p. 197)

This work is an exploration of teenagers who experience homosexual feelings but it is also intended to be an exploration of the ways in which they choose, or do not choose, to build a relationship to their inner selves. When Danny said he thought he might be gay and when he cried, he spoke of inner truth and the consequences of holding tightly to it while he engaged the world. How Danny and others like him navigate this challenge, the struggle for personality and towards individuation, is a central focus of this book.

Adolescent boys who struggle with homosexuality are also in the midst of a discovery of themselves played out in the fabric that surrounds them, the parents and peers, the teachers and friends, the minister or priest, the drug store owner or the voices of celebrities and politicians on television. They are contained in a culture, a society, a religion and a set of values handed to them, integrated within them at birth. How the world has reacted to them in the past has been incorporated within their self image and sense of identity. As they develop an identity that includes homosexuality and begin to express it externally, these teens are likely to have an increased sensitivity to how the world around them views homosexuality. Adolescents may have heard that homosexuality is immoral or may have heard that it is normal and acceptable. They may be aware of the gay community and may have formed opinions about the nature of homosexuality on the basis of images from television or from the words of their parents and peers about that community. How teenagers navigate their entry into the world, when their homosexuality is consciously intact, depends to some extent on such experience. In some ways, the process might be easier for them if the world around them held one consistent view of homosexuality. At least then, they could anticipate the world's response to them, for better or worse. Yet, as will be seen in the following chapters, the collective, cultural, scientific, psychological, and religious views of homosexuality are not now, nor have they been, either static or uniform. To the contrary, they represent a variety of perspectives that therapists working with these teens should contemplate so that they may, in turn, broaden the lens through which they see their young clients.

CHAPTER I

HOMOSEXUALITY, SCIENCE AND PSYCHOLOGY

Danny had been to therapy before. He didn't like it. He was fourteen at the time and recalled that his mother had become so frustrated by the family's behavior at home, especially Danny's, that she had arranged for the family to go to therapy as a group. Danny recalled that he sat in the corner of the therapist's room and that his mother did most of the talking at first. She was upset by her husband, who yelled at Danny "too often." No longer, she said, was the father communicating. Danny's younger sister was continually upset by the fighting and had become timid and quiet at home. Danny had changed, she said. He used to make excellent grades, was polite, and helped around the house. It was as if Danny had "fallen off a cliff."

Over time, after Danny's mother had aired her complaints and concerns, the therapist "made" everyone speak and, generally, the group agreed that Danny was the major concern. Hearing that, the therapist had asked Danny if he thought he was the problem. "I just broke" he recalls. He cried but agreed with the group that he was a problem. He remembered the smiles on the faces of his family, especially his dad's, as if they were pleased by his confession. He remembers the awful feeling inside, one of humiliation, and now remembers that day with anger. He had said he was the problem that day because he had no choice. There was no other way out of all the criticism. Inside, he never really thought he was the problem or at least not all of it.

After a few sessions, his sister's attendance was no longer thought to be useful and after a few more, Danny's father concluded it was a waste of time. Danny and his mother continued for a few more sessions and Danny thought those sessions were all right. He and his mother resumed communication and Danny agreed to change his attitude.

Just over a year later, Danny came to the school clinic asking to see a therapist, voluntarily, and was assigned to me. His reasons were vague. He "just wanted to talk to somebody." He preferred that his mother not know, that no one know, but agreed to take home a form to gain her consent for treatment once I had explained the ways in which our conversations would be confidential.

In our sessions, Danny acknowledged that he had, at the time, been acting poorly and that he was responsible for some of the fights at home. His grades had plummeted from his straight A performance in grade school and middle school to near straight F's by the time he reached high school. His parents had tried to make him study more but they had finally "given up" on him. Danny recalled that by the time his mother had "made" him see his first therapist, he had started staying out at nights and he had stopped seeing many of his old friends. He recalled the night he took a bottle of vodka from home and drank much of it before sneaking back into the house undetected. He drank vodka on other occasions, especially when his parents left home to visit his extended family across town. He liked those days because he could just relax, alone, in the silent darkened house.

Danny felt that his parents were responsible for many of the problems. Although he struggled to articulate in what ways, Danny felt that his parents had changed too. His father was cold and angry now. They used to be close when Danny was a child and they spent time together. Somewhere along the way, and Danny did not know when it happened, he and his father had grown apart. The things his father liked to do Danny did not enjoy. His dad liked to sit with Danny's uncles, drink beer on Sunday afternoon, and watch televised sports. Danny preferred to be alone. His dad had, for a while, tried to engage Danny in discussions about the girls at school. Danny felt both pressured and embarrassed by those discussions. He avoided them at all costs and, eventually, his father stopped asking. Danny thought his Dad was disappointed in him but, to Danny, his father was the disappointment. Now, they avoided one another or fought.

Danny and his mother fought often but usually made up soon after. Only a few of their fights seemed to end in long periods of estrangement. There were times when his mother came close to him and reassured him just as she had done when he was young. She seemed to care again about him in a deeper way and in those moments, he felt like himself again. At other times, she seemed somehow detached and would side with his father. She chose her husband over her child on those days. On other days, she blamed them both equally, siding with neither. She was in between.

Danny no longer wished to fight and had instead withdrawn as much as possible. He preferred now to sit in his room and play video games for hours on end. His parents did not like it, preferring that he engage in family activities at least sometimes, but they too had become weary of the fights. They left him alone.

Danny found school to be boring, something that he dragged himself through. He liked one class, his art class, and was proud of the grade he was getting there. He knew a few friends but mostly found that he was most peaceful when he was alone. He said he didn't "get" kids his age. Among the best parts of his week was coming to therapy with me. He could talk about anything he liked.

The thing Danny could speak about privately, in individual therapy, that had been hidden in family therapy, was his homosexuality. Privately, Danny could share his "certainty" that his family would reject him for it. It cannot be known how family therapy would have unfolded had Danny spoken of his sexual feelings but it seems clear that the direction and content of that therapy might have been dramatically different. Had he spoken about it, his father's dislike for homosexuals might have been discussed. The reasons that his mother was caught in a struggle between father and son, while protecting a daughter from chaos at home, might have been more clear if the nature of Danny's sexual feelings and his fear of rejection, his "certainty" that he would be rejected, had been discussed. The therapist might have gained tremendous insight and might have been able to conceptualize the family disturbance differently as well as devise different interventions.

Perhaps the essential quality in Danny's individual therapy that allowed him to disclose and explore his emerging homosexuality was safety. Without it, Danny could not share what was hidden inside and his deep concern about it. Without that context, Danny's experience of therapy and with his family was that he was a problem child in an otherwise good family. With safety and in his disclosure, Danny could begin to associate his behavior, his feelings, his relationships to his family and his depressed moods with something tangible and specific. In many ways, when Danny began to speak about homosexuality he also began to attach again to himself, to his feelings, and to his questions. He did not need to speak of it in every session, and did not, but therapy was a place where he could when he wished to, and by doing so, could begin to understand his sexual feelings, his attraction to other boys, and what that meant to him as he moved into the world around him.

Therapists must consider how to clinically treat young men like Danny and their families when the issue of homosexuality is presented.

How they proceed will depend in large measure on how well they understand homosexuality, how it forms, and how it is understood as a psychological issue. To that end, a discussion of the major contributors, past and present, to a psychological understanding of homosexuality is important for all therapists to have available. Given that conversations about homosexuality have been integrated within the works of many major theorists in the past, and especially because many of those views about homosexuality conflict with modern ones, a review of those writings is especially important. Because much of the psychological literature of the past posited a psychological cause for homosexuality, theories that may conflict with recent scientific findings, the discussion begins with the current genetic and neurobiological understanding about the nature of homosexuality.

Biology, brain structure and neurobiology

John Money, in *Gay, Straight and In-Between: The Sexology of Erotic Orientation* (1988), described in exhaustive detail the development of sexuality from a biological perspective. To Money, sexuality begins as bisexual potential.

> Any theory of the genesis of either exclusive homosexuality or exclusive heterosexuality must address primarily the genesis of bisexuality. Monosexuality, whether homosexual or heterosexual, is secondary and a derivative of the primary bisexual or ambisexual potential. (p. 13)

To Money, the mammalian embryo is sexually bipotential and slowly develops into either masculine or feminine, based on the introduction or absence of hormones. The development of sexual orientation is a complex interaction of chromosomes, the development

5

of ovaries or testicles in the fetus, prenatal hormones, the development of the body after birth, and hormones at puberty, while allowing for the effects of child- rearing and the influence of gender identity and social gender role. Further, Money made the important point that what forms pre-birth will be influenced by a variety of factors after birth. Just as the quality of nutrition given an infant promotes or diminishes the growth of the body, a variety of external factors will impact the development of sexuality after birth (p. 50).

Money's research, presented to the American Psychological Association's annual conference in 1985, described the scientific attitudes prior to the development of sophisticated applications of genetic research. Yet, his contribution to understanding the biological development of sexuality remains important if for no other reason that it clearly shows that the development of sexuality is informed by many biological, prenatal processes.

Following Money's work, and especially since the early 1990s, other researchers have established specific and strong links between homosexuality and brain structure, genetics and fetal development.

Brain structure and neurobiology

In general, scientists have investigated the relationship of homosexuality to the structure and functionality of the brain, and to genetic construction, by locating participants who self-identified as either homosexual or heterosexual. In that way, the findings of the research can be understood as applying to people who have formed an identity, perhaps because of their experience of sexuality over time. In general, the research can claim to be valid in that it shows distinctive characteristics in the brain structure and genetic make-up of each self-identified group, homosexual or heterosexual. At this stage, research of this type does not fully explain the variations of feelings that occur in individuals, such as those experienced for bisexual people. The research is somewhat vulnerable to the criticism that individuals may incorrectly identify their true sexual orientation to researchers so that, for instance, a man who feels homosexual attractions may identify himself as heterosexual for the purpose of the study and, therefore, compromise the findings. At the same time, given the strength of the findings and the number of different studies completed, these studies show compelling evidence that sexual orientation has a biological and genetic basis.

Early research on differences in the brain structures of heterosexual men, heterosexual women and homosexual men has found differences in a small section of the brain, the suprachiasmic nucleus, which is found in the hypothalamus. Swaab and Hofman (1990) found that this region, the suprachiasmatic nucleus, was 1.7 times larger in homosexual men and contained 2.1 times as many cells as were found in heterosexual men. Simon LeVay (1991) dissected the brains of deceased people who could be presumed to be homosexual or heterosexual, based on their personal life histories, and found that the anterior region of the hypothalamus was the same size in women and homosexual men but that this region was much larger in heterosexual men. Allen and Gorski (1992) noticed significant differences in the anterior commissure of the brains of gay men which supported the growing evidence that differences in certain areas of the brain were partially determinant of homosexuality.

Later researchers have supported, refined and duplicated many of the findings of the early 1990s. Swaab, Chung, Kruijver, Hofman, and Ishunina (2002), in their continuing research into the nature of the relationship between areas of the brain and sexuality, stated that the functional differences in reproduction, gender, and sexual orientation are to be found in the structural and functional differences in the hypothalamus. Beyond these structural and functional differences, researchers at the University of Chicago ("Sexual Orientation Among

Men," 2003) also found that the hypothalamus metabolizes glucose differently in homosexual men and heterosexual men, building additional evidence that the way in which the hypothalamus operates is different based on sexual orientation.

While differences have been noticed in the brain structures of adults, noted above, Rahman (2005) cited significant evidence that sexual orientation is actually laid down in neural circuitry during early fetal development. Garcia-Falgueras and Swaab (2010) have found strong evidence that gender identity and sexual orientation are actually organized into the brain of the human fetus at two months and four months respectively.

Cognitive differences which might suggest neurobiological differences have been done using fluency and spatial recognition tests. In the findings of McCormick and Witelson (1991), the cognitive patterns of homosexual men were not significantly different from that of heterosexual women but were noticeably different from heterosexual men, prompting the researchers to conclude that "there is a neurobiological factor related to sexual differentiation in the etiology of homosexuality" ("A Cognitive Profile").

In a study measuring the hemispheres of the brain, Sanders and Wright (1997) concluded that, generally, the groups of homosexual men and heterosexual women had more similarity in their results than either group did with heterosexual men. Savic and Lindstrom (2008), using MRI and PET technology, studied cerebral symmetry and connectivity between spheres of the brain in heterosexual men and women and homosexual men and women. They found that heterosexual men and homosexual women had a rightward cerebral asymmetry (larger right hemisphere) whereas homosexual men and heterosexual women had hemispheres that were more symmetrical. Beyond that, heterosexual men and homosexual women had different connectivity in the amygdala, an important structure in the brain related to sexuality, than did homosexual men and heterosexual women.

This research was also confirmed in a study by the Karolinska Institute in Sweden ("Scans See 'Gay Brain Differences,'" 2008), which found that heterosexual men and homosexual women had a larger right hemisphere than left while both homosexual men and heterosexual women had brain hemispheres that were equally sized. The Swedish study also confirmed differences in connectivity in the amygdala.

Genetics

In 1993, Hamer, Hu, Magnuson, and Pattatucci launched a separate line of inquiry into the biological and genetic aspects of homosexuality when, by studying the families of gay men, they noticed that gay men had significantly more gay uncles and gay cousins on the maternal side of the family than on the paternal side. To these researchers, such findings suggested that homosexuality might be related to markers on the X chromosome inherited from the mother. Subsequent genetic research done by them found a "99% chance that at least one subtype of male sexual orientation is genetically influenced" ("A Linkage Between DNA"). Research by Hu et al. (1995) confirmed the linkage between markers on the X chromosome and male homosexuality. Mustanski et al. (2005) performed full genome scans on gay men and their families that identified which markers on the X chromosome most likely related to homosexuality, in large measure confirming that homosexuality may be related to markers on the X chromosome.

In a separate line of inquiry into the genetic etiology of homosexuality, Herschberger (2001) and Bailey, Dunne, and Martin (2000) have all conducted studies of twins that have suggested a strong link between genetic make-up and the occurrence of homosexuality. Swedish researchers Langstrom, Rahman, Carlstrom, and Lichtenstein

(2010) conducted a comprehensive study of all adult twins in Sweden (7,600 twins), finding that environmental factors explained only 0-17% of the choice of sexual partner, while between 18% and 39% of that choice could be related to genetic factors.

Scientists have also begun to look into the fetal environment and the relationship of hormonal influences on the development of homosexuality specifically and sexual orientation in general. Blanchard and Klassen (1997) have found that sexual orientation correlates with the number of older brothers such that each older brother increases the odds of homosexuality in a younger brother by 33%. According to Blanchard (as cited in Abrams, 2007, p. 3), the chance a first son will be homosexual could be reasonably estimated to be 2%. Because of hormonal changes in the mother, the probability that a fifth son by her would be homosexual increases to approximately 6%. If that same mother had 15 children, the probability that her 15th child would be homosexual would rise to something approaching 50%. Blanchard assigns this "birth order effect" to changes in the mother after each birth that result in her introduction of different levels of hormones to each succeeding fetus. In a later study, Blanchard and Lippa (2007) surveyed 87,798 men in a web-based study and found additional, supporting evidence of the birth order effect in their much larger sample. Bogaert (2006) directly pitted prenatal against postnatal mechanisms in an effort to determine whether biological or social/child rearing practices were most likely to explain the birth order effect and concluded it was of a prenatal origin.

Suzanne Huwiler (Huwiler & Remafedi, 1998) summarized much of the most recent research findings regarding the genetic and neurobiological foundations of homosexuality. They found that there now exists a large body of scientific evidence that demonstrates biological differences between heterosexual and homosexual people.

Emerging from the data is a unifying theory that the expression of orientation is controlled by one or more genes, whose effects are mediated by pre-natal sex steroids, impacting the central nervous system's development, organization, and structure in a manner that ultimately directs sexual arousal, gender role, and possibly other neuropsychological functions. (p. 120)

Genetics and prevalence

For the most part, the research outlined above has studied the physiology and genetics of people who have identified themselves as either homosexual or heterosexual. It does not, generally, explore the question of what role genes play in the experience of homosexuality in people regardless of how they identify, nor does it account for the question of how prevalent homosexuality may be. One group of genetic researchers interested in this area of study, Santilla et al. (2008), noticed that in many studies, significant numbers of men acknowledged homosexual feelings and had engaged in some homosexual sexual activity while the number of those who identify as "gay" was typically much lower. In a study designed to consider both genetic make-up and homosexual feelings and behavior, Santilla et al. interviewed over 3,000 male twins and their siblings to survey the extent to which each person had homosexual feelings or had engaged in homosexual behavior. They then conducted research on markers on the X chromosomes in each participant.

Santilla et al. (2008) found that 32.8% of the men acknowledged homosexual feelings or fantasies but that only 3.1% had engaged in homosexual sex. Their analysis of the genetic markers of the participants confirmed a significant correlation between certain markers on the X chromosome and both the occurrence of homosexual feelings and in homosexual activity. They concluded that there is a significant potential for homosexuality in a large percentage of men and, further, that the potential for homosexuality, regardless of activity or identity, is genetically influenced.

Providing a recent summary of findings, LeVay (2011) surveyed a wide variety of scientific studies conducted over the last two decades, many of which are detailed above, in order to clarify the role of genetics and neurobiology in the formation of homosexuality.

> Biological research has advanced to the point where it can offer ideas about the development of traits that used to fall squarely within the province of psychology. Biological Psychology (or psychobiology) is the name of the hybrid discipline that has grown up around these ideas . . . . With regard to sexual orientation, biological psychologists have made a variety of important observations:

> - Homosexual behavior is common among nonhuman animals. In a few species, individual animals have a durable preference for same-sex partners.
> - Both in childhood and during adult life, gay people differ from straight people of the same sex in a variety of mental traits that fall under the general label of gender.
> - Evidence suggests that the levels of sex hormones circulating during fetal life influence those gendered traits.
> - Evidence suggests that genes influence sexual orientation and other aspects of gender.

- Structural and functional differences exist between the brains of gay and straight people . . . .
- Differences exist in the structure and function of the bodies of gay and straight people.
- Birth order influences sexual orientation in men, and this influence appears to operate through biological mechanisms rather than social ones. (LeVay, 2011, pp. 42-43)

In summary, researchers have established which regions of the brain are most involved in the development of sexuality and sexual orientation and have established that those regions, especially the hypothalamus and amgdyla, are significantly different in size, metabolism and connectivity in homosexual men. They have provided significant evidence that these differences develop in the first 4 months of fetal development. There is, additionally, important evidence that homosexuality is linked to the X chromosome and more specifically to certain markers on it, which suggests that homosexuality is at least partially formed as a result of genetic influence. There is also strong evidence that the mother's hormones during pregnancy shape a homosexual orientation in the fetus. Finally, some researchers have concluded that homosexuality, in feeling states and in activity, is common to many men who do not identify as gay and that those feelings are linked to a genetic cause as well.

Prevalence

Beyond the issues of genetics and biology, another important way in which homosexuality must be considered relates to the prevalence of homosexuality in the population. If, on one hand, homosexuality is an experience of the group who identify as gay, psychology must consider theories and treatment strategies for a small group within the broad population. If, on the other hand, as Santilla et al. (2008) suggest above, homosexuality is prevalent in a much wider percentage of the population, much of which identifies as heterosexual, homosexuality must be considered as being highly relevant to understanding the psychological and sexual issues for that broad population. The discussion of prevalence studies below, done in the United States and around the world, suggests the latter.

> A considerable portion, perhaps the major portion of the male population, has at least some homosexual experience between adolescence and old age . . . . In these terms (of physical contact to the point of orgasm), the data in the present study indicate that at least 37% of the male population has some homosexual experience between the beginning of adolescence and old age. This is more than one male in three of the persons that one may meet as he passes along the street. (Kinsey, Pomeroy, & Martin, 1948, p. 895)

In his landmark studies of human sexuality in the 1940s and 1950s, Alfred Kinsey established himself as a leading expert in the field of human sexuality. In his works, including *Sexual Behavior in the Human Male* (Kinsey et al., 1948), Kinsey described the responses of men he had interviewed about their sexual feelings and behaviors. Kinsey found that in his private interviews with male participants, a very large percentage, 37%, stated that they had engaged in homosexual activity that had resulted in orgasm at some point in their lives. His findings established that homosexuality, as feeling and behavior, exists in a wide segment of the population and in numbers far beyond the small group that are exclusively homosexual.

It should be noted at the outset that Kinsey's findings were criticized as being based on convenience samples, not random samples, and as such, were subject to bias (Cochran, Mosteller, & Tukey, 1954). These criticisms were especially focused on Kinsey's estimate that 37% of the population had experienced homosexual sex in their life times. Cochran et al. (1954) suggested that because of sampling errors, Kinsey's estimate could be exaggerated and unreliable. They did not dispute Kinsey's general premise that homosexuality exists among heterosexuals. Years later, and after years of reviewing Kinsey's data, Gebhard and Johnson (1979) found that Kinsey's findings were fundamentally accurate, revising Kinsey's estimate that 37% of men had engaged in homosexual sex downward to 36.4%.

Regardless of the actual numbers involved, Kinsey's research is perhaps most important in that it conveys an important aspect of homosexuality that is often overlooked. Homosexual experience is not unusual in the lives of many men and very often is experienced by men who consider themselves heterosexual and who are thought of as heterosexual by others. According to Kinsey (1948): "There is only about half of the male population whose behavior is exclusively heterosexual and there are a few percent who are exclusively homosexual" (p. 895).

Kinsey found that approximately half of all males were exclusively heterosexual, that a small percent were exclusively homosexual and that the remainder of the male population had both homosexual and heterosexual experiences. His work established that homosexuality existed in "every social level, to persons in every occupation and of every age" and that the incidence of homosexuality was similar whether interviews were done "in large towns, small towns, private institutions or state universities, church schools or other environments" (1948, pp. 896-898).

The police force and the court officials who attempt to enforce the sex laws, the clergy and the business men and every other group in the city which periodically calls for the enforcement of the laws—particularly against the laws against "perversion"—have given a record of incidences and frequencies in the homosexual which are as high as those of the social level to which they belong. (p. 898)

Kinsey's research suggested that regardless of how men behaved socially and despite their condemnation of homosexuality publicly, including the prosecution of homosexual behavior, these men themselves confided privately that their histories included homosexual feelings and acts. This inconsistency, to Kinsey, was not a matter of simple hypocrisy. Instead, Kinsey felt that these men were as much victims of the impact of social mores, those social customs that were inconsistent with normal human sexuality, as were the men who were caught and prosecuted for homosexual acts. To Kinsey (1948), "They themselves are the victims of the mores. As long as there are such gaps between the traditional custom and the actual behavior of the population, such inconsistencies will continue to exist" (p. 898).

His research indicated that the "heterosexuality or homosexuality of many individuals is not an all-or-none proposition" (Kinsey, 1948, p. 897). Rather, to Kinsey, male sexuality was best viewed as falling on a continuum from exclusive homosexuality to exclusive heterosexuality with the understanding that many men will feel and act in both heterosexual and homosexual ways during their life times. Kinsey (1948) dismissed the notion that human sexuality can be neatly segmented into either homosexual or heterosexual categories and he illustrated the limitations of using taxonomic categories when dealing with human sexual or psychological experience.

It is fundamental of taxonomy that nature rarely deals with discreet categories. Only the human mind invents categories and tries to force facts into separated pigeon-holes. The living world is a continuum in each and every one of its aspects. The sooner we learn this concerning human sexual behavior the sooner we shall reach a sound understanding of the realities of sex. (p. 897)

To Kinsey, male sexuality must be understood in its variations. His research found that sexual variance, including both homosexual and heterosexual attractions and behavior, was the norm for nearly 40% of American men. While the human mind may tend to categorize sexuality into groups, by doing so, the "realities" of what actually occurs is lost.

Kinsey's work is significant in many ways. First, he was the first researcher of note to establish the degree to which homosexuality is present in American men. By establishing a range of sexual expressions including homosexuality, heterosexuality and bisexuality, Kinsey allowed for a much broader understanding of sexuality. While his numerical percentages have been criticized, Kinsey established a benchmark for other researchers attempting to establish how male sexuality is expressed among men so that further research might notice different variations of sexuality beyond heterosexuality.

Kinsey's work is also important for the field of psychology. While not directly addressed by him, Kinsey's work opens the door to questions about how men relate to their sexuality. While issues surrounding homosexuality are typically associated with men who are "gay," it is rarely thought of as a clinical issue for the large portion of the male population who identify as heterosexual. Yet, Kinsey found that men who identified as heterosexual and who have homosexual feelings may experience significant emotional conflicts, and at the same time, may go to great lengths to shield them. In short, Kinsey's work suggests that homosexuality, as a clinical issue, may pertain to far more men who identify as heterosexual than to the much smaller group who identify as gay.

Another major implication of Kinsey's work is that his findings tend to undermine the contemporary notion that categories of gay, straight, or bisexual are sufficiently broad and flexible for a deeper understanding of male sexuality. While it can be said that a man who is sexual will express it toward the same sex, opposite sex, or both, it is not true that the categories gay, straight, or bisexual capture an individual man's experience fully. Kinsey's research clearly demonstrates that many men experience considerable variations in their sexuality, both emotionally and behaviorally, over a lifetime. Some may have homosexual experiences periodically, perhaps spaced over years, while others may experience homosexual feelings more briefly. Some men may feel attracted homosexually and not act on it while others may act homosexually on occasion without an emotional or psychological attraction to their partner. The categorization of these individual variances, at least to Kinsey, was not useful and if done, was not accurate. At the individual level, taxonomic categories, as Kinsey suggested, fail to capture naturally occurring variations in human sexuality.

A great many other studies have been conducted in the years since Kinsey worked, and in many ways they confirm his basic assumptions, although figures vary from Kinsey's estimates. In general, the research establishes that, as Kinsey found, far more men have homosexual experience, feelings and fantasies than the number of men who identify as gay. It is important to consider in all research below that research participants may, or may not be, influenced by what Kinsey found in his participants, a reluctance to describe publicly the true nature of their sexual feelings. Additionally, it should be noted that surveys may ask about sexual behavior in a number of contexts and by using various questions so that data is expressed in different ways.

A study in the United States by McWhirter et al. (1990) found that 13.95% of males had "either extensive or more than incidental homosexual experience." The National Survey of Sexual Health and Behavior interviewed over 6,000 people in the United States and found that 15% of men had at least one oral sex encounter with another man (1992). In a review of prevalence studies across culture and age ranges, Savin-Williams (2006) found that among American adult men, 8% reported same-sex attractions, 8% reported same-sex behavior but only 2% identified as gay. Additionally, 15% of Australian men reported same-sex attractions, 16% reported same-sex behavior but only 7% identified as gay while in Turkey, among young adults, 6% reported attractions, 4% reported homosexual behavior, and 2% identified as gay.

Suzanne Huwiler (1998, pp. 108-111) summarized a variety of other research projects studying the prevalence of homosexuality in the male populations, finding similar results. Fay et al. concluded that 20.3% of adult American men had at least one sexual contact to orgasm with another man in their lives. More than 3% of men reported that sex with another man had been occasional or often; and 1.6% - 2% had such contact in the preceding year. Seidman and Riederall's survey conducted between 1970 and 1991 estimated that between 12% and 25% of American men had at least one homosexual experience and that 10% reported homosexual activity after age 15 but that homosexual activity within the last year was reported by only 1% to 6% of the respondents. Sell et al. found that 20.8% of American men, 16.3% of men from the United Kingdom and 18.5% of men from France had reported either homosexual attraction or behavior after age 15. Within the past five years, 6.2% of American men, 4.5 % of men from the United Kingdom and 10.7% of men from France had reported homosexual attractions or behaviors.

Among these studies, and many others not reviewed here, considerable variance exists in figures on the prevalence of homosexuality. To some extent, these problems relate to the nature of questions beings asked and how researchers define what homosexuality involves. Addressing this problem, Savin-Williams (2006) states that there are many aspects to homosexuality including feelings of attraction, same-sex behaviors and identity as gay. How any research study is structured and what questions are asked determines to a large measure the findings.

> When researchers assess the number or characteristics of homosexual individuals, they base their findings on a single sexual-orientation component—usually identity. Those who self ascribe a gay/lesbian label are neither exhaustive nor representative of those with a same-sex orientation. (p. 40)

To Savin-Williams (2006), when research into homosexuality is constructed so that a broader definition of homosexuality is used, homosexuality is much more prevalent in the broader male population.

> In general, requesting information about attraction elicits the greatest prevalence of homosexuality, occasionally doubling or tripling the proportion of individuals that report same-sex behavior or identity as gay/lesbian/bisexual. In turn, reports of same-sex behavior usually exceed those of homosexual identification. The majority of people attracted to their own sex or engaging in same-sex sexual behavior do not identify as homosexual. (p. 41)

Beyond the construction of surveys and the parameters used in each, these findings are also affected by several other important considerations. First, all such research depends on the self report of the participants and while not easily quantified, the participant's attitudes about homosexuality, their consciousness of their own feelings, and their comfort in telling others about those feelings may have an impact on the reliability of prevalence studies. The personal feelings of the participants about homosexuality may skew research results and may be, to some extent, influenced by predominant social attitudes. As an example, the impact of social discussions on how males responded to questions about homosexuality was considered in a longitudinal study done by The Hamburg Institute in 1990. According to their findings, a survey of boys, aged 16 and 17, done in 1970 found that 18% of them reported same-sex behavior. The same survey done in 1990 found that only 2% reported same-sex behavior. To the director of the Institute, Volkmar Sigush ("Scans See 'Gay Brain Differences,'" 2008), a fear of being seen as gay has increased among German boys "ever since homosexuality became publicly argued to be an innate sexual orientation." Participants, and, in general, men may be reluctant to acknowledge homosexual feelings if by doing so they must be characterized as being gay or self identify as gay. The nature of social discussion and social debates about being gay, or homosexuality, may play an important role in other surveys although it is a matter of speculation as to how much.

Beyond that, researchers studying the prevalence of homosexuality may need to consider the ambivalence of some men or adolescents to acknowledge homosexual feelings even at the technical level of their research design. As an example, a 1998 study by Turner et al. considered the question of research techniques and found that when young men were asked to use a computer they reported homosexual feelings at a rate 400% higher than when the same participants responded in writing, using paper and pencils, suggesting that anonymity was a powerful factor in assessing homosexuality among young men.

In short, prevalence studies that rely on self reports may be affected by a variety of influences including technical aspects of research, ambivalence of participants to express homosexual feelings, or what Savin-Williams (2006) calls "self-or-other deception, social conditions and variable meanings" (p. 43).

In summary, a review of prevalence studies from Alfred Kinsey's work through the present suggests with remarkable consistency that homosexuality is widely experienced among the broad male population although only a small fraction of that population identifies as gay. When researchers consider homosexual attraction, homosexual behavior and identity separately, it becomes clear that a large percentage of men who do not identify as gay have homosexual attractions or have had some homosexual experience. Beyond that, how one quantifies the prevalence of homosexuality depends on whether one includes feeling states, behavior, or identity among other considerations.

Importantly, the literature described above also demonstrates, with tremendous consistency, that homosexuality is an important psychological consideration for men who identify as heterosexual. While much of the material discussed in this work relates to men who identify as gay, heterosexual men who have homosexual feelings and cannot express them without emotional conflict are worthy of much more consideration. How they reconcile the sexual feelings that are homosexual with an identity that is heterosexual and how therapists can successfully help them in that reconciliation is an important question for the psychological community.

Additionally, as Kinsey noticed, some men in his research who were among the harshest in their attitudes about homosexual people also expressed privately that they had homosexual experience. As will be discussed later in this chapter, Freud, according to Downing

(1989), noticed a connection between homophobic attitudes expressed outwardly by individuals and their own repressed or denied homosexual feelings internally. If true, psychological discussions of homosexuality must consider how homosexuality exists in the heterosexual population if the nature of homophobia is to be considered, as it may be to some extent rooted in the shame and guilt experienced in that population.

In summary, contemporary research has established a biological basis for homosexuality. Prevalence studies demonstrate that homosexuality is experienced by a large percentage of men regardless of how they identify personally or in the world. The research also suggests that only a small percentage of men who have homosexual attractions identify as gay. Given that psychology, as a profession, has held many different views of homosexuality over the last century, it is important that these recent discoveries about genetics, neurobiology and prevalence be used to assess the validity and importance of psychological theories developed over those years.

Homosexuality and psychological theories

Sigmund Freud, the "founding father" of psychoanalysis and a critical theorist in the wider field of psychology, considered sexuality a central drive in human life and a central component of psychological development. Because Freud wrote extensively about human sexuality and its role in psychological development, not to mention his stature in psychology more broadly, Freud may be of singular importance in understanding how the profession of psychology has viewed homosexuality in the last century. His theories continue to be the guiding force in modern psychoanalytic practice and have provided the foundation for the development of many other theoretical models including object relations theory and Erik Erikson's work on life stages.

No simple and comprehensive survey of Freudian thought is possible here. His work spans many decades. The exploration of his work has been underway for more than a century and many volumes of work have been published about Freud's theories by some of the world's leading thinkers in psychology. Yet several of his key concepts related to homosexuality are essential for this work and are reviewed very briefly here.

First, Freud's understanding of the relationship of psychology and biological sciences provides clarity and can, to some extent, serve to synthesize his view about homosexuality with more recent scientific discoveries about it. Second, his writing related to the bisexuality of all human beings is important in any consideration of homosexuality because it leads inevitably to the question of how sexual identity forms, or to what Christine Downing (1989) calls, the "mystery of sexual identification" (p. 41).

Third, Freud's discussion of the psychological etiology of homosexuality in the case of Leonardo da Vinci is important because that description, repeated in much the same way in *The Three Essays* (1949/2000), represents his view of how homosexuality forms as a psychological process in some cases. This configuration has been often repeated in the last century in psychoanalytic literature and is integrated in some form or another within other theoretical models (Isay, 1989). Yet, the caveats Freud used to clarify this theory are often not included in that same literature. A broader review of Freud's thoughts in *Leonardo da Vinci and a Memory of His Childhood* (1910/1961) and *The Three Essays* (1949/2000) provides essential clarifications about his overall attitudes about homosexuality, often missing in the writing of those who followed him.

Freud recognized that psychological life was intricately connected to biological life. In his work *The Psychical Apparatus* (1938/1969), he synthesized much of his thinking on psycho-analysis and how, from that view, our mental life could be understood. At the heart of his thinking is the simple recognition that human psychological life begins with the biological constructs of life. "We know two kinds of things about what we call our psyche (or mental life): firstly, its bodily organ and scene of action, the brain (or nervous system) and, on the other hand, our acts of consciousness" (p. 13). Additionally, Freud considered the limits of psychological inquiry. "Instincts and their transformations are at the limit of what is discernable by psycho-analysis. From that point it gives way to biological research" (1910/1989, p. 98). Freud believed that biological aspects of human life were foundational even if not fully understood by the science of the time. Psychoanalysis was able to observe the manifestations of instinctual drives and notice the transformations in consciousness that they generated. Recent discoveries of the genetic and neurobiological aspects of homosexuality represent direct evidence that homosexuality can no longer be seen as a purely psychological matter as Freud and others theorized. At the same time, Freud was clear that psychoanalysis was interested in the transformations of instinctual drives and research on the biological etiology of homosexuality does nothing to minimize that aspect of Freud's work. Although his theory of a psychical genesis of homosexuality can no longer be seen as the cause of homosexuality, his observations into the psychological transformations of libidinal energy remain powerful, intriguing, and important.

A second important consideration for this work, which relates to Freud's theories of homosexuality, is Freud's bisexual hypothesis. Detailed thoroughly in Christine Downing's *Myths and Mysteries of Same-Sex Love* (1989), Freud's early theory of human bisexuality suggested that all humans, as children, were drawn to both the same sex and the opposite sex and that psychological influences determined the eventual expression of sexual drives in the adult. Over time, according to Downing, Freud's theory evolved into something more sophisticated and profound.

But by 1915 . . . . The "bisexual hypothesis" no longer means that each of us has as part of our given psychical make-up a bit of the opposite sex but rather that to begin with we are not defined sexually.... Our bisexuality refers not only to the fact that we are really subject to both homosexual and heterosexual impulses but that our sexuality comes to have both a conscious and unconscious component. Freud sees us as beginning with an undifferentiated sexual nature. We are then forced (by culture, by language) to line up on one side or other of the sexual division—but anyone "can cross over and inscribe themselves on the opposite side from that which they are anatomically destined" . . . . Thus the discussion of inversion leads Freud not to an easy distinction between homosexuality and normal sexuality but rather to the *mystery* of sexual identification. Heterosexuality turns out to be as problematical as homosexuality. (p. 41)

Freud's theories of homosexuality start with his view that humans begin with an undifferentiated bisexuality that is then directed either in a same-sex or heterosexual direction. Freud suggested that all who are consciously heterosexual are unconsciously homosexual to some extent and that those who are consciously homosexual retain unconscious heterosexual impulses. What aspects of one's sexuality are allowed into consciousness depends to some extent on cultural influences. Understood this way, both heterosexuality and homosexuality are formed psychologically. As such, Freud did not believe that homosexuality was formed in a distinctly different way from heterosexuality or that it should be viewed pathologically.

Psycho-analytic research is most decidedly opposed to any attempt at separating off homosexuals from the rest of mankind as a group of a special character . . . it has found that all human beings are capable of making a homosexual object choice and have in fact made one in their unconscious. Indeed, libidinal attachments to persons of the same sex play not less a part as factors in normal mental life . . . . than do similar attachments to the opposite sex. On the contrary, psycho-analysis considers that a choice of an object independently of its sex . . . . is the original basis from which, as a result of restriction in one direction or another, both the normal and inverted types develop. Thus from the point of view of psycho-analysis the exclusive sexual interest felt by men for women is also a problem that needs elucidating. (Freud, 1962, pp. 145-146)

To Freud, homosexuality is innate in all humans. Even if that aspect of one's sexuality remains in the unconscious, as is the case for those who have an "exclusive sexual interest" heterosexually, homosexuality is a factor in the development of one's mental life. This aspect of Freud's work provides an important foundation to understanding his views on how homosexuality comes to be the dominant means of sexual attraction in some men.

In *Leonardo da Vinci and a Memory of His Childhood* (1910/1989), Freud wrote comprehensively about homosexuality using the life of Leonardo da Vinci as a basis for discussion. In it, Freud outlines his belief that Leonardo had become homosexual as a result of his early childhood psychological experience. On this basis, Freud articulated both a psychoanalytic understanding of homosexuality and a theory for its development.

Using a dream from Leonardo's childhood and accessing historical information about his life, Freud noticed the relationship of Leonardo to both his mother and father. From these particulars, and based on his previous works and theoretical perspectives, Freud formulated the theory that homosexuality was psychologically formed in the following ways.

> In all our homosexual cases the subjects had had a very intense erotic attachment to a female person, as a rule their mother ... this attachment was evoked or encouraged by too much tenderness on the part of the mother herself ... the father was absent from the beginning or left the scene at an early age, so that the boy found himself left entirely under feminine influence. (1910/1989, p. 54)

Freud positioned the development of Leonardo's homosexuality in a family constellation in which Leonardo was exposed to and attached to the mother and without a father to balance her psychological influence. Based on these familial relationships, Freud imagined a series of psychological processes that inhibited a heterosexual object choice, causing Leonardo and others like him to choose homosexually.

> The child's love for his mother cannot continue consciously any further; it succumbs to repression. The boy represses his love for his mother; he puts himself in her place, identifies himself with her, and takes his own person as a model in whose likeness he chooses the new objects of his love. In this way he has become homosexual. (pp. 54-55)

Homosexuality of this type, to Freud, develops out of love for, and identification with, the mother, made possible by the absence or minimal influence of a father. While attracted to women as are other men, the homosexual man must repress his heterosexual feelings in order to preserve his love for his mother and to remain faithful. Retreating to autoeroticism, the homosexual man loves other men in the way his mother loved him, and transfers all erotic feelings away from love objects like his mother on to those men. In this way, he continues to make homosexual object choices throughout his life.

Yet, Freud (1910/1989) also points out that his theory does not account for all types of homosexuality and he specifically does not rule out that homosexuality may be constitutional.

> We are far from wishing to exaggerate the importance of these explanations of the psychical genesis of homosexuality.... We know that they are not sufficiently comprehensive to make a conclusive explanation of the problem possible. What is for practical reasons called homosexuality may arise from a whole variety of psychosexual inhibitory processes ... we too cannot reject the part played by constitutional factors, to which the whole of homosexuality is usually traced. (p. 56)

That Freud could offer a comprehensive theory of a psychological genesis of homosexuality and, at the same time, provide caveats that allowed for other explanations of it, including the idea that homosexuality is "constitutional," speaks to the complexity and nuance of his theoretical approaches. In Downing's (1989) comprehensive review of his theories about homosexuality, a more complex view of Freud's thinking emerges.

According to Downing (1989), to Freud, homosexuality was an important consideration in many aspects of psychological life and in psychoanalysis (p. 49).

> For Freud we are all in some sense homosexuals . . . . Freud is also persuaded that the fear of one's denied homosexual longings constitutes one of the most powerful elements in resistance to analysis . . . . Homophobia, too, is seen as an expression of repressed homosexuality. Freud regards it as the individual's attempt to reject admission of his own unconscious homosexual desires with "vigorous counter-attitudes." (p. 49)

To Freud, the denial of homosexual feelings results in not only a defensiveness that undermines psychoanalysis but is also a central driving force behind "vigorous" homophobia.

To Downing (1989), although Freud often used terms like "perversion" to describe homosexuality, he did not use that term in the derogatory sense it came to mean later. As Downing noted, Freud "makes clear that what we call normal channels of sexuality are the socially approved or conventionally defined ones" (p. 42). Quoting Freud from the *Introductory Lectures and An Autobiographical Study*, Downing noticed Freud's belief that those who we call homosexual are often people "of high intellectual and ethical development" and that regarding homosexuality, he made no moral judgment or "judgments of value" (p. 42). According to Downing, "since he did not regard homosexuality as a pathology or illness . . . . Freud regarded as pointless attempts to 'cure' it" (p. 43). In 1935, Freud wrote a letter to an American mother who asked for his guidance for her homosexual son, a letter that illuminates Freud's attitudes clearly.

Wien IX, Berggasse 19, April 9th, 1935

Dear Mrs....

I gather from your letter that your son is a homosexual. I am most impressed by the fact that you do not mention this term yourself in your information about him. May I question you why you avoid it? Homosexuality is assuredly no advantage, but it is nothing to be ashamed of, no vice, no degradation; it cannot be classified as an illness; we consider it to be a variation of the sexual function, produced by a certain arrest of sexual development. Many highly respectable individuals of ancient and modern times have been homosexuals, several of the greatest men among them. (Plato, Michelangelo, Leonardo da Vinci, etc). It is a great injustice to persecute homosexuality as a crime and a cruelty too. If you do not believe me, read the books of Havelock Ellis.

By asking me if I can help, you mean, I suppose, if I can abolish homosexuality and make normal heterosexuality take its place. The answer is, in a general way, we cannot promise to achieve it. In a certain number of cases we succeed in developing the blighted germs of heterosexual tendencies, which are present in every homosexual; in the majority of cases, it is no more possible. It is a question of the quality and the age of the person. The result of the treatment cannot be predicted.

What analysis can do for your son runs in a different line. If he is unhappy, neurotic, torn by conflicts, inhibited in his social life, analysis may bring him harmony, peace of mind, full efficiency, whether he remains homosexual or gets changed.

If you made up your mind that he should have analysis with me, I don't expect you will, he has to come over to Vienna. I have no intention of leaving here. However, don't neglect to give me your answer.

Sincerely yours with kind wishes

Freud

P.S. I did not find it difficult to read your handwriting. I hope you will not find my writing and my English a harder task. (Freud, 1951)

Speaking in lay terms, Freud conveyed his understanding that homosexuality is no vice, nothing to be ashamed of and that it represents no degradation. He was clear that the persecution of homosexuality was cruel and that to abolish homosexuality in any individual was unlikely. Given his view that all humans have an innate bisexuality, to Freud, helping someone "become" heterosexual involved a process of retrieving unconscious latent heterosexual fragments. It is a matter of speculation but it seems doubtful that in such cases Freud would have imagined it to be useful to abolish homosexual feelings. To do so, presumably, would require that homosexual feelings be returned to the realm of the unconscious.

Sigmund Freud is among the most important theorists in the field of psychology and the pre-eminent theorist for the understanding of psycho-sexual development. Of all major theorists, Freud was perhaps the most prolific writer about homosexuality. Freud did not have access to recent studies of genetics and neurobiology that identify the biological determinants of sexual orientation yet he honored the fact that our biological lives set the stage for our psychological lives. In that sense, given the genetic basis of homosexuality, it is possible to understand Freud as describing the psychological transformations that occur for homosexual men because of their biological lives. In other words, Freud may well have been noticing the psychological effects of inborn homosexuality, not the cause of homosexuality itself.

It also must be noted that psychological studies have been performed to test Freud's theories and those of other psychological theorists regarding a possible psychological etiology of homosexuality and have found generally that such theories are not supported.

> Weak or absent fathers, emotionally demanding mothers, being an only child and subject to parental pampering, have all been blamed by psychotherapists of different schools, but carefully controlled studies of heterosexual and homosexual men and women, together with their family histories, have failed to substantiate these contentions. Neither paternal nor maternal personality traits or parental relationships, sibling constellations or early experiences of many kinds have been shown to be significantly different between the two groups. (Stevens & Price, 1996, p. 178)

Jung and homosexuality

Interestingly, Carl Jung, whose theories and ideas are important considerations throughout this work, wrote very little about homosexuality. Robert Hopke's (1989) exhaustive examination of Jung's discussions of homosexuality demonstrates that Jung wrote sparingly about homosexuality as a specific topic of interest. To the extent he did write about it, Jung posited three different theories about homosexuality, according to Hopke (1989), over the course of his life's work. In some writings, Jung suggested that male homosexuality relates to a specific relationship to the feminine. Originally, Jung felt this relationship stemmed from unresolved conflicts from the personal mother but, in later writings, widened his perspective so that he understood the relationship to be with the anima, and still later, to be with the matriarchal consciousness (p. 60). A second theory briefly discussed by Jung is that homosexuality may result from an incomplete attachment to the archetype of the Hermaphrodite, "the unbroken state of nondifferentiation that comes, psychologically and mythically, before all else" (p. 64). Hopke considers this theory to be especially important as it relates to the archetypal movement within an individual toward wholeness psychologically (p. 64). Jung's third "theory" of homosexuality, according to Hopke (1989), sprang from Jung's "intuition of how fundamental one's sexual orientation seems to be." That theory was Jung's suggestion that homosexuality is constitutional (p. 66).

Other psychological theories

While Jung's specific writings on homosexuality are sparse, many other authors in the field of psychology have written extensively about homosexuality for at least the last 100 years. According to John Money (1988), K. M. Beckert, an early psychologist who wrote before Freud, was the person who originally coined the term "homosexual," and he is among the first psychologists to offer a theory for why men were attracted sexually to other men. Beckert believed their behavior resulted from a "horror" of women which then caused the physical problem of erectile dysfunction. These men, not able to perform heterosexually, then chose other men for sexual gratification (p. 9).

As was the case with Beckert, and notwithstanding the more nuanced views of Freud and Jung, the field of psychology generally considered homosexuality to be a disorder and to be pathological from the time Beckert's writing in 1869 to 1973 when the American Psychiatric Association released the third revision of the *Diagnostic and Statistical Manual*. In the 3rd edition, for the first time, homosexuality was not listed as a mental illness (Isay, 1989). Throughout most of the history of modern psychology, many of the most prominent writers in the field of psychology, some of whom created highly respected theoretical models and traditions in psychology, spoke of homosexuality as disease.

In his survey of the relationship of psychoanalysis and homosexuality, Richard Isay (1985, 1986, 1989) describes the evolution of psychoanalytic perspectives from Freud through the 1980s. In general, Isay states that psychoanalytic theory posits that when normal development occurs, it results in heterosexuality. Often, psychoanalytic theory holds that homosexuals suffer from a deficit of masculinity.

> All psychoanalytic theories of homosexuality suggest that homosexual men suffer from a deficiency in their masculinity. Either a distant father fails to help his son separate from his mother, or the mother pathologically binds the boy to her . . . . To put it simply, traditional analysts believe a man cannot be homosexual without also being and/or feeling effeminate. (1989, pp. 17-18)

Within this line of thinking in psychoanalysis, according to Isay, early childhood developmental problems which prevent heterosexuality and normal functioning result in a defensive same-sex attraction. As development continues, the homosexual develops other pathological symptoms, often severe, and may develop personality disorders that last a lifetime (Isay, 1985). The nature of these problems, as described in psychoanalytic literature, represent among the most severe psychological problems known. A sampling of some of those descriptions is described in Isay's (1989) review.

> The number and kind of pathological deficits attributed to homosexuals are very large, and I have selected only a few for illustrative purposes. Bergler (1956) wrote of six traits: masochistic provocation and injustice collecting, defensive malice, flippancy, hypernarcissim, refusal to acknowledge accepted standards in nonsexual matters, and general unreliability .... Socarides (1968) wrote that approximately half of the patients who engage in homosexual practices have a concomitant schizophrenia, paranoia, are latent or psuedoneurotic schizophrenics or are in the throes of a manic-depressive reaction. The other half, when neurotic, may be of the obsessional or, occasionally, of the phobic type. (p. 2)

Other highly respected and well-known psychiatrists agreed. According to Isay (1985), when the country of England considered the decriminalization of homosexuality in the 1950s, the government relied on a commissioned study called the Wolfendon Report which criticized the view that homosexuality was a disease. In its American edition, Karl Menninger wrote the introduction and added his perspective, stating "Homosexuality . . . constitutes evidence of immature sexuality and either arrested psychological development or regression. Whatever it be called by the public, there is no question in the minds of psychiatrists regarding the abnormality of such behavior (Isay, 1985, p. 3).

Other theorists from different schools of psychological thought also contended that homosexuality was pathological. John Bowlby, according to Peel et al. (2007), felt that while a homosexual's internal psychological systems might be in working order, they were not "functionally" in order so that they caused a misdirection from the normal functioning of sexuality, or heterosexuality.

According to Peel et al. (2007), object relations theorist Ronald Fairbairn considered homosexuality to be a failure of both heterosexuality and social responsibility.

> Fairbairn maintained that the distress homosexuals feel is from their forfeiture of social and marital advantages rather than from guilt or remorse and that typically they resent society's attitude toward them. Ultimately, the homosexual does not want cure but acceptance. Therefore, homosexuality is the naturally occurring expression of a psychopathic personality. (p. 81)

Erik Erikson, a highly regarded and well-known theorist best known for his theories related to psychological stages of life, considered homosexuality to be deviant (1968). While Erikson based his theories of stages on psychoanalytic theories, he originated many popular and widely known concepts about identity formation in adolescence. While he may well have agreed that homosexuality was a failure in early childhood development, he also considered that the formation of homosexuality could come during an adolescent struggle with "bisexual confusion."

> But there are also aspects of identity formation which anticipate future development. The first of these is what we may call a polarization of sexual differences . . . the elaboration of a particular ratio of masculinity and

femininity in line with identity development. Some of our patients suffer more lastingly and malignantly from a state not uncommon in a milder and transient form in all adolescence; the young person does not feel himself clearly to be a member of one sex or the other, which may make him the easy victim of the pressure emanating, for example, from homosexual cliques. (p. 186)

To Erikson, in adolescence, there was a naturally occurring process of differentiation of masculinity and femininity and, during this period, a boy begins to gain the correct amount of masculinity for adult life. An unsuccessful process of differentiation might cause a boy to be confused, feeling not part of either sex, which might allow him to slip into homosexual groups for support. Erikson considered this phenomenon to be the establishment of a negative identity and to be pathological in nature. In short, such a young man chooses to identify with what he should not be.

Even in individual disturbances usually called prepsychotic or psychopathic or otherwise diagnosed in line with adult psychopathology, an almost willful *Umschaltung* to a negative identity ... can be studied. On a somewhat larger scale, an analogous turn toward a negative identity prevails in the delinquent (addictive, homosexual youth) of our larger cities .... often sought collectively in cliques and gangs of young homosexuals, addicts and social cynics. (1968, pp. 88-176)

It is of some historical interest, according to Shelby (1994) and Isay (1989), that the tone of the discussion of homosexuality became more hostile after the end of World War II, especially within the American psychiatric community. Isay (1989) explained that many American analysts served within the military during the war, returning to the United States afterward. This experience, in part, informed a particular view of how "healthy" masculinity appears in a man. These analysts often became influential members of psychiatric institutions throughout the country and began to bring psychoanalysis into the mainstream of America's broader health care system. Psychoanalysis found significantly more legitimacy as it "strengthened its ties to psychiatry, medicine and the disease model" (p. 6). Isay noticed that during this period, America was in the midst of the McCarthy era which, among other things, resulted in the purging of homosexuals from government. It was, to Isay (1989), a period when non-conformist attitudes, and attitudes of acceptance of homosexuality, were suspect. According to Isay (1989), "During this time, when there were purges of homosexuals from government, there was also a consolidation within psychoanalysis of the theory of the pathological adaptation of homosexuals, and the exclusion of homosexuals from analytic institutes became customary" (p. 6).

Shelby (1994) agreed that American psychoanalysis, the medical profession, and social influences became enmeshed after World War II in a way which altered the profession's attitudes and behaviors toward homosexuality. Some within the psychological community took advocacy positions outside professional circles. According to Shelby (1994), "After World War II, American analysts presented some of their most virulent statements regarding the homosexual psyche, often writing in the popular press rather than in scientific journals. The emphasis shifted to the issue of changing homosexual orientation" (p. 5).

Isay (1989) reviewed some of that public dialogue, written by psychoanalysts decades after Freud (1951) wrote to an American mother that homosexuality was no vice.

Sixty years later, two American psychoanalysts, concerned by the increasingly aggressive attempts of homosexuals to achieve civil rights, were quoted in the *New York Times*. Irving Bieber stated that "he does not approve the attempt by organized homosexuals to promote the idea that they represent just another minority, since the minority status is based on illness . . . " The second analyst, Charles Socarides, who still writes extensively about homosexuality, is quoted as saying: "The homosexual is ill, and anything that tends to hide that fact reduces his chances of seeking and obtaining treatment . . . . If they were to achieve social acceptance it would increase this difficulty." (p. 4)

To these authors, homosexuality was an illness that psychiatry could treat. Any tendency, social or personal, that allowed homosexuals to find acceptance was itself a perpetuation of the illness. That these authors wrote in *The New York Times* speaks to both psychiatry's active involvement in social issues and public policy as well as the power and influence that both psychoanalysis and psychiatry had obtained in American society.

That homosexuality had become defined as a form of serious mental illness within the broad health professions is evident in the fact that it was listed as such in the *Diagnostic and Statistical Manual* during the 1960s and early 1970s. According to Isay (1989), "In the first *Diagnostic and Statistical Manual* of the American Psychiatric Association, *DSM-1*, homosexuality was listed in the category "sociopathic personality disturbance." It was listed under "personality disorders and certain other nonpsychotic mental disorders" in *DSM-II* (1989, p. 6).

Isay (1989), Shelby (1994), and Hopke (1989) all suggest that a combination of factors altered the psychological community's view about homosexuality in the late 1960s and early 1970s. All three authors suggest that, in part, change occurred as a result of the emergence of a more or less formal gay community in the late 1960s that actively sought social change. It is perhaps ironic that by coalescing around what Erikson (1968) called a "negative identity," an identity of being homosexual, homosexuals began to find increasing acceptance. Ronald Long (2004) describes the events at the Stonewall Inn that set in motion the social change that psychologists like Hopke (1989) and Isay (1989) suggest also led to changing attitudes within the psychological community.

> The Stonewall Inn was a gay bar located in New York's Greenwich Village. In late June of 1969, a police bust for illegal sale of alcohol—an unfortunately common event at the time—resulted in the arrest of several patrons and the bar's staff. The released patrons, numbering about 200, were witness to the arrests and became incensed. The ensuing melee and subsequent rioting raised the Stonewall resistance to mythic status as the event that founded the modern movements for lesbian and gay liberation and civil rights. Men and women in large numbers came out of the closet and identified themselves publicly as lesbian and gay, refusing to acquiesce to a social practice that held their sexual orientation to be something they should be ashamed about. (Long, 2004, p. 4)

Obviously, increased levels of acceptance and the elimination of the belief that homosexuality was a psychological disease also came about as a result of changes from within the psychological community. Eventually, the professional standard for the identification of mental disorders, the *Diagnostic and Statistical Manual*, was changed. According to Isay (1989), the American Psychiatric Association, in 1973, removed homosexuality from the *DSM-III* as a mental disorder (p. 6).

In the nearly four decades since the revision of the *Diagnostic and Statistical Manual* in 1973, attitudes about homosexuality and therapeutic approaches for the treatment of homosexual people have changed dramatically. Authors such as Isay, (1989), Hopke (1989), Shelby (1994), and Peel et al. (2007) suggest that homosexuality is now considered to be a normal variation of sexuality. Each of these authors, among many others, has written about homosexuality in a way which attempts to address historical misconceptions about the nature of homosexuality. These authors each represent a different tradition in psychology and, although they represent only a small sample, their work is a testament to the broad nature of the change that has occurred.

Isay (1985, 1986, 1989), writing from a psychoanalytic perspective, has written extensively and originally to reexamine long-held attitudes within that tradition about the early childhood experiences of homosexual men. Hopke (1989) has built upon Jungian concepts of the archetypal dimensions of masculine, feminine and the androgynous to incorporate new understandings of homosexuality for the analytic psychology tradition. Likewise, Shelby (1994) has clarified many significant therapeutic issues in the treatment of gay men using self psychology as a basis. Peel et al. (2007) have provided similar clarifications using object relations theory as a basis. These examples illustrate the wide ranging effort within the broad psychological community to understand homosexuality and the psychological lives of homosexual people.

Contemporary definition

No comprehensive theory about the nature of homosexuality or any that fully describes the psychological experience of homosexual people exists. While there have been many viewpoints in the past and many newer perspectives, the literature does not include a standard, largely accepted psychological perspective about homosexuality. Absent that, the general description of how homosexuality is conceptualized by the American Psychological Association, herein referred to as the APA, is useful. The APA is one of the nation's leading associations for mental health professionals and a clearing house for much of today's psychological thought.

To the APA, homosexuality is a normal variation of sexuality directed in a same-sex direction. How one's sexual attraction is directed, homosexually, heterosexually or bisexually, is thought of as one's sexual orientation. According to the APA (American Psychological Association, 2009, "Sexual Orientation and Homosexuality"), sexual orientation is considered "an enduring emotional, romantic, sexual or affectional attraction toward others." It begins to emerge in adolescence without previous sexual experience in the vast majority of cases. Sexual orientation includes exclusively heterosexuality, exclusive homosexuality and "various forms of bisexuality." It is not a choice.

In its summary statement cited above, the APA provides our profession's current psychological perspective, a perspective that may put to rest many important questions adolescents, families, therapists, and the broader society may ask. First, the APA locates the emergence of sexual orientation at early adolescence, an especially important consideration for this work and the subject of more thorough discussion later in it. Beyond that, one's sexual orientation, the direction of one's enduring emotional, psychological and sexual attractions, is not chosen. The direction of these attractions may be homosexual, heterosexual or both.

While clarifying some important areas of inquiry, the APA statement also implies significant psychological complexity in any discussion of sexual orientation or of homosexuality. Specifically, to consider homosexuality as a psychological experience, it is necessary to consider feeling states, one's self concept, and one's behavior. According to the APA (2009), "Sexual Orientation is different from sexual behavior because it refers to feelings and self concept. Individuals may or may not express their sexual orientation in their behavior" ("Sexual Orientation and Homosexuality").

The APA (2009) also alludes to a fourth major aspect of the psychological experience of homosexuality, which is to identify oneself publicly or to "come out." The APA describes some historical and current ways in which homosexuality has been encountered in the broader society.

> Some homosexual or bisexual people may seek to change their sexual orientation through therapy, often coerced by family members or religious groups. The reality is that homosexuality is not an illness. It does not require treatment and is not changeable . . . . Homosexuality was once thought to be a mental illness because mental health professionals and society had biased information. ("Sexual Orientation and Homosexuality")

Until 1973, when the American Psychiatric Association removed homosexuality as a mental and emotional disorder, the field of psychology relied on biased information and treated homosexuality as an illness. While the profession now considers it to be healthy, and has for more than 35 years, it is clear from the APA that bias continues to exist in families, religious groups and others. While the nature of social bias will be discussed later in this work, it is important here to notice that the development of a homosexual orientation involves the expression of one's homosexuality to the world and any challenges experienced in that process.

The APA (2009) summary also addresses the question of how sexual orientation develops.

> Most scientists today agree that sexual orientation is most likely the result of a complex interaction of environmental, cognitive and biological factors. In most people, sexual orientation is shaped at an early age. There is also considerable recent evidence to suggest that biology, including genetic and inborn hormonal factors, play a significant role in a person's sexuality. ("Sexual Orientation and Homosexuality")

Sexual orientation, whether homosexual, heterosexual or bisexual, forms through a complex interaction of many factors at an early age, including the strong possibility that it may develop pre-birth and as a result of innate, biological or genetic factors.

Using the American Psychological Association literature as a basis, homosexuality can be understood as an innate and natural expression of sexuality where the direction of one's sexual and emotional attractions are directed primarily toward members of the same sex. It is likely that homosexuality is formed as a result of genetic and prenatal developmental processes but, in any case, homosexuality forms at an early age. It is not changeable. At adolescence, typically, homosexuality emerges as a psychological challenge involving the development of a "sexual orientation." That process involves important psychological challenges. First, one must experience homosexual feelings over time, or in an "enduring way." One must allow those feelings to help form a personal identity in relationship to sexuality. One must choose in what way he will express himself behaviorally and, finally, one must face the challenge of telling others or of "coming out."

In what ways this developmental process occurs is explored later in this work but, at this point, it is important to recognize the implications of the APA summary. Feelings, self concept, behavior, and identity in the world are distinct, different, and important components of the psychological experience of homosexuality. As such, the possibility exists that in any individual, these components may conflict with each other. What happens if innate and naturally occurring feelings are unwanted or result in guilt? What impact does that conflict have on the development of identity? What occurs when a teenager's sexual feelings and their conceptualization of themselves differ? What conflicts arise when a teenager behaves heterosexually when their naturally occurring feelings are homosexual? In other words, the developmental challenge of homosexuality must also include the challenge to integrate feelings, personal identity, behavior and external identity so that they are congruent.

CHAPTER 11

HOMOSEXUALITY, CULTURE AND HISTORY

Danny had no roots. In his homosexuality, Danny had no heritage. He had never heard of the Stonewall Inn nor had he known that Leonardo da Vinci was homosexual. He scarcely knew who Leonardo was. Danny was unaware that he had something in common with Socrates, something important, or that throughout the history of mankind there have been homosexuals like him. For Danny, homosexuality made him different from others, not similar to Michelangelo.

In private moments, when no one noticed his activities, Danny had discovered what homosexuality was and who homosexuals were. He explored web sites online, some explicitly sexual and others that offered support for gay teens. His mother liked television comedies, several of which featured gay characters. Danny watched those shows and gained an image of homosexual lives from them. Other shows with characters who were gay teenagers provided messages that stated that he might have to struggle with harassment but that, in the end, he could accept himself and be proud of his nature. There were other shows, mostly talk shows or news shows, where Danny heard that homosexuality was controversial and that much of his society condemned it. When his mother or father watched television with him, Danny pretended that he was disinterested but he heard every word being spoken when the words gay or homosexual were topics of conversation. He and his life were being discussed and he was learning about his nature.

Over time, Danny's understanding of homosexuality coalesced. Danny developed a narrative about homosexuality gleaned from all his secret investigations. There were people, a small group, who were different. There were gay men and lesbians, bisexual people who liked both men and women sexually, and then transgendered people who seemed very different because "they were somehow both male and female." These people wanted the right to marry, wanted an end to being harassed, and wanted to see an end to the discrimination they faced in the world. Some of these people seemed outrageous in their behavior, men dressing as women in outrageous attire at gay events, and although that is not what Danny meant by homosexual, he thought it was a matter of personal choice that should be accepted. To Danny, being gay was a matter of personal choice and civil rights. Much of the rest of the world seemed to criticize gay and lesbian people. To Danny, it was possible the criticisms might be right but people, even those who are different, had every right to be who they were.

Just as Danny had imagined homosexuality in a particular way, and just as psychology has done over the past 100 years, societies and cultures have also conceptualized homosexuality in specific ways. Danny was not yet aware of those differences. He based his conception of homosexuality on the present and local narratives available to him. Absent any historical context, the experience of gay people, as seen by Danny, is primarily a matter of the personal choices made by a small minority of people that have been criticized as being in defiance of the majority's wishes. Being gay was largely a social struggle and he could advocate for being gay because all people should be treated equally. Without a broader perspective, one gained through a cultural and historical lens, Danny was not yet prepared to advocate for homosexuality because it has, and has had, intrinsic value. Yet, as seen below, in many times in history and in many cultures, the value of homosexuality was articulated in absolute and specific ways.

Just as is the case with Danny, one way in which modern psychological therapies can be broadened and enhanced is by informing them with a wider variety of perspectives. A review of the patterns and trends of social and cultural attitudes about homosexuality throughout history can clarify both the nature of homosexuality and the nature of hostility toward it. Discussions of homosexuality often involve a wide range of corresponding issues including those related to how masculinity and femininity are defined, how societal attitudes shift and impact homosexual people, and the nature of love among others. A review of historical attitudes about homosexuality can bring new insight to these discussions and may help to inform psychological attitudes about them.

To understand historical perspectives about homosexuality and how they differ from contemporary ones, some attention must first be paid to two broad issues. Specifically, the modern concept of categorizing sexual preferences as gay or straight stands in sharp contrast to historical views. Second, the notion that homosexuals represent a minority, one grouped by the nature of their sexual attraction, represents a sharp distinction from many eras of the past.

Categorization of erotic life

When K. M. Beckert coined the term "homosexual" in 1869 (Money, 1989), he established for the first time, within our modern vocabulary, formal and distinct categories of erotic life and sexual expression. The gender of the person a man was attracted to, male or female, defined that man's sexuality and the state of his mental health. In subsequent decades, as noticed above, categories of sexual attraction have been further split into gay, lesbian, bisexual and heterosexual.

These distinctions have become an aspect of personal and social identity so that the gender of the person to whom one is attracted has become a significant issue related to social discussions, psychological discussions, mental health, legal matters, issues of discrimination, and many other contemporary social concerns.

In some ways, Beckert's coining of the term homosexual can be seen as a watershed in thinking about sexuality. At least symbolically, he created a point of separation between past and present. The separation of human erotic life into categories would have been, according to historian John Boswell (1980), a foreign concept to those who lived before the modern era.

> It can be well argued that the homosexual/heterosexual dichotomy is not a real one, and this would have been the response of most ancient authorities. At best, these categories group together according to one arbitrarily chosen aspect of sexual action—the gender of the parties involved . . . The homosexual/ heterosexual dichotomy is crude and imprecise and often obscures more than it clarifies. (p. 42)

To some extent, John Boswell, who surveyed the relationship of Christianity and homosexuality throughout history, bridges past attitudes about homosexuality and contemporary ones within western cultures. Seen historically by Boswell (1980), sexual activity throughout the ages has often been based on issues other than the gender of the partner. "Many people are more aroused by the acts themselves, (penetration, oral stimulation etc.) than by the persons involved" (p. 42). Categorizing sexual activity based on the gender of the partner, either homosexual or heterosexual, does not account for sexual activity and preferences that are driven by social norms, by body type or attractiveness, specific sexual activities or a host of other considerations (p. 42).

Boswell (1980) recognized a limited value in using the term homosexual in that it does, in fact, describe one specific aspect of sexual behavior or attraction but he stated that the value of using the term is inherently limited by the "inevitable weakness of taxonomic arrangement of human behavior" (p. 42). Just as Alfred Kinsey (1948) noticed in surveying the prevalence of homosexuality in the United States, Boswell noticed that human sexual behavior throughout history has been innately filled with variation that "categories" or descriptive terms like homosexual must exclude for the sake of communication and discussion (p. 42).

Homosexuals as a minority

Just as the separation of sexuality into gay and straight orientations has split the human experience of sexuality into categories, modern social constructions have defined heterosexuality as a majority orientation and homosexuality, or gay people, as being part of a minority. The separation of homosexuals as a class of people, and as a minority, has not been typical of societies throughout much of recorded human history, according to Boswell (1980, p. 58). Over the course of many centuries, no distinction between homosexuality and heterosexuality was common and without such a distinction, no social grouping, or minority status, was created for those with same-sex attraction. Yet, during some periods in history, like this century, homosexuals became a part of a minority within the broader society. Boswell (1980) suggested that, in many ways, the creation of a minority class for homosexuals develops in societies when, for some reason, the majority wishes to make such distinctions. "Majorities, in other words, create minorities, in one very real sense, by deciding to categorize them" (pp. 58-59).

While much of Boswell's work illuminated how societies have

constructed a minority class for homosexuals, Boswell suggested that during periods when homosexuals were classed as a minority, and often demeaned, social intolerance increased for other minorities as well, including Jews, gypsies, certain Christian sects, the poor, or people whose race deviated from the majority. In other words, Boswell tied the creation of minorities to a majority's desire to distinguish them and attempts to suppress or eradicate them, and he noticed the complex collective attitudes that underpin that effort. Any modern conception of homosexuality, one that is consistent with historical expressions of homosexuality, must include an understanding that many high functioning societies and cultures have not considered homosexuals to represent a minority. In fact, many cultures and societies in the West, and outside Western societies, have included homosexuality as a necessary and valuable aspect of social construction and the personal development of societal members.

Homosexuality in culture and history

Goethe wrote that homosexuality is as old as humanity itself and can therefore be considered natural, and human history lends his statement the ring of truth. (Ford & Beach, 1952, p. 125)

Homosexuality has existed in most societies for as long as recorded descriptions of sexual beliefs and practices have been available. Societal attitudes toward homosexuality have had a decisive impact on the extent to which individuals have hidden or made known their sexual orientation. (American Academy of Pediatrics Committee on Adolescence, 1993, p. 631)

In their sweeping review of culture and sexuality, anthropologist Clellan Ford and psychologist Frank Beach (1952) surveyed 76 cultures around the world, assessing each culture's sexual attitudes and practices, including the degree to which homosexuality was expressed. The cultures surveyed included both small and relatively obscure tribes and larger societies like the United States. Their work assessed sexual practices including heterosexuality and homosexuality, as well as child rearing practices, initiation rites involving sexuality, and many other characteristics of these cultures related to sexuality. They surveyed societies around the globe including those in Africa, Asia, North and South America, the Pacific region and Australia.

In general, Ford and Beach (1952) found that homosexuality is widespread across many societies and cultures. Out of the 76 cultures they investigated, 49, or 64%, viewed homosexuality favorably, at least for some members of the culture or in some circumstances. While no comprehensive discussion is possible of their extensive research here, examples provided by Ford and Beach illustrate the variety of ways in which homosexuality has been expressed culturally (pp. 129-131).

The most common form of institutionalized homosexuality, according to Ford and Beach (1952) is that of the Native American berdache, a man who "dresses like a woman, performs women's tasks and adopts some aspects of the feminine role in sexual behavior" (p.130). In some societies, including the Siberian Chukchee, men who adopt such a feminine role are considered to be powerful Shaman who enjoy "considerable prestige" while holding a position of power in the society (p 131). These men are considered to be transformed by supernatural powers. Some societies, like the Koniag tribe of Alaska, rear some children from infancy to occupy a female role and when mature, these men became the wives of prominent men, were held in high esteem and were credited with magical powers (p. 132). In other societies, homosexuality has been expected and institutionalized.

Among the Siwans of Africa . . . all men and boys engage in anal intercourse . . . and males are singled out as peculiar if they do not engage in these homosexual practices. Prominent Siwan men lend their sons to each other and they talk about their masculine love affairs as openly as they discuss their love of women. (p. 132)

Among the Aranda tribe of Australia, pederasty, or sexual relations between a man and a pubescent boy, was a recognized custom in which an unmarried man took a younger boy as his wife until he married a women. While still bachelors, the Keraki tribesmen of New Guinea universally practiced sodomy with younger males and anal intercourse was seen as part of the younger man's puberty rites of passage. "This practice is believed by the natives to be necessary for the growing boy" (Ford & Beach, 1952, p. 132). Among the men of the Dahomean and Nama tribes in Africa, mutual masturbation is practiced and is the primary form of accepted homosexuality (p. 133).

Beyond the societies with institutionalized homosexuality or those with favorable attitudes about it, Ford and Beach (1952) also found 28 societies which reported that homosexuality was being absent or rare. They note that the reports of prevalence in these societies should be expected to be lower because in all of them, homosexuality was condemned, restricted or punished. According to the authors, "Among all the societies in which adult homosexual activities are said to be rare, definite and specific social pressure is directed against such behavior" (p. 129).

Restrictions against homosexual behavior begin to be imposed in childhood among the Cuna tribe of Panama and in some North American Native American tribes. Other cultures restrict homosexual behavior to prostitutes but do not condone it among others, while still other cultures, like the Rwala Bedouins of the Arabian desert, sentenced homosexuals to death. Of the 28 societies surveyed, only one, the Siriana people of Bolivia, reported homosexuality to be rare despite not having sanctions or prohibitions against it (Ford & Beach, 1952, pp. 129-130). Ford and Beach (1952) classified the United States as being in the minority of cultures surveyed in that it disapproves of homosexuality.

> Our own society disapproves of any form of homosexual behavior for males and females of all ages. In this it differs from the majority of human societies. Some people resemble us in the respect, but a larger number condone or even encourage homosexuality for at least some members of the population. (p. 125)

In *Patterns of Sexual Behavior* (1952), Ford and Beach concluded that homosexuality is present in virtually all societies, that it is approved of in most but restricted and condemned in some, including the United States. Beyond that, their work demonstrates that the expression of homosexuality is in many ways controlled and directed by prevailing social attitudes. Regardless of those attitudes, it is also clear that homosexuality exists, is common, is naturally occurring, and is experienced by men in a wide range of cultures and societies.

Ronald Long, in *Men, Homosexuality, and the Gods* (2004), also explored cultural attitudes around the world. While Long's work relates specifically to religious attitudes about homosexuality, discussed later in this work, his survey of cultural attitudes is important here.

According to Long (2004), some non-western cultures, including that of ancient China, found acceptance of homosexuality based on the behaviors of cultural legends and the stories about ancestral heroes. Legendary figures and rulers who embraced homosexuality conveyed to the general population that same-sex attractions and behavior were natural aspects of life.

Once, when the emperor Ai was resting with his favorite, Dong Xian, he was called away to attend to some urgent matters. As a token of his love, he preferred to cut off the sleeve of his garment rather than awaken his companion whose head was resting on it. Thus, homosexual love came to be known as the "passion of the cut sleeve" . . . Knowledge of, and lack of moral outrage about, such male favorites among the political elite of the Zhou, the legendary heroes of Chinese civilization, bespeaks a climate that has no particular moral objection to male-male love and sex merely because of the gender of the parties involved. (p. 22)

Just as homosexuality has a history of acceptance in different eras in Chinese history, acceptance of homosexuality can also be found within Japanese history and as part of Buddhist history.

Monkish sexual desire was typically that of an older monk for a younger. Indeed, among the Japanese . . . homosexual love was thought of as something that transpired between an older man and a younger . . . . We are not speaking here of an adventitious development within Japanese Buddhism, but indeed of an established, recognized spiritual path, the way of *shudo* or "boy love", which owes its origins to one of the great cultural figures not only in Japanese Buddhism, but in Japanese culture as well. None other than Kukai (774-835), the founder of the Shingon sect of Buddhism, is supposedly to have introduced the way of *shudo* into Japan. (Long, 2004, p. 112)

In some cultures, homosexual behavior has been mandated and institutionalized for the sake of creating masculinity within their male populations. This type of homosexual behavior was required regardless of whether or not love or same-sex sexual attraction was present among the societal members. As examples, Long (2004) described the Azande and Nzema tribes of Africa. "In the African cultures of Azande and the Nzema, young men might form 'marriages' with teenage boys until the former take wives and the latter take 'boy wives' themselves" (p. 5). Among these tribes, adolescent homosexuality is a central aspect for the development of masculinity and for their preparation, marriage, fatherhood, and the tasks of manhood. Even in the warrior tribe, the Sambians of Papua New Guinea, all prepubescent boys were required to have oral sex with older boys as a necessary part of their development into adult men (p. 20).

In striking contrast to many contemporary attitudes that have associated homosexuality with weakness and effeminacy, including those expressed by psychologists (Isay, 1989), to the Azanda, Mzemic, and Sambian tribes, homosexuality was an experience in which young men discovered the essence of masculinity. To these tribes, homosexuality was a mandated activity, a necessary part of adolescent initiation into adulthood, and an experience essential for manhood (p. 20).

The works of Ford and Beach (1952) and Long (2004) contribute new perspectives into the relationship of homosexuality and culture. In some cases, as seen above, homosexuality can be understood as a social benefit, or as a means by which young men become adults, and homosexual behavior is mandated for that purpose. In other cases, homosexuality that stems from same-sex attractions by individual men is embraced broadly within cultures. Still other cultures have held negative and restrictive attitudes about all forms of homosexuality. This pattern, in fact, can be seen throughout history, according to Louis Crompton (2003).

The history of civilization reveals, above all, how differently homosexuality has been perceived and judged at different times in different cultures. In classical Greece male love . . . was associated with courage in battle, philosophical mentorship and the defense of democracy . . . In Arab Spain and medieval France perceptions diverged . . . In the former, love between men was a romantic possibility constrained by a strict religious code; in the latter, sodomy was a filthy and unmentionable vice punishable at the stake. In China, the "southern fashion" called to mind the love of emperors . . . in Japan, *nanshoku* (male love) was associated with Buddhist saints, samurai warriors and the kabuki theatre . . . In eighteenth-century France . . . it was associated with the fashionable world, with Italy and with Greek philosophers. In the Netherlands, in the same age, it was a threat to national survival. (pp. xiii-xiv)

While no comprehensive coverage of homosexuality in history is possible in this brief summary, examples are useful and instructive in that they can broaden contemporary attitudes. Because this work is a study that examines homosexuality in the United States, a special emphasis is made below on the historical attitudes in Western civilizations out of which American attitudes have grown.

Homosexuality in the West

Socrates, born nearly 2500 years ago in ancient Greece, is today considered "one of the most powerful, intriguing, annoying, inspiring and widely known figures in the history of philosophy" (Soccio, 1998, p. 76). He is considered one of the chief architects of philosophical thought in Western civilization. He wrote nothing, and what we know of his thinking comes primarily from the writings of Plato (p. 76).

Plato's *The Symposium* (1999) is "one of the most striking and famous studies of love in Western thought" and has "been immensely influential on thinking about love from antiquity to the present day" (Gill, 1999, p. vii). Socrates, and the other men whose dialogue is recorded in *The Symposium* (1999), speak about the nature of love with a marked "emphasis on sexual relations between males" (p. vii). In fact, *The Symposium* (1999) is a dialogue about the nature of love told within the context of homoeroticism. Socrates, husband to Xanthippe and father of three (Soccio, 1998, p. 76), was also a lover of younger men. Through his dialogues about homosexual love, captured in the words of Plato, Socrates explored the depths of love, and subsequently, informed others about the nature of love for centuries to follow.

The Symposium (1999) is best known for its powerful philosophical implications but is also distinctive in its straightforward discussions about the homosexual feelings of its speakers. Plato's dialogues are full of allusions to Socrates' love of young men (Downing, 1989, p. 238). In one example noticed by Christine Downing (1989), Socrates is being teased about his infatuation with Alcibiades when the much older Socrates responds, "Then I saw what was inside his garments and I was aflame and beside myself" (p. 238). Later in his speech, the younger Alcibiades tells his audience "You see that Socrates is erotically attracted to beautiful boys, and is always hanging around them in a state of excitement" (Plato, 1999, p. 55). In fact, each of the men speaking in the dialogues, like Socrates, speaks about the nature of love in the context of the physical, sexual and emotional aspects of homosexual love.

To Plato and Socrates, as expressed in *The Symposium* (1999), the physical and sexual experience of homosexuality was a "stepping stone" toward a deeper and transcendent experience of love, a "necessary stepping stone whose absence would make that higher level impossible" (Downing, 1989, pg. 239). According to Downing (1989), "For the Platonic Socrates male love becomes the privileged path that leads to the growth of the soul, to creativity, and to the species of immortality available to humans (p. 240).

Sexual and emotional love between men was a necessary part of the experience of love and was part of a "privileged path" that led to the discovery of love's deeper nature. Through the experience of homosexual love, a man was on the path to the growth of his soul, was fully engaged in an act of creation, and had before him the potential of discovery of what could be known about immortal truth. This possibility existed in part because love, or Eros, was itself at the core of all things.

> The God (Eros), he said, is held in honor because he is one of the most ancient, as is provided by the fact: Eros has no parents and none are ascribed to him by prose writers or poets. Hersiod says that first Chaos came into existence and then,
>
> Broad-breasted Earth, a secure seat for everything for ever, and Eros. Acusilas agrees with Hersiod, saying that after Chaos two things came into existence, Earth and Eros. (Plato, 1999, pp. 9-10)

In Greek mythology, out of chaos, out of nothing-ness, came the earth and then came the creative force that caused all other things, Eros, or love. Eros, the energy of creation, was combined with the raw material of earth to form all of life and all things that could be known, seen or experienced. Among the greatest benefits of Eros, according to Plato's character Phaedrus, was the love between two men.

> On his origin, Parminides says that the very first God
> she devised was Eros, so Eros's great antiquity is widely
> accepted. Because of his antiquity, he is the source of our
> greatest benefits. I would claim that there is no greater
> benefit for a young man than a good lover and no greater
> for a lover than his boyfriend. (Plato, 1999, pp. 9-10)

Eros, the creative force of the world, the God who was the source of life's greatest benefits, was also the source of homosexual love to the Greeks of Plato's *The Symposium* (1999) and to their guide, Socrates. Such love was at the threshold, a "stepping stone" (Downing, 1989, p. 239) to wisdom and the discovery of love's nature. While volumes have been written about Plato's works, and much debate is possible about the role of homosexuality in them, it is clear that, among the ancient Greeks, homoeroticism was practiced, enjoyed, honored, fully part of the natural world, and above all, an expression of Eros, the creative energy of the world.

Among the ancient Greeks, Alexander the Great, born in 356 BCE, is considered one of the greatest generals and warriors in history, having conquered much of the known world in that time, and having accomplished that task before his death at age 33 (O'Brien, 1992, p. 223). Alexander and his life-long friend Hephaestion were homosexual lovers, according to O'Brien (1992). The relationship between Alexander and Hephaestion, a king and his close lieutenant, began in their youth and ended only upon Hephaestion's death. The loss devastated Alexander who wrote "my dear companion has perished . . . whom I loved beyond all other companions as well as my own life" (p. 58). While Alexander loved Hephaestion, he also married three women although at least two of those marriages were "blatantly political," done to some extent in order that the king should have an heir (p. 59). Homosexuality can be understood as an enduring aspect of Alexander's emotional life, perhaps the focus of his love and sexual life, yet it was merged with heterosexuality as well. As with many historical figures, Alexander's sexuality was not the source of his identification as an individual, gay or straight, but rather, sexuality was expressed in different directions for different purposes.

Homosexuality in Roman culture

> Julius Caesar incurred considerable disrespect for his relations with Nicomedes, King of Bithynia, because he was widely rumored to have been passive. Suetonius says that Dolabella called Caesar "the queen's rival". (Boswell, 1980, p. 75)

That Julius Caesar, among the most famous persons in Roman history, was widely known by his peers as having homosexual sexual relations is testament to John Boswell's (1980) assertion that the Roman era can be viewed as the "base period" of social tolerance in the Western world. "Roman society almost unanimously assumed that adult males would be capable of, if not interested in, sexual relations with both sexes" (p. 73). That Julius Caesar was ridiculed for being passive in homosexual relations is an indication that even in Rome, a society of enormous tolerance for sexuality, sexuality was in some ways directed and controlled. Aside from gender expectations, according to Boswell, (1980), "the major cause of the prejudice appears to have been a popular association of sexual passivity with political impotence" (p. 74).

The example of Julius Caesar's sexual affair with a foreign king suggests not only that the Roman era was a period of tolerance in which homosexuality was considered a natural expression of sexuality among men but also that homosexuality, like all sexuality, must be considered in the context of social attitudes. Like many other cultures listed above, Roman culture considered different aspects of sexual behavior with different levels of acceptance. Julius Caesar's passivity in sexual relations with another man generated significant social criticism, not because it was homosexual but, rather, because of the passive position he took during his sexual encounters. While generally considered a signal of political impotence on the part of adult male Romans, that stigma could not have been too severe as it did not affect the power wielded by Caesar. In fact, in part because of homosexuality's general acceptance as an aspect of male sexuality, it was integrated within the lives of some of Rome's most admired and powerful men.

> Nero married two men in succession, both in public ceremonies with the ritual appropriate to legal marriages . . . . Probably the most famous pair of lovers in the Roman world was Hadrian and Antinous. Hadrian (r.117-38) was the most outstanding of the "five good emperors" …. He appears to have been exclusively gay. (Boswell, 1980, pp. 81- 84)

The suggestion made in modern discussions of homosexuality that it is somehow antithetical to power, social order, institutional stability, or that it is uniformly disapproved of by majority populations in high functioning societies can be easily put to rest by the consideration of Rome during the era of the emperor Hadrian and his lover Antinous. According to Boswell, (1980), the emperor fell deeply in love with the young Greek. When Antinous died crossing the Nile, Hadrian "was heartbroken and wept like a woman." Antinous was deified. Hadrian had statues built in his honor throughout the empire and games were held in his honor for two centuries after his death (p. 84). In one of the most peaceful and prosperous periods of Roman civilizations, the emperor of Rome was exclusively homosexual. For two centuries after his death, Rome celebrated the life of the emperor's lover, another man.

Such public acceptance of homosexuality suggests that Roman society had little anxiety about homosexuality and that homosexuality was in no way considered to be the behavior of a minority. In fact, according to Boswell (1980), during the rule of Augustus, the government taxed homosexual prostitution and afforded boy prostitutes their own legal holiday (p. 84). To conclude, Boswell stated that "Neither the Roman religion nor Roman law recognized homosexual eroticism as distinct from—much less inferior to—heterosexual eroticism" (1980, p. 84).

Homosexuality throughout the centuries

Briefly, it is worth noting that shifts in attitudes about homosexuality during and after the fall of the Roman Empire occur with regularity throughout the centuries. In the first three centuries after Christ, according to Boswell (1980, p. 121), the Roman Empire was characterized by an "increasing absolutism" which resulted in a "greater and greater totalitarian control over personal aspects" including intolerance in sexual matters like homosexuality. Yet, the interference of the state in personal matters met resistance. Boswell (1980) cites many examples of the social debates of the time including the many passionate expressions of the value of homosexual love (pp. 124-136). Legal issues related to homosexuality changed slowly over time. In 342 CE, marriage between two men, which had been allowed previously, was outlawed (p. 123) but homosexual prostitution in Eastern Europe remained legal until the sixth century (p. 124). Throughout this period, Christian thought and attitudes varied as well, contrary to popular notions that Christianity's negative attitudes regarding homosexuality have been consistent over time. In fact, Christianity and homosexuality were often integrated. The first law outlawing homosexuality, placing it in the category of adultery, was not passed until 533 CE and was passed by civil authorities to undermine the bishops of the church who routinely engaged in homosexual activity (p. 171).

Shifts in attitudes about homosexuality, developing over the period of decades and centuries, are well documented by historians Crompton (2003) and Boswell (1980). Their discussions of homosexuality in history demonstrate that neither the total acceptance of homosexuality nor the denigration of it can be understood as a consistent social attitude over time. While there were some periods of intense hostility towards homosexuality, in other periods, homosexuality was celebrated and in some ways became an integral part of flourishing societies. An example of a period in history when homosexuality was especially celebrated, Boswell (1980) described the period between 1100 CE and 1250 CE as a period during which there was not only extraordinary achievement in many aspects of society but also a high degree of tolerance and admiration of gay people (p. 221).

Sprinkled throughout periods of history, both in times when homosexuality was expressed freely and those when it was disparaged, are the stories of individuals who were homosexual and acclaimed. As Freud (1910/1989) noticed, homosexuality and creative genius go hand-in-hand in the person of Leonardo da Vinci who, according to Freud, was a "universal genius whose outline can only be surmised, never defined" (p. 9). Likewise, Michelangelo, born on March 6, 1475, was a "colossus" of imagination. Michelangelo was homosexual and had an important and lasting relationship with one of his younger models, according to Rictor Norton (1973, pp. 148-149). Famed composer Tchaikovsky, 1840-1893, also found his first true love homosexually when, at 32 he fell deeply in love with Vladimir Shilofsky. At the younger man's death, Tchaikovsky married a woman, although the marriage was generally non-sexual and ended unhappily (Rowse, 1977, pp. 136-40).

Among the most famous men whose homosexuality became a public controversy, according to Rowse (1977), was Oscar Wilde (1856-1900), a married man, father of two, and famed playwright. At the height of his career and with the premier of *The Importance of Being Earnest* completed, Wilde fell in love with Lord Alfred Douglas, a young nobleman. The young man's father objected and Wilde was criminally charged for his sexual relations with the younger man. Wilde was convicted and sentenced to years of hard labor. His family, deeply shamed by his open expression of love for another male and by the public humiliation of the trial, disowned him, changing their last name to avoid any associations. Wilde was forced into bankruptcy and never wrote anything of significance after his years in prison. Although Wilde and Douglas renewed their relationship after his release from prison, Wilde was a "broken man" and died three years later (pp. 164-169).

Whether one speaks of the sadness in the story of a broken man like Oscar Wilde, of the heroics of Alexander the Great, the genius of Leonardo or the wisdom of Socrates, it is clear that homosexuality has been an important aspect in the lives of some of history's greatest figures. Homosexuality was an integrated part of their lives, who they were, what they accomplished, in what ways they failed, and of their legacies.

In the same way, homosexuality can be understood as an enduring part of cultural and social life throughout history, integrated and ever-present, and part of the legacy of those societies. In some cultures, homosexuality has prospered. In some cultures, homosexual acts have even been mandated for adolescents as part of their maturation. In others, homosexuality has been ridiculed and punished. Yet, it is clear that homosexuality has been part of the *prima materia* of social conversation and organization since the beginning of recorded history.

The influence of culture and society, no matter how restrictive, does not eliminate the appearance of homosexuality, as Ford and Beach (1952) noted. Homosexuality, as a natural part of human sexuality, appears in all cultures throughout history. At the same time, how homosexuality is understood by a society varies dramatically. As Ford and Beach (1952) stated, "Along with other members of his society each person finds certain opportunities and restriction provided by his culture which tend to mold his sexual behavior into a particular pattern" (p.17). The expression of homosexuality, whether freely and openly, with pride, defiance, or guilt, can be understood as a personal and psychological matter because each person relates to the environment in different ways. But, as the above demonstrates, every homosexual man or adolescent makes those choices within the context of his society.

Why different cultures respond to homosexuality in such different ways is unclear and the reasons for such disparate attitudes are no doubt highly complex. Some insight can be gained by reviewing surveys designed to evaluate contemporary cultural attitudes about sexuality, across many cultures, and to notice what factors influence permissive attitudes about sexuality today.

Widmer, Treas, and Newcomb (1998) surveyed attitudes of permissiveness about sexuality in 24 countries. Their survey considered attitudes in each country about extramarital sex, sex before marriage, and homosexual sex, combining answers within categories ranging from "always wrong" to "not at all wrong." In general, they found that the United States ranked as one of the least permissive countries in its attitudes about homosexuality, tied with Slovenia as the 19th least permissive country of the 24 countries surveyed. The United States ranked slightly above Bulgaria, Ireland, Hungary, and Northern Ireland as countries where large portions of the population considered homosexual sex as being "always wrong." The study concludes that "American sexual values are strikingly nonpermissive."

The authors considered religious attitudes as a possibility for the development of non-permissiveness but were struck by the number of countries, like Italy, with strong Catholic influence, that were more permissive than the United States. The authors concluded that non-permissive attitudes are not associated with Christian beliefs but are strongly associated with regular church attendance. In those countries where people participate directly in the institutions of Christianity, through regular attendance at church, attitudes have become less permissive. Countries where religion remains an important aspect of life, but where religious attitudes are more personally developed and maintained, outside formal church attendance, attitudes about sexuality are more permissive (Widmer et al., 1998).

While in no way does this research fully explain how non-permissive attitudes develop in society, the work of Widmer et al. (1998) does point to how important religion and religious beliefs may be in the formation of cultural attitudes. As is seen in the next chapter, the relationship between religion and homosexuality is complex and, for adolescents who struggle with homosexuality, a powerful relationship to be considered.

CHAPTER III

HOMOSEXUALITY, CHRISTIANITY AND MYTHOLOGY

Danny stopped going to church when he was 13. He recalled that it "just happened" one day as his family engaged in their usual Sunday morning routine. Sunday was a time to sleep in and breakfast seemed a more casual affair than on other days. The pace of the day was slower on Sundays at least until Danny's mother began to corral the family and instruct them to get ready for Mass. That day, as his siblings began to shower and dress, Danny stayed in his room. As his mother passed by the door he said simply, "I'm not going." His mother tried to change his mind and his father shouted at him, ordering him to go, but Danny did not. His father was "deeply disappointed" in him and their ongoing rift seemed to deepen as if Danny had now done something especially serious. Danny did not go that day or the next Sunday or any others but the fights began to dissipate over time and his parents eventually stopped asking him to go. "I don't believe in any of it," Danny confided to me. "It's all bullshit," he said, adding emphasis. In our conversations together, Danny did not associate his being gay with his loss of interest in going to church. Rather, Danny seemed to be investigating the whole notion of God and religion, exploring alternatives to Catholicism just as he was exploring alternatives in many areas of his psychological and physical life.

Known or unknown to him, Danny seemed engaged in a series of psychological explorations that had powerful ramifications. His exploration of homosexuality was both a point of self knowledge and affirmation but, also, a separation from the norm, from the majority, and from how he had imagined his life before. His exploration of God, beyond the confines of Catholicism, allowed him to say "I am independent" but with that statement came the correlate "I am a transgressor." Danny was a transgressor in the eyes of his mother and father, defiant in the face of the priest, the Church and perhaps God. Like all transgressors, Danny suffered the consequence of scorn but gained the freedom of seeing things from the outside. He allowed himself psychological space to explore alternatives, to play in the field of imagination, and to play and imagine about something as serious and powerful as God, the Father. It was play that was nearly unimaginable from inside Catholicism. With the conviction of adolescent courage, Danny could declare that God did not exist at all, or that God was just a silly story, or on one warm spring day, to say that God was like the sun and the trees and nature itself. "It is in everything," he said that day.

In the end, Danny did not settle on a new concept of God and his efforts to discover a new God did little to remove the remnants of the God he had known. Danny still referred to God as him. Danny still used the word sin. He continued to say that God was inside him and he continued to imagine that God believed homosexuality was sinful and wrong. Outside Catholicism and outside family, Danny was free to imagine but was not free to discard the seamlessly integrated ideas about God that had been incorporated since birth. "I think it's a sin," he said referring to homosexuality. "But, since everyone is a sinner anyway, what's the difference?" Danny was a sinner because of innate feelings he could not control. He hoped everyone else was as sinful.

Therapists wishing to help young men like Danny face an immediate question. In matters of religion, what is the role of psychotherapy? Is it appropriate to encourage Danny to reconsider his religious beliefs? Clearly, therapists might support any client in their consideration of religious alternatives yet advocacy of such a search is different. If Danny's school allowed active harassment of homosexual teens, many therapists might advocate a change in schools. If one parent was actively aggressive or violent towards Danny because he is gay, many therapists might feel it appropriate to advocate that Danny live with a more tolerant parent or other family member. Yet, if Danny's religious affiliation caused him shame, while other religious groups accepted him, is it appropriate to advocate that Danny change religions? Or should therapists accept the idea that religion is beyond the scope of psychology and that matters of spirituality are not changeable in the way other influences in his life are? Are therapists resigned to attempt to mitigate the effects of the shame and guilt that may result from religious beliefs and to do so in deference to any person's right to believe?

To some extent, the answer to these questions relates to a deeper one. Are religion and psychology separate fields of inquiry, separated by tradition, belief and practice or are they so integrated as to be inseparable? No answer to those questions is possible here but it is important to articulate the perspective of this work. Using the work of Carl Jung, Edward Edinger, Joseph Campbell, Christine Downing and others as a foundation, this work takes no position on the nature of God nor on the value of any religious tradition but does assume that all religious and spiritual beliefs are psychologically important and in many ways, are psychologically based. From this perspective, Danny's struggles with his religious beliefs, and especially when those beliefs collide with his homosexuality, can be seen as deeply internal and essential psychological questions that require the attention of psychotherapists.

As will be seen below, religious or spiritual stories, provided through institutional religions or mythological material, convey guidance to the human internal world. Sometimes, how we are to feel, what we are to value and cherish, and how we are to behave is given to us through the direct instruction of institutional religious leaders. In other cases, we are provided stories with which we must struggle to create meaning through interpretation. Homosexuality is described in many ways by various spiritual traditions and, to some extent, those teachings provide guidance to teenagers who have homosexual feelings, guidance that may either reassure them or cause them to resist their own internal world. Examples of male-male love, both physical and spiritual, abound in the stories and practices of Christianity, other religious institutions, different cultural legends and stories, and in mythology. Condemnations of homosexuality abound as well. Because Danny, and other teens, may use such material to guide their internal world, their decisions, the development of self-esteem or self-loathing, and the development of their relationship to themselves, a survey of this material is highly relevant to this work.

As mentioned previously, this work is focused on homosexuality in western cultures and the survey of religious and mythology below is largely restricted to western cultures as well. Beyond that, the survey of religious material is confined to Christianity for several important reasons. First, a thorough review of all major religions and their views about homosexuality is far too extensive a subject to be done accurately in this short work. Second, the teenagers upon which the composite cases are drawn for later chapters in this book were born into families who were Christian so that a discussion of Christianity is a useful foundation for those studies.

A third reason to focus on Christianity in this work is that, according to James Hillman (2004), Christianity has a deep influence on the lives of all westerners, believers and non-believers, known or not, conscious and unconscious. Because in many ways that influence is unconscious, Hillman (2004) believed that psychologically, "We are all Christians, regardless of the faith you profess, the church you attend, or whether you declare yourself utterly atheistic" (p. 190).

> You may be Jew or Muslim, pay tribute to your god in Santeria fashion, join with other Wiccas, but wherever you are in the Western world, you are psychologically Christian, indelibly marked with the sign of the cross in your mind and in the corpuscles of your habits. Christianity is all about us, in the words we speak, the curses we utter, the repressions we fortify, the numbing we seek . . . Once you feel your personal soul to be distinct from the world out there, and that consciousness and conscience are lodged in that soul (and not in the world out there) . . . you are psychologically Christian. Once your first response to a dream, a bit of news, an idea divides immediately into "good" or "bad", psychologically you are Christian . . . When you turn from books and learning and instead to your feelings to find simple answers to complexities, you are Christian, for the Kingdom of God and the voice of His true Word lies within. Once you feel sin in connection with your flesh and its impulses, again you are Christian. (p. 190)

Christianity, to Hillman (2004), is more than a faith to be practiced. Its messages, its formulation of feelings and sexuality into "good and bad," and its way of speaking about young men like Danny are deeply ingrained into the consciousness of all westerners. They are embedded in Danny's internal world as well. By examining Christianity, and other spiritual traditions and their mythologies, some clarity may be possible about not only the nature of homosexuality but also the hidden, embedded, seeds of doubt Danny has about himself. It can also be said that, in this review, young homosexual boys like Danny may find examples of male-male love in Christianity and throughout many cultures in the West that may help deepen their appreciation of their innate sexuality and its expression.

Homosexuality and Catholicism

The Catholic Church is an institution that can claim continuity throughout the centuries and therefore maintains that it has a unique capacity to speak on matters of spirituality. As the one continuous guardian of Christian theology, the Church has established its theological stance over centuries. As such, the Church regards itself as being integrated with tradition and scripture from the earliest days of Christianity and, therefore, in a way which is divinely guided.

> It is clear, therefore, that in the supremely wise arrangement of God, sacred Tradition, sacred Scripture, and the Magisterium of the Church are so connected and associated that one of them cannot stand without the others. (Vatican II: Dei Verbum 10, as cited by John Paul II, 1986, para. 10)

> It is likewise essential to recognize that the scriptures are not properly understood when they are interpreted in a way which contradicts the Church's living tradition. (John Paul II, 1986, para. 11)

While recognizing the findings of science, the Church considers its views on matters of morality, spirituality and Christianity to be grounded in "human reason illumined by faith" which, to the Church, provides a richer perspective on human life (John Paul II, 1986, para. 3). Given the biological and genetic findings of science about homosexuality, discussed previously, understanding the Church's viewpoint on the relationship of the Church and the science of homosexuality is useful. According to John Paul II (1986), the Church may learn from scientific discovery but is also able to "transcend the horizons of science," feeling confident that its vision "does greater justice" to the human experience (para. 3). In this way, the Church considers that its viewpoint may, in some cases, disregard even the findings of science. With this in mind, the views of the Church represent, especially to Catholics, a profound and powerful voice that defines what Christianity represents and how one is to live within a Christian context.

The Catholic Church, under the leadership of John Paul II, issued the *Letter to the Bishops of the Catholic Church on the Pastoral Care of Homosexual Persons* in 1986, which set out the Church's views on homosexuality. In it, John Paul II recounts that in 1975, the Church's *Declaration on Certain Questions Concerning Sexual Ethics* had made a distinction between homosexual tendencies and homosexual acts and had noted that homosexual acts were in "no case to be approved of" (para. 5). According to John Paul II, after the release of that document, discussions in the Catholic community had begun to make an "overly benign" interpretation of homosexuality so much so that some had gone so far as to "call it neutral or even good" (para. 6). John Paul II's 1986 letter was intended to clarify the Church's view about homosexuality and to redirect the clergy from that more "benign" view. In it, he stated "Therefore special concern and pastoral attention should be toward those who have this condition, lest they be led to believe that the living out of this orientation in homosexual activity is a morally acceptable option. It is not" (para. 7).

In his letter, John Paul II seeks to establish a comprehensive statement on homosexuality. In 2003, he also issued *Considerations Regarding Proposals to Give Legal Recognition to Unions Between Homosexual Persons*, which addressed the issue of same-sex marriages. Between the two documents, supplemented by the Catechism of the Catholic Church, John Paul II sought to clarify issues related to many aspects of the "troubling moral and social phenomenon" of homosexuality (Introduction section, para. 1).

First, John Paul II recognizes that homosexuality has existed throughout history and suggests that it may be constitutional for some.

> Homosexuality . . . . has taken a great variety of forms through the centuries and in different cultures . . . . The number of men and women who have deep-seated homosexual tendencies is not negligible. (*Catechism of the Catholic Church*, Part 3, Sec 2, Chapter 2).

> This judgment of Scripture does not, of course, permit us to conclude that all those who suffer from this anomaly are personally responsible for it. (John Paul II, 1986, "The Nature of Marriage," para. 8)

A second tenet of the Catholic view of homosexuality, described in the 1975 *Declaration on Certain Questions Concerning Sexual Ethics* and in Pope John Paul's letters, is that a distinction must be made between homosexual feelings, or an orientation, and homosexual behavior or sex. To John Paul II (1986), "the particular inclination of the homosexual person is not a sin" but the inclination is "ordered toward an intrinsic moral evil," the act of sex between men (para. 6). "Sacred Scripture condemns homosexual acts 'as a serious depravity' . . . homosexual acts are intrinsically disordered" (John Paul II, 2003, "The Nature of Marriage," para. 8). Further, although a homosexual inclination is not sinful, to John Paul II, it is a tendency that is "ordered toward" something intrinsically evil and therefore, the inclination is considered an objective disorder (Para. 6).

In general, then, Catholicism accepts that homosexuality is "not negligible", has been within the human population for centuries, and that it may be constitutional as a sexual orientation. The Church accepts that homosexual orientations in themselves are not sinful but are directed so completely toward a sin that they must be considered morally objectionable. Homosexual sex is intrinsically disordered and a moral evil.

The Church, through its communications to the clergy, prescribes the Catholic solution for homosexual persons.

> As in every conversion from evil, the abandonment of homosexual activity will require a profound collaboration of the individual with God's liberating grace . . . They are called to enact the will of God in their life by joining whatever sufferings and difficulties they experience in virtue of their condition to the sacrifice of the Lord's Cross . . . . The Cross is a denial of self, but in service to the will of God himself who makes life come from death and empowers those who trust in him to practice virtue in place of vice . . . . To refuse to sacrifice one's own will in obedience to the will of the Lord is effectively to prevent salvation. (John Paul II, 1988, para. 28-32)

Homosexuality, as a spiritual matter within Catholicism, is evil and immoral, especially when sexual feelings are acted upon. Through a denial of one's own feelings and actions, in the way Christ sacrificed himself on the Cross, a homosexual person must endure suffering in this life to find salvation. According to the *Catechism of the Catholic Church*, homosexuals are called to chastity and perfection. "Homosexual persons are called to chastity. By the virtues of self-mastery that teach them inner freedom . . . . they can and should gradually and resolutely approach Christian perfection" (2006, Part 3, Section 2, Chapter 2, Article 6).

To give some context, it should be noted that the Catholic Church uses similar language to describe other sexual activity outside of marriage. As examples, the *Catechism* addresses other common human issues involving sex.

> Lust is disordered desire for inordinate enjoyment of sexual pleasure. Sexual pleasure is morally disordered when sought for itself . . . Both the Magesterium of the Church . . . and the moral sense of the faithful have been in no doubt and have firmly maintained that masturbation is an intrinsically and gravely disordered action . . . Pornography . . . is a grave offense. (2006, Part Three, Section Two, Chapter Two, Article 6)

Homosexuality and all non-procreative sexual acts are objected to by the Church because they do not reflect or perpetuate God's creation through procreation. Specifically, homosexuals are not reflective of God's nature because they do not reflect God's inner unity.

> God, in his infinite wisdom and love, brings into existence all of reality as a reflection of his goodness. He fashions mankind, male and female, in his own image and likeness. Human beings, therefore, are nothing less that the work of God himself; and in the complimentary of

the sexes, they are called to reflect the inner unity of the Creator. (John Paul II, 1988, para. 12)

Homosexual acts close the sexual act to the gift of life. They do not proceed from a genuine affective and complimentarity. Under no circumstances can they be approved" (John Paul II, 2003, "The Nature of Marriage," para. 7).

John Paul II links heterosexuality with the divine image of God and in the complimentary relationship of man and women, John Paul II sees the act of procreation as the extension of God's creation. From this point of view, homosexual sex is not reflective of God.

John Paul II (1986) cites Biblical references in support of the Church's prohibition against homosexual sex. Among those citations are Leviticus and the Gospel of St. Paul in Corinthians and Romans, among others.

The Church's doctrine regarding this issue is thus based ... on the solid foundation of a constant Biblical testimony. The community of faith today, in unbroken continuity with the Jewish and Christian communities within which the ancient Scriptures were written, continues to be nourished by those same Scriptures and by the Spirit of Truth whose Words they are. (para. 10)

Following John Paul II, Pope Benedict XVI continued to consider homosexuality a "strong tendency ordered toward an intrinsic evil." According to Donadio (2013), the most recent Pope, Francis, took a much more compassionate tone when speaking about homosexuality in 2013. In fact, Pope Francis made headlines throughout the world when he used the word gay and said "If someone is gay and he searches for the Lord and has good will, who am I to judge?" This new tone represents, according to Donadio (2013), a revolutionary change in tone although Vatican officials, soon after Pope Francis spoke, were quick to point out that Francis never veered from church doctrine opposing homosexuality (Donadio, 2013).

As a psychological matter, the question of how a Catholic homosexual man or adolescent is to see himself in relation to God must be asked. Clearly, such a question depends on the individual and many possible answers are possible. Yet, on the surface, it is likely that he must consider that he does not and cannot mirror God's essence when that essence is described in the context of the further creation of mankind through procreation and marriage. Catholic homosexual men and teens must accept that, at the Church's direction, their feelings are a serious depravity that will lead them to acts which are disordered. Psychologically, their bodies generate "disordered" feelings which, like all sexuality, occur spontaneously and from a place beyond conscious control. In this way, homosexuals engage in an inner warfare, pitting their natural and bodily lives against their spiritual lives, pitting the nature of what has been created against the wishes of the Creator. Catholic homosexuals are provided a path that includes the denial of self, a life of suffering, and the obligation to strive for perfection.

Homosexuality and other Christian faiths

Other Christian religious institutions continue to debate the meaning of Biblical references and how Christianity should view homosexuality. Within the Anglican Church, for instance, a series of conferences have occurred over the past decades in which many differing views have been expressed and honored. As an example, the 1998 Lambeth Conference issued a statement that stated it could not agree on the scriptural, theological, historical and scientific issues raised by the study of homosexuality. The report then summarized the differing views without privileging any one.

> Our variety of understanding encompasses: Those who believe that homosexual orientation is a disorder . . . Those who believe that relationships between people of the same gender should not include genital expression . . . Those who believe that committed homosexual relationships fall short of the Biblical norm, but are to be preferred to relationships that are anonymous and transient . . . Those who believe that the Church should accept and support or bless monogamous covenant relationships between homosexual people and that they may be ordained. (Anglican House of Bishops, 2003, p. 30)

In its book, *Some Issues in Human Sexuality: A Guide to the Debate* (2003), the Anglican House of Bishops discusses the many differing views that guide current Christian thinking about homosexuality and notices that some churches such as the Church of Christ in the USA and the United Church of Canada "have moved to an official acceptance of homosexual relationships and a willingness to ordain those in such relationships" (p. 21). Perhaps among the most publicized such ordination was the ordination of Gene Robinson as the first openly gay Bishop in the Episcopal Church, the Anglican body in the United States, in 2003. The ordination of Robinson created a significant split within the Anglican Church and rival Episcopalian churches have developed as alternatives in the United States ("Episcopal Church Ordains," 2010).

Debate about homosexuality within the Christian community is widespread. In June, 2006, the governing body of the Presbyterian

Church (USA) met to debate differing views on gay clergy and same-sex unions and whether the denominational rulings or local churches should have the ultimate say (Grossman, 2006, p. 2). The former head of the Presbyterian Church USA, the Rev. Jack Rogers, saw these struggles with homosexuality as being similar to theological arguments of the past about African Americans and women among others. "They were all cursed by God in Scriptures, inferior in moral character and willfully sinful and deserving punishment. Eventually, most churches found a biblical basis for changing their stance on race and gender but not on homosexuality" (Grossman, 2006, p. 2). The Evangelical Lutheran Church in America began a four-year process in 2008 to consider its views on ordaining gay clergy and blessings for same sex unions. In other Christian communities, including the largest denominations in the United States, Roman Catholics, Southern Baptists, and the Church of Jesus Christ of Latter Day Saints, there is a firm belief that homosexuality is sinful (p. 2).

As mentioned, religious denunciation of homosexuality is typically based on two primary issues. First, Christian groups base their objections to homosexuality on the idea of the complementary nature of man and women. In this view, it is only through the bonding of the opposite sexes that God's creation of mankind can be continued through procreation. The second major basis for the criticism of homosexuality is the citation of passages within Scripture.

It should be noted that only a few of the many thousands of scriptural verses in the Bible deal with homosexuality directly (Helminiak, 2000). It should also be noted that many theologians and historians interpret those scriptural passages in very different ways (Boswell, 1980; Helminiak, 2000; Anglican House of Bishops, 2003). Yet, some scriptural passages declare that homosexuality is sinful or wrong and, as such, they provide a basis for those who condemn homosexuality as unnatural or sinful.

While no extensive review of these scriptural arguments is possible here, an example of how one such passage can be understood is useful. Perhaps the most often cited denunciation of homosexuality in the Bible is Leviticus in which the teaching is direct and clear. "You will not have intercourse with a man as you would a woman" (Lev. 18:22). While many argue that this admonition is clear and determinative of how Christianity views homosexuals, others argue that when the Bible is interpreted in such literal ways, modern Christians face a problem of consistency. If Christians are to accept Leviticus's statement on homosexuality in a literal way, then they must, the argument goes, accept the other statements contained in Leviticus.

> You will not wear a garment made from two kinds of fabric (19:19). You may eat any animal that has a cloven hoof, divided into two parts . . . the following which either chew the cud or have a cloven foot, are the ones you may not eat (3:3). If anyone vows the value of a person to Yahweh and wishes to discharge the value . . . a man between twenty and sixty will be valued at fifty silver shekels . . . between five and twenty years, a boy will be valued at twenty shekels, a girl at ten shekels . . . (27:3). The man who commits adultery with his neighbor's wife will be put to death, he and the woman (20:10).

As author and Episcopal Priest Daniel Helminiak explains, any interpretation of the Bible requires some consideration about the context in which it was written and therefore, how it is "read." Literal readings of Scripture can often lead to the problem posed by the above citation of Leviticus. Modern Christians who claim that Leviticus must be accepted in an exclusively literal way about homosexuality are generally unlikely to suggest that modern society should value a boy or a girl in monetary ways nor are they likely to suggest that the death penalty is appropriate for adultery. To Helminiak (2000), a more useful approach to the understanding of the Bible's meaning is to approach it through "historical-critical reading" (pg. 33).

> The literal reading claims to take the text simply for what it says. This is the approach of Biblical Fundamentalism...The rule is that a text means whatever it means to somebody reading it today . . . . Compare the other approach, the historical-critical reading. The rule is that the text means whatever it meant to the people who wrote it long ago. To say what a biblical text teaches us today, you have to first understand the text in its original situation and then apply meaning to the present situation . . . Although on TV and radio we generally hear only the fundamentalist approach, all the mainline Christian churches support the historical-critical method . . . . Of course, some of the churches back off the critical- historical method when it comes to the Bible texts on homosexuality and some other questions—like divorce, the place of women in society and church. (p. 33)

Another consideration to be made when using Biblical references about homosexuality is that in many such conversations, as seen below, there remains a perception that what is contained in modern versions of the Bible is the exact content of the Biblical documents and Christian teachings of 2,000 years ago. According to Boswell (1980), the content of the Bible has changed over centuries.

The "Bible" was not disseminated in the early church in the form in which it came to be known later. Early Christians read and venerated many books now rejected as apocryphal.... Roman Catholicism did not officially establish the canon of the Bible until the Council of Trent in 1546. (p. 92)

Christian fundamentalism in the United States typically accepts literal readings of the Bible regarding homosexuality. The late Jerry Falwell, a leading social and religious critic of homosexuality throughout the 1980s and 1990s, understood the Bible to be the literal word of God and accepted the idea that the modern version of the Bible contains the word of God transcribed exactly. From that standpoint, Falwell (2000) considered homosexuality to be unnatural.

I believe with all my heart that the Bible is the infallible word of God. Men wrote as God dictated it through them. Forty men wrote and recorded scripture—they were the instruments—the Holy Spirit was the author, and every word is therefore pure . . . . I believe that we are all born heterosexual—physically created with a plumbing that's heterosexual, and comes with instincts and desires that are basically heterosexual. (pp. 5-7)

Falwell created the Moral Majority, a social, religious and political organization dedicated to the preservation of what it considers to be Christian values (2000, p. 5). Other groups, such as the Family Research Council, which combine conservative Christian religious attitudes and social activism, have followed Falwell's lead. They too condemn homosexuality.

Family Research Council believes that homosexual conduct is harmful to the persons who engage in it and to society at large, and can never be affirmed. It is by definition unnatural, and as such is associated with negative physical and psychological health effects. ("Homosexuality," 2011)

To some extent, these conservative Christian and fundamentalist groups see homosexuality as a personal problem. At the same time, these groups, by actively working for a broader social rejection of homosexuality, suggest that homosexuality is a social problem as well. They tend to believe, sometimes emphatically, that their beliefs are in line with God's. As an example, when asked if it was possible that he was mistaken about homosexuality, Jerry Falwell (2006) replied, "Only if God is mistaken" (p. 5). Groups like the Moral Majority or Family Research Council typically articulate that their group's views are the views of many people, if not the majority of people, and that those views are completely consistent with God's wishes. In this way, the group's views are empowered by both the people, a majority, and God's wishes. In other words, the majority of people's view of homosexuality is the same as God's and all agree with the denunciation of homosexuality. Such a trend, according to historian John Boswell (1980), is not new.

In the Middle Ages this development was captured in the shibboleth *Vox populi vox Dei*—"The voice of the people is the voice of God" … this principle also proved fatal to persons—like Jews, gay people and "witches"— whose life-styles differed from those of the majority: a voice not in harmony with that of "the people" was ipso facto out of harmony with God's preferences, and

86

if a majority of people disliked gay people, then so did God (p. 38).

When social attitudes against homosexuality are merged with the "word of God" in this way, young men like Danny and other gay people, Christian or not, face a powerful combination of negativity with which they must contend.

That Christianity is the source of criticism about sexuality was of interest to authors like Carl Jung. He noticed the ongoing difficulty western religion has with the problem of sexuality in general and saw it as a conflict contained in the depths of the psyche. To Jung, instinct and the desire for a spiritual life were both contained within the individual and expressed collectively. Instinct and sexuality came first.

> The conflict between ethics and sex today is not just a collision between instinctuality and morality, but a struggle to give an instinct its rightful place in our lives and to recognize in this instinct a power which seeks expression . . . cannot be trifled with . . . and cannot be made to fit within our well meaning moral laws. We could call sexuality a spokesman for the instincts which is why from the spiritual standpoint sexuality is the chief antagonist . . . because the spirit senses in sexuality a counterpart equal and indeed akin to itself. For just as the spirit would press sexuality into its service, so sexuality has an ancient claim upon the spirit which it once—in procreation, pregnancy, birth and childhood—contained within itself. (Jung, 1948/1960b, p. 57)

According to Jung, a child is born with an "immense split" in his make-up. On one hand, he is the container of instinct and on the other, the carrier of an "age old" capacity for consciousness, including consciousness of the divine. "Thus in the child- psyche the natural condition is already opposed by a spiritual one and this opposition is the expression, and perhaps also the basis, of the tension we call psychic energy" (1948/1960b, pp. 51-52).

Gilbert Herdt (2005) wrote extensively about religious and spiritual practices that have incorporated sexuality symbolically. He agreed with Jung that sexuality has been perceived by religion to be a difficult force to control and define, stating that "indeed, much of the religious concern with sexuality boils down to the question of how sexuality can be canalized" (p. 4111).

Male love and Christianity

Theologically, liturgically and institutionally, Catholicism privileges an all-male structure whose goal is to encourage and nurture, through a series of male controlled practices and beliefs, a profound love for another male (deity). (Kripal, 2005, pp. 8241-8247)

Some authors, like Kripal (2005) argue that male-male love is present in much of Christianity and its religious ceremonies, although clearly not explicitly sexual in nature. Much of the Christian tradition is organized around the love between masculine figures, both spiritual entities and human beings. Christianity begins with God, the Father whom all men are called to love. It includes, Christ the Son, who loves all humans and loves the father. Even Satan, the dark force of Christian thought, is a man, the fallen son of God. The Catholic Mass is conducted by men who through their presence provide an intermediary between the people and the masculine Christ and Father-God. Given that Catholic clergy are required to be celibate, one essential aspect of Catholicism can be thought of as love between men absent sexual acts. According to Boisvert and Goss (2005), "Traditional Roman Catholic theology supports the concept of priest as the liturgical impersonation of Christ . . . and the Catholic laity is . . . to understand Christ as sexless" (pp. 128-129).

Love between men and the masculine, without sex, is seen symbolically as the path to the divine. While largely a masculine affair, Christian mythology includes aspects of the feminine that are required for the love between the masculine to occur. According to John Boswell (1980), just as the Virgin Mary was the way in which Christ was delivered in earthly form, Catholic Priests are to be seen as incorporating the feminine as a means to deliver the congregation to the masculine divine. "The priest, like the figure of Mary . . . gives birth to Christ's presence on the altar" (p. 130).

Jungian analyst Robert Hopke (1989) stated that in some ways, priests represent the androgynous aspect of the psyche in that the priest, symbolically, merges both masculine and feminine into the integrated psychological whole. Because the priest not only attends to the spiritual aspect of a congregation but also to social issues, educational needs and the caretaking of the community, the role of the Catholic priest is in many ways comparable to the androgynous, Native American Berdache who provide such duties to the community (p.182).

In other words, throughout Catholic symbolism, one finds the suggestion that masculine love can be transcendent. Such love is masculine but sexless. Catholic theology provides a mechanism for the inclusion of the feminine through the androgynous priest. More importantly, Christianity provides for the direct involvement of the feminine, and women symbolically, through the Virgin Mary, who is the necessary conduit for the experience of this transcendent love.

In some ways, this symbolism of love between masculine figures, facilitated by the feminine, is not dissimilar to the discussion of love in *The Symposium* (1999) discussed previously. In *The Symposium*, Socrates describes love between men as transcendent and he states that he learned his knowledge of love's transcendent quality from the feminine figure Diotoma (Plato, 1999, p. 44). In some ways, in both *The Symposium* and in Catholic symbolism, one can see a predominantly male version of love that transcends the body which is made known and made possible only through the intervention of the feminine. One obvious distinction between these two views of masculine love, of course, is that in Catholicism sexual love between men is considered immoral (Pope John Paul II, 1986, p.1), while in the Socratic version, sex between men is a necessary "stepping stone" to transcendent love (Downing, 1989, p. 239).

God-imagery

What one means by the word God and in what context that word is used are important considerations for this work. As mentioned before, this work takes no position whatsoever on the nature of God but must allow for the discussion of the psychological aspects of religion and of an individual's relationship to "God." As a psychological matter, how an individual conceptualizes God and how that image changes over time is significant in its implications for many other aspects of the individual's life. Psychologically, those images of God are not the same thing as God but are created from within the individual person. Authors like Campbell and Jung have attempted to clarify this issue.

> But the transcendent is unknowable and unknown.
> God is transcendent, finally, of anything like the name
> of "God." God is beyond name and forms. (Campbell,
> 1988, p. 49)

It is the fault of the everlasting contamination of object and imago that people can make no conceptual distinction between "god" and "god-image" and therefore think that when one speaks of god image one is speaking of god. (Jung, 1948/1960a, p. 278)

From a psychological perspective, as Carl Jung (1948/1960b) noted, a fundamental distinction must first be made between God, an unknowable entity, and the image of God humans create psychologically. As noticed above and throughout this work, the way different religious groups imagine God varies from group to group although all Christian groups would agree there is a God. Likewise, God images vary from culture to culture and collective God images vary throughout history told through myths and religious stories that evolve over centuries. Yet, the image one holds of God, despite not being the same thing as God, remains a powerful influence in many lives. How one imagines God may well give direction to a life and may determine what is meaningful. How one imagines God may provide guidance for the resolution of crisis' and life's problems. As such, God images are powerful aspects of psychological life and an important aspect for psychological investigation. A considerable number of theoretical works and quantitative studies have been done to investigate how humans form God images and while the literature listed below is not comprehensive, it does support the concept that psychological influences are profoundly important.

Both Sigmund Freud and Erik Erikson postulated theories that suggest that the formation of God-images occurs very early in child development (Goodwin, 1998, p. 96). In *Freud and Erikson: Their contribution to the Psychology of God-Image Formation*, Antoinette Goodwin (1998) notes Freud believed that an infant's mother and father, and the movement of feeling between them, created what he termed "the father of personal pre-history" which then became the basis for a child's concept of God. This image creates an "ideal" image to which the child's ego relates internally (p. 97).

Erik Erikson believed, according to Goodwin (1998), that in order to develop, an infant must first develop trust in his parents and in the external world. Erikson believed that an infant carried a deep desire to build a bond of unity with a "maternal matrix," based on the mother, which translated psychologically into a desire for wholeness. This movement toward wholeness becomes, to Erikson, the basis for the search for spirituality. Concurrently, a child develops a relationship to the paternal influence in his family, based psychologically on the father, which Erikson suggests creates a sense of conscience. Based on the child's relationship to this "conscience," the child may feel confident and able to show initiative, or conversely, may struggle with issues like guilt and shame (pp. 111-112).

In *A Developmental Perspective on the God-Image*, Louis Hoffman (2005) suggested that the formation of God-imagery is "primarily based on the process of experience and maybe mostly unconscious" (p. 129). He noted that humans develop concepts of mother, father, siblings, and the world around them through experience that modifies those concepts over time. Through the senses, through communication and interaction, one's understanding of others and their environment evolve over time. In the case of the concept of God, no such direct interaction, in a physical way, is possible. To Hoffman, the development of God-imagery must therefore be the result of one's intuitive, abstract thinking and unconscious processes (p. 130).

Other theorists and researchers have offered other perspectives, sometimes through quantitative studies, in order to understand the psychological formation of God- imagery.

Dickie et al. (1997) explored the family structure and parental influences in relationship to the way God was imagined. In *Parent-Child*

Relationships and Children's Images of God, the authors noted that the characteristics one imagines in God are closely tied to the relationships and perceptions one has of one's parents.

> For men, mothers were responsible, more than fathers, for creating a climate for son's self-esteem through nurturance and discipline, which in turn contributed to seeing God as nurturing and powerful, feeling close to God, and being more religious. Punishing/judging parents directly affected punishing/judging God-images in these young adults. Men perceived God to be more punishing/judging than did women . . . . Parents do influence directly and indirectly the ways in which children perceive God. Regardless of race, socioeconomic status, or religious affiliation, children in our studies reported thinking about God often and perceiving God as similar to their parents in qualities of nurturance and power. (p. 25)

Other authors suggest that the image one has of God may also be formed out of life experience itself. For example, Sharon Shakel (2001) in *The Effects of Parental Death During Childhood On Adult Experience of God,* researched the effects of loss of a parent on how participants in her study imagined God. To Shakel, "Those people who lost a parent to death . . . were more likely than controls to experience God as more distant, inaccessible, impersonal and mythical" (p. 6149).

Dimitris Pnevmatikos (2002) in *Conceptual Changes in Religious Concepts of Elementary Schoolchildren: The Case of the House Where God Lives* studied the ways in which children imagined God and how those images shifted in childhood and in adolescence. Pnevmatikos studied the relationship of children in Christian primary school to their image of

God by asking them to draw the house where God lived. He found that children often drew images of God's house based on the teachings they had heard from parents, church or school so that in early childhood, images of God and his house were seen literally. God was drawn in human form and he lived in an actual house, often a church (p. 103). By late childhood, God was more often symbolized using a crucifix or star but was also depicted as a supervisor, or a special, helping man (p. 106). By adolescence, God was thought of in a highly individualistic way and was generally described in abstract terms and often as spirit. While children in early childhood imagined God as external, living in a house some other place, by adolescence, God was imagined more often as being spiritual energy and internal to the individual (p. 107).

While not discussed by these authors, the research suggests that homosexual teenagers are faced with an internalization of God imagery at puberty, a time of sexual awakening. The research suggests that their image of God will have been informed unconsciously based on their parents and social attitudes, including their beliefs about homosexuality. A psychological conflict of enormous difficulty is suggested for teens who believe that God disapproves of homosexuality when both God and homosexual feelings are internally experienced and beyond conscious control. In short, gay teens face a struggle of "me versus me" where sexuality and God are at war.

Homosexuality and mythology

Another way to understand the relationship of an individual—in this case a young man like Danny—to God, the Creator, is to consider Danny's relationship to the stories about the divine told as myth and religious story. As seen throughout this work, as a result of the effort of many authors, all cultures and religions have guiding mythologies that tell the stories of how life began and how human beings relate to the power of the cosmos. Mythologies vary from culture to culture and change over time. Mythologies and religious stories are created and abandoned, but to authors like Joseph Campbell (1988), myth, including religious myth, represents a profound need and desire in human life.

> I think what we are looking for is a way of experiencing the world that will open to us the transcendent that informs it, and at the same time forms ourselves within it. (p. 53)

> Every mythology has to do with the wisdom of life as related to a specific culture at a specific time. It integrates the individual into his society and the society into the field of nature. It unites the field of nature with my nature. (p. 55)

Seen from Campbell's perspective, myth integrates the individual, culture and the transcendent. It expresses the wisdom that guides a life and a culture. Myth allows humans to see their own nature as being consistent with the nature of all things. In many ways, religious stories from Christianity can be seen as mythology because when one is Christian, the divine, human nature and wisdom are expressed in the stories of Christ and others. The stories of Christianity guide the Christian faithful. As Campbell (1988) noticed, mythology is specific to culture and time but all cultures have guiding myths (p. 55). Integrated within mythology are typically stories of how all things were created.

Discussing creation mythology, Marie Louise von Franz (1995) emphasized the special significance that creation myths have had for human beings.

> Creation myths are the deepest and most important of all myths . . . they refer to the most basic problems

of human life, for they are concerned with ultimate meaning, not only of our existence, but of the existence of the whole cosmos. (p. 1)

The story of creation in Christianity tells the story of the Father-God who created the world and all humans. It does not address sexuality, much less homosexuality.

> In the beginning, God created heaven and earth . . . God said, 'Let there be light' . . . God said, 'Let there be a vault through the middle of the waters to divide the waters into two' . . . . God said 'Let the waters under heaven come together in a single mass, and let dry land appear' . . . God said 'Let there be lights in the vault in heaven to divide day from night' . . . God said 'Let the waters be alive with a swarm of living creatures' . . . God said 'Let the earth produce every kind of living creature' . . . God said ' Let us make man in our own image, in the likeness of ourselves' . . . On the seventh day God completed the work he had been doing. He rested on the seventh day after all the work he had been doing. God blessed the seventh day and made it holy, because on that day he rested after all his work of creating. [Genesis: 1:1]

In comparison, as mentioned previously, Greek mythology describes the fundamental creative force of the universe as being love, or Eros, out of which sexuality and homosexuality emerge (Plato, 1999).

> The God (Eros), he said, is held in honor because he is one of the most ancient, as is provided by the fact: Eros

has no parents and none are ascribed to him by prose writers or poets. Hersiod says that first Chaos came into existence and then, Broad-breasted Earth, a secure seat for everything for ever, and Eros. Acusilas agrees with Hersiod, saying that after Chaos two things came into existence, Earth and Eros. (Plato, 1999, pp. 9-10)

From Eros and matter came the story of how humans came to be and how they experienced love thereafter. Told by Aristophanes in *The Symposium* (Plato, 1999), the creation of human beings is a matter of love, sexuality including homosexuality, and the erotic yearning for another person that is divinely inspired. In his story, once upon a time, human beings were originally round figures with four arms and four legs who rolled instead of walking. Each human had one head with two faces and two sets of genitals. Some had both male and female genitals, others had two sets of female genitals, and the rest had two sets of male genitals. Fearful of the pride and power of the humans, the gods decided to keep humans preoccupied so that they would not storm the heavens. Zeus split each round, double sided human into two beings, with one set of genitals each, with the faces and genitals positioned on the front of their bodies. Humans, thereafter, became focused on the search for their other half, so much so that they no longer disturbed the gods. Those beings that originally had the genitals of both sexes had been split into humans of opposite sexes and therefore sought to unify with a member of the opposite sex. Those who originally had two sets of female genitals became female beings who sought out the sexual company of other females and those with male genitals became males who sought out other males for love and sex. Quoting *The Symposium*, "While they're boys, because they were sliced from the male gender, they fall in love with men, they enjoy sex with men and they like to be embraced by men" (Plato, 1999, pp. 24-27).

The mythologies of ancient Greece expressed the idea that Eros was the force of creation and that love, heterosexual and homosexual, is fully part of the divine. While Christianity addresses sexuality in its broader religious stories, human sexuality is not part of the story of creation cited above. One must look to the institutions of Christianity, or read the stories of the Bible, to begin to consider how humans are to relate to human sexuality. As interpreted today, the institutions of Christianity state that their religious stories, or myths, demonstrate that homosexuality is immoral (Pope John Paul II, 1988).

Mythology, beyond creation myth, has another important function in human experience in that each culture, through its mythology, provides guidance for how one is to understand the experience of being alive. In many ways, mythological stories articulate the nature of consciousness in human life. According to Christine Downing (1989), Greek mythology expresses both the light and dark aspects of human experience as well as the divine. The gods and goddesses represented the "eternal aspects of human experience," both pleasing and displeasing. To Downing, the gods and goddesses "illumine our lives" (p. 147).

Greek mythology articulates a view that the divine and humans were in constant interaction so that human experience included the divine in daily life. The divine was part of homosexual love, just as humans were. To Downing, (1989), "None of the Greek gods or goddesses is a homosexual, but most are seen as attracted to members of their own sex and to members of the other" (p. 147). The most famous such story involves Zeus, "the dominant figure in the Greek pantheon." In the story, Zeus becomes enamored by the youthful beauty of the young, blond Ganymede "who was the loveliest born of the race of mortals." Zeus abducts the young Ganymede, taking him to the heavens to be forever with the gods (P. 149).

As it is expressed throughout its mythology, the culture of ancient Greece understood homosexuality as being more than simply a sexual act. Homosexuality was an expression of creation, a natural state of affairs for both men and gods, and youthful males could well be the objects of desire for the gods. The expression of love between men was more than romantic. It was also an act of creation and an extension of the cosmos.

It is important to recognize here that adolescents today, young men like Danny who are homosexual, belong to a different culture than the one experienced by Socrates and Aristophanes. They live in a culture dominated largely by Christianity and its stories. Those stories are generally interpreted in a way that excludes their sexual nature from the forces of creation. Modern mythologies, especially Christian ones, do not provide guidance to Danny for a life that includes the affirmation of his homosexuality in the way other guiding mythologies have. To the contrary, the dominant mythologies today denigrate the inner emotional experience of adolescent homosexuals as being immoral. A crisis, both spiritual and psychological, may exist for Danny and others who find that they are no longer included in the myths that their parents and society embrace. Danny's preliminary attitude, formed at his young age, was to question the nature of God but to retain some of his Christian mythology so that he was still "a sinner."

Danny is not alone in his questioning. That many men and women today, far beyond the small group who identify as gay, have found themselves without a guiding mythology has been noticed by many authors including Lionel Corbett (1996).

> Widespread disenchantment exists both with traditional notions about God and also with the doctrinal systems to which these ideas belong. Orthodox systems of thought are often out of harmony with individual needs for and experiences of the sacred. We have long had to rethink the traditional ideas about God as an old man in the sky who is benevolently watching over

us . . . There have been many attempts to tell people what God requires of them that are based on authority rather than personal knowledge. The illusory image of a God, who's an all good protective but invisible spirit, can no longer be maintained. (p. 1)

The continuing accumulation of scientific knowledge about the nature of the universe, not to mention our understanding of evolution, makes the belief in Christianity's creation story untenable for many and, with that, the images of God as an old man in the sky have fallen. The story of a Father-God who created all things in six days, before resting on the seventh, no longer fully supports Danny and his emerging homosexuality and he searches for new ways to understand how he fits within the cosmos.

By dismissing the Christian idea of God, by agreeing with it in some ways, or by exploring the idea of God as being in all things, Danny is in the process of making myth. His efforts can be understood as an effort, as Joseph Campbell (1988) put it, to integrate himself into the field of nature and to unite "the field of nature with my nature" (p. 55). Danny's effort to create a personally meaningful myth in which he is part of the whole, and the whole is in him, represents an effort to create meaning. The creation of mythology need not be collective, and as the example below demonstrates, it may be personal.

In the Beginning....

In a flash, a big bang, dust and rock, helium and hydrogen, in staggering amounts, blew into the dark void of space. How it happened, why it happened is a mystery. Perhaps it was an isolated occurrence, perhaps one of many big bangs. No one knows. The rocks and dust still race 14 billion years later. For some reason, the expansion of the universe is occurring at a faster and faster pace, not at a steady rate the way science would imagine, the way reason would have it. We do not know why. Perhaps the material is moving to a universal edge, within a container of some sort. Perhaps there is no edge, no end to it. The material racing through space created stars, and planets and galaxies of extraordinary complexity, with unknown rhythms of their own, unknown interiors, unknown life forms. Different stars used the material born of the Big Bang and created other elements that one day coalesced, with dust and rock from the Big Bang, on our small planet Earth. Still billions of years later, something unknown happened, perhaps a reaction from a bolt of lightning, perhaps something more subtle, but life began in an elemental form. It survived somehow. It is a miracle it survived at all. Life forms multiplied and adapted. Life changed and became many forms, each adapting, many surviving, many unable to make it to their tomorrow.

Man evolved from those humble, tentative beginnings and mankind adapted well. One day, at some unknowable time in our collective history, mankind woke up from unconsciousness and could see himself. He developed consciousness of himself. He could see others and knew he was different from them. He was also different from that which created him. Once he was conscious of himself as separate, he could begin to wonder out loud how he had come to be. What power was so great it could create such beauty in the world, could create him, and could cause him to think and feel and be afraid of dying? What should he do, he must have wondered, now that he could choose? What was the purpose of him?

Millions of years later, I walked in the bright sunshine of Santa Fe, NM, deep in a dry arroyo, watching Buster, an Akita, chase groundhogs into their holes in the soft sand. Buster and I and the groundhog were born of the material of a mysterious, unknown and unknowable event 14 billion years earlier, tied to it by the chemicals in our body, in our cells and the oxygen in our lungs. We were an expression of the Big Bang, an expression of its potential. It was Buster's nature to chase the groundhog and the groundhog's nature to run, to taunt him by throwing dirt out of the tiny hole. They were a fine expression of the potential of an event billions of years before. The flowers too had done their job, blossoming, as a reminder of what beauty the Big Bang could create.

Life would go on, I thought, but what a terrible tragedy it would be if Buster had not been born, had not shown the universe what it means to stand at rigid attention, to wait patiently, to show a fierce determination, to want to catch a groundhog. And what a missed opportunity for the full expression of creation it would be if the groundhog denied his nature, refused to participate in the chase. What a sad day, a missed opportunity it would be if I did not live my life with all my might, to explore every turn, to look within, to express my potential. It was not mine alone. It belonged to the universe as well. I was a reflection of the universe, a tiny, short-lived moment that expressed it. The universe needed me. Without me, without Buster, the groundhog and all those who live to express its beauty, the universe would have no purpose at all. (Chabin, 2006, pp. 51-53)

Such personal mythology can be grounding. It can incorporate science, consciousness and the lived experience of one person into a seamless expression that provides a foundation for that individual's life. Because such a story emanates from within the person's psyche, it provides an inner consistency as well as consistency with how the universal is imagined. While true of one person's myth, to many authors, all mythology begins in the inner world. To authors like Joseph Campbell (1988), many people today, like Danny, are engaged in a search for a mythology that not only includes them, but ultimately, the divine that includes them.

The old gods are dead or dying and people everywhere are searching, asking: What is the new mythology to be, the mythology of this unified earth as one of harmonious being? . . . . One cannot predict the next mythology any more than one can predict tonight's dream; for a mythology is not an ideology. It is not something projected from the brain, but something experienced from the heart, from recognitions of identities behind or within the appearances of nature; perceiving with love a "thou" where there would have been otherwise only an "it." As stated already centuries ago in the Indian Kena Upanishad: "That which in the lightening flashes forth, makes one blink, and say 'Ah!'—that 'Ah!' refers to divinity. (Campbell, 1988, p. 17)

While teenagers like Danny are, at a fragile and early stage of life, presented with the enormous question of how they and God relate, according to Richard Frankel (1998), adolescents embrace that overwhelming question with passion.

G. Stanley Hall (1904), who coined the term adolescence to mean a discreet developmental period, understood it as a time of religious enthusiasm. There is a search for meaning beyond the self in the cosmological contemplation of where one fits into the universe. A genuine opening to matters of the spirit arises as an adolescent immerses himself in the religion of his parents, adopts a new religion, or begins studying spiritual texts or engaging in spiritual rituals. (p. 123)

Danny, according to Frankel (1998), has a psychological propensity and need to discover his place in the cosmos but Danny's homosexuality and what he knows of God suggest to him that he cannot be wholly contained, and loved, by the Creator of his life. He is faced with a challenge of how to ground his life and whether or not that grounding can be sculpted from the elements of his Catholicism. Without Catholicism, Danny is faced with the question of where to look for guidance. One possible way, a suggestion from depth psychology, is for Danny to choose his own way.

> Yet the development of personality means more than just the fear of hatching forth monsters, or of isolation. It also means fidelity to one's own being. For the word "fidelity" I should prefer, in this context, the Greek word . . . which is erroneously translated as "faith". It really means "trust", trustful loyalty, a loyal perseverance and confident hope . . . personality can never develop unless the individual chooses his own way, consciously and with moral deliberation . . . a man can make a moral decision to go his own way only if he holds that way to be best. (1934/1983, p. 197)

Danny has many choices to make. He must first decide if his homosexual attractions mean that he is gay and must then choose whether or not to declare himself gay, fully and confidently, to others. He must choose how to navigate his life and how to navigate through the further development of his relationships to his family and friends. Danny must decide whether or not to go boldly into a sometimes hostile world around him or to do so with timidity and reserve. He must decide his relationship with God, and ultimately, what he imagines God to be. To answer those questions, Danny must first have a foundation and must locate a guiding force that is reliable. To Jung (1934/1983), Danny might wish to consider having a "trustful loyalty, a loyal perseverance and confident hope" in himself.

CHAPTER IV

ADOLESCENT DEVELOPMENT

The previous chapters demonstrate that homosexuality has been present throughout the history of civilization and that it has often been defined in different ways in different cultures and in different ages. The field of psychology has viewed it, at different times, as a natural aspect of human sexuality, as a psychologically formed phenomenon, as pathological and sociopathic, and as a type of sexual orientation. In history and throughout a variety of cultures, homosexuality has been both reviled and exalted, seen as both deviant and as the path to transcendence. Some cultures have integrated homosexuality into adolescent initiation rites, other cultures have allowed homosexuality to be expressed freely, while still others have condemned and restricted the expression of same sex love and sexuality. Religious attitudes have also been diverse. Some religious attitudes condemn homosexuality as immoral while other religious institutions ordain homosexual priests. Homosexuality has been a central aspect in many mythologies, in some conveying that it is an eternal aspect of human experience while others exclude stories of sexuality and homosexuality altogether. Homosexuality, what is fundamentally a love between men, is defined by the multiple ways it is seen by others.

Adolescents who have homosexual feelings must reconcile their sexual feelings with many other aspects of their emotional lives including their self concept, identity, their behavior and their identity in the world. To do so, they will encounter the many diverse definitions of their homosexuality that the world has created. They will meet with the attitudes of their family, their friends, their society and their religion, all of whom may have differing views about homosexuality. At the same time, these adolescents, like all teens, will undergo a great many other, remarkable biological and psychological transformations that place additional and significant pressure on them emotionally. Therapists working with these teens are well served by understanding the transformations underway including and beyond their sexuality.

Brain development

In his article *Beautiful Brains* in *National Geographic* (2011), David Dobbs surveyed recent findings on the development of the brain in teenagers, finding that between the 12th and 25th years of life, the brain undergoes a massive restructuring. "As we move through adolescence, the brain undergoes extensive remodeling, resembling a network and wiring upgrade" (p. 43). In a series of complex changes involving the brain's axons, myelin, dendrites, and synapses, which are all involved in the brain's transmission of information, the teenage brain changes in ways that "make the entire brain a much faster and more sophisticated organ . . . . These physical changes move in a slow way from the brain's rear to the front," beginning in the areas of the brain that control basic functions such as vision and movement and moving, over time, to the areas in the brain's front that control complex thinking (p. 43).

Considering a series of research projects studying teenage brains, including projects that have monitored changes over time, Dobbs (2011) noticed that these findings help explain many teen behaviors, including those that are often seen by adults as most troubling.

When this development proceeds normally, we get better at balancing impulse, desire, goals, self-interest, rules, ethics and even altruism, generating behavior that is more complex, and sometimes at least, more sensible . . . . These studies help explain why teens behave with such vexing inconsistency: beguiling at breakfast, disgusting at dinner, masterful on Monday, sleepwalking on Saturday. Along with lacking experience generally, they're still learning to use their brain's new network. Stress, fatigue or challenges can cause a misfire. (p. 48)

Dobbs recognized that much of the literature that has discussed the brains of teenagers in the last decade have focused on the "immature brains" of teens as a major reason for issues like risk taking or poor impulse control. Because the frontal lobe is the last to develop fully, and because it controls executive decision-making which, in turn, moderates impulsivity, many theorists have focused on the late development of the frontal lobe as a primary cause of many of adolescents' most troubling behaviors. At the same time, according to Dobbs (2011), this lack of development also allows, in a more positive way, flexibility that is necessary as adolescents encounter the often difficult and challenging broader world (p. 59). More recent theorizing has suggested that the teen brain is adaptive and "casts teens less as a rough draft than as an exquisitely sensitive, highly adaptable creature wired perfectly for the job of moving from the safety of home into the complicated world outside" (p. 49). As examples of the adaptive qualities in teens, Dobbs suggested that typical complaints about teenagers such as their capacity for thrill seeking or even impulsivity may be necessary qualities for the movement into the world, despite their sometimes dangerous nature.

"A love of novelty leads directly to new experience . . . and the hunt for sensation provides the inspiration to leave the home" (p. 49).

Citing work done at Temple University, Dobbs (2011) stated that teens are well aware of mortality, use the same basic cognitive strategies adults use in assessing risk, and contrary to popular belief, actually overestimate risk. Teens take more risks because they value the reward that is possible more than adults, especially social rewards. "Physiologically, adolescence brings a peak to the brain's sensitivity to dopamine, a neurotransmitter that appears to prime and fire reward circuits and aids in learning patterns and making decisions" (p. 55).

According to Dobbs (2011), other neural hormones associated with social connections are also especially important in the adolescent brain which helps explain why teens prefer the company of their own age group with an often deep intensity. "Some brain-scan studies, in fact, suggest that our brains react to peer exclusion much as they respond to threats to physical health or food supply" (p. 55). In other words, according to Dobbs (2011), "At a neural level . . . we perceive social rejection as a threat to existence" (pp. 54-55). This may be an especially important consideration for gay teens who often face harassment, bullying or isolation as is discussed more fully later in this work.

Dobbs is careful, throughout his work, to recognize that many of the behaviors of teenagers, including their risky behaviors, their sometimes dangerous activities, and their frequent mood swings, are often difficult for adults to tolerate. In many ways, those behaviors and moods can be attributed to the developing brain in teens, not to mention the many other psychological challenges and influences in their lives. At the same time, Dobbs showed that the teen brain may well be precisely what evolution had in mind for young people who are tasked with exploration, leaving the comfort of home, finding novelty and new ideas, and getting prepared to encounter the broader world.

The move outward from home is the most difficult thing that humans do, as well as the most critical— not just for individuals but for a species that has shown an unmatched ability to master challenging new environments. In scientific terms, teenagers can be a pain in the ass. But they are quite possibly the most fully, crucially adaptive human beings around. Without them, humanity might not have so readily spread across the globe. (2011, pp. 55-59)

Research into the developing brain of adolescents is an important aid to understanding the psychological difficulties and behaviors of teenagers who have same- sex feelings. While Dobbs' work is by no means comprehensive, it suggests that these young people are biologically prone to risky behavior that is guided by reward-seeking, especially the reward of connection to peers. It suggests that teens are susceptible to emotional struggles due to fatigue and crisis in part because their brains are undergoing a massive reorganization. As will be seen throughout this work, teens who face a crisis emotionally due to their homosexuality may well be especially vulnerable to these issues.

Adolescent psychology—identity formation

For, indeed, in the social jungle of human existence there is no feeling of being alive without a sense of identity. (Erikson, 1968, p. 130)

Erik Erikson, one of the most prominent psychological theorists on adolescent development considered "identity formation" to be the central psychological task of adolescence. The challenge of adolescence, according to Erikson (1968), was the formation of an identity that included "both a persistent sameness within oneself . . . and a persistent sharing of some essential character with others" (p. 109). To

Erikson, identity referred to three separate psychological components. First, identity referred to an "individual identity" so that a person understood a sense of who they are. Second, "identity" referred to a "continuity of character" so that one's sense of oneself was understood as continuous over time. Finally, Erikson considered "identity" to be the maintenance of an inner solidarity with the ideals of the group or broader society (p. 109).

Erikson (1968) saw adolescence as the last stage of childhood and adolescence as a period during which a new identity emerged that was new and different from childhood identity. During childhood, according to Erikson (1968), the child developed tentative aspects of an identity that made him feel as if he knew approximately who he was. As the child continues to develop, in Erikson's view, the experience of life challenges and frustrates those tentative notions until adolescence when childhood identities are abandoned in exchange for something more permanent (pp. 19-123).

To Erikson (1968), identity formation, the central psychological challenge of adolescents, required the individual to alter and change those early childhood identities because of new psychological experiences including those brought about through puberty. The adolescent must repudiate some childhood identities, or assimilate others, then integrate those identifications into a new version of one's identity that includes a new-found sexual maturity after puberty. To be successful in creating a new and more complete identity, the adolescent must find recognition for his new identity by society and must be welcomed into the world of adulthood by it.

> It is of great relevance to the young individual's identity formation that he is responded to . . . such recognition provides an entirely indispensable support to the ego in the specific tasks of adolescing. (p.120)

To Erikson, the formation of identity required that the adolescent find acceptance by society so that he could find a role in it. The "requirement" of social acceptance and recognition may be especially difficult for young people whose homosexuality may be unacceptable in their immediate environment. As mentioned previously, Erikson, who was not aware of the many new insights into homosexuality that confirm it as part of normal sexuality, considered homosexuality to be a negative identity similar to those held by other "social deviants." His work does not fully address the challenges of identity formation in gay teens, yet his theories about adolescent development are important in this discussion.

Using Erikson's model of development, and because his model recognizes the enormous significance of social acceptance in adolescent development, the difficulties gay teens face can be better understood. Young gay people are asked, in the completion of their psychological tasks, to form a sense of themselves in a way that is felt as authentic internally, continuous over time and harmonious in the world. Many young people, as will be seen, have heard derogatory statements about homosexuality throughout childhood. For them, familial, social, and religious condemnations they have encountered may well have been internalized so that the inner identity relating to their sexual feelings may contain shame, doubt, or guilt. Given the hostility they may have already experienced, to imagine that they are gay and will have a gay identity throughout their lives, on a continuous basis, may cause pessimism in many. Given the social criticism of homosexuality they encounter, they may easily doubt the possibility of finding a "harmony" between their identity and the world around them. Erikson's model is especially useful in that it not only defines what is psychologically important in adolescence generally but, also, it defines some of the deeper psychological challenges involved in establishing an identity in adolescence that includes homosexuality.

Identity formation—gay teens

Gay adolescence is a modern invention . . . adolescents who are romantically and erotically attracted to others of their biological sex have always existed, in every recorded culture and in every historic time. Only recently, however, have young people incorporated these attractions into their sense of self, publicly announced their attractions to friends and relatives, and formed a personal identity based on their attractions. Gay adolescence is a modern invention. (Savin-Williams, 2005, p. 50)

Just as the term homosexual is a modern invention, as Boswell (1980) noticed, the concept of gay adolescence is also a very recent concept. As Savin-Williams (2005) noted, young people today are asked to categorize their sexual feelings into the categories of gay, straight, or bisexual, then integrate that into their identity and publicly announce it to the world.

Building on the work of Erikson on the nature of identity formation, Vivienne Cass (1984) theorized that there was a formal process for the development of a gay identity. Other authors since them, notably Savin-Williams (2005), have both summarized that work and critiqued it. As discussed by Savin-Williams (2005), the Cass stages are useful to consider because they describe a series of processes that may well be common to many young people, and adults, as they first consider their homosexual feelings and eventually build an identity that includes them.

The first stage, Identity Confusion, is understood to begin when the young person becomes aware that their sexual feelings are homosexual. Typically, the young person either resists/denies them or accepts them. This stage is usually accompanied by confusion or anxiety. In stage 2, Identity Comparison, the young person begins to evaluate his sexual feelings in comparison to the experiences of others and begins to consider the possibility that he is gay. Through self-reflection, and in comparison to others, the young person may see this new awareness as desirable, may think it is too costly in that it may cause alienation from friends and family, or may think it is a temporary condition. By the time the young person has fully begun Stage 3, Identity Tolerance, he has developed a tentative acceptance that he is gay but has done so without a desire to be gay. He has developed a sense of how homosexuality may affect other areas of his emotional life and self-concept. He may begin to make contact with other homosexuals and may accept them or devalue them. Stage 4, Identity Acceptance, refers to the stage when the young person accepts that he is gay and accepts that it is ok for him to be gay. This acceptance leads the young person to notice the discrepancy between his own feelings and those around him who may criticize homosexuality. This stage, stage 5, when the young person is proud of his nature, is called Identity Pride. Stage 6, Identity Synthesis occurs when the young person has integrated his sexual identity into his broader sense of self so that he is more than gay, is not defensive, and feels self-actualized (pp. 73-74).

Cass's model (1984) of identity formation in LGBT teens fills in many gaps in the work of Erikson because it directly considers the experience of people with same-sex attractions and those who identify as gay. The model clarifies many of the internal questions, doubts and crisis' experienced by young people, and in some cases adults, as they begin to integrate sexual feelings that fall outside the heterosexual norm. Among the many benefits of the Cass model is that parents, teachers, and therapists are given insight into many aspects of homosexual psychological development that were, before Cass, completely unavailable to them. Cass's pioneering work, much of which was completed in the 1970s, opened a window into the experience of gay people unlike any of her predecessors.

While Cass's model is useful and is generally recognized as the most articulate of all developmental theories about the stages of identity formation among homosexual people, Savin-Williams (2005) found that there is an inherent problem in all such models.

> Unless a sexual identity model explicitly rejects universalism and includes contextual, cultural, and historic considerations, it is doomed as an obsolete relic of a time when development was perceived as predetermined and universal. . . An individual's life is more than a category, and is always in a state of flux and self-discovery. Life is dynamic, in perpetual reinvention rather than sitting at a concluding point. (p. 81)

As is seen throughout this work, individuals respond in many different ways to homosexual feelings and the stories included within this work demonstrate that those individual stories cannot be easily crystallized into or contained within one theory of development. In fact, many who have homosexual feelings or attractions, or participate in homosexual sex, do not identify as gay. Much can be learned about homosexuality and the process of individual development in the stories of those who have not concluded they are gay, are not proud of their feelings, or who identify as heterosexual despite their feelings. This work includes many stories of those who, within Cass's construct, have come to a sense of pride about their homosexuality and their identity but by no means can that pattern be said to apply to all who have homosexual feelings.

As Kinsey noted in 1948, a majority of men who had homosexual experience in his studies identified as heterosexual. Savin-Williams (2005), noticed the same phenomenon in adolescence. "It is true that the majority of young people who engage in gay sex are heterosexual— at least by self definition—according to a study of Massachusetts and Minnesota public schools" (p. 29). When considering all aspects of homosexuality, including feelings, fantasies, attractions and behaviors, the discrepancy between those teenagers who experience homosexuality in some form and those who identify as gay is striking.

> Despite the substantial number of young people who have some component of a same-sex sexuality, less than two percent of high school students actually identify as lesbian, gay or bisexual . . . . it is safe to conclude that at least 15 percent and maybe as high as 20 percent of all adolescents have some degree of same-sex orientation. (Savin-Williams, 2005, pp. 41-44)

Any discussion of adolescent homosexuality must begin with an awareness that individuals respond in an endless variety of ways to it. How they respond to it, whether or not they identify with it, how they communicate to the world about it, and how they view themselves are all individual decisions and models of development that do not account for that variance are inherently limited by these facts. A broader view of identity formation, one that considers other aspects of adolescent psychology, is required. Quoting Winnicott (1963), Richard Frankel (1998) conveys something of that broader view.

> Adolescents can be . . . "seen searching for a form of identification which does not let them down in their struggle, the struggle for identity, the struggle to feel real, the struggle not to fit into an adult-assigned role, but to go through whatever has to be gone through" (Winnicott, 1963a, p. 152) . . . The search to discover a sense of self that feels real in the world is at the center of identity formation. (p. 214)

For young men who have same-sex attractions, the crisis of identity formation, according to Frankel (2005), may well be more than the acceptance of being gay or the announcement of that fact to the world. Reconciling homosexuality with their broader personalities may require that they struggle with many different parts of themselves and with many aspects of the world around them, both in ways related to homosexuality and in ways not directly related to it. In the broadest sense, these young men must struggle to "go through whatever has to be gone through" in order to feel real in the world.

Adolescent psychology beyond identity formation

No comprehensive review of the theories of adolescent psychology is possible in this short work, but, at the same time, material that broadens the conceptualization of adolescence beyond the process of identity formation is important. Richard Frankel (1998) considered the works of many authors in psychology who considered adolescence from a depth psychological point of view and who noticed the deeper trends at play within adolescent psychological life. Frankel's work (1995), as described here, both deepens and broadens the discussion of adolescent psychology, and while not comprehensive, it adds an important dimension to the consideration of what teenagers who have same-sex attractions may experience.

Persona

Among the many concepts outlined by Jung and others within the depth psychological tradition is the role of persona. Frankel (1998) discussed its role in adolescent psychology. Noting that the term derives from the Latin word referring to the masks worn by actors, Frankel describes persona as the outer face a person puts on to confront the world. Persona "functions in the psyche by mediating between the ego and the external world ... The shaping of one's worldly identity is a central task of adolescent individuation" (p. 129).

To Frankel (1998), adolescence is a period during which the individual is actively working through the inner experiences of development even while meeting the world and attempting to navigate its demands. Theories of identity formation can, if misread, imply that when one completes the formation of identity, that identity is expressed directly to the world without any other mediating psychological factor. In some ways, these models may imply that the inner and outer identities are synonymous. Depth psychology suggests that an intermediary function, the persona, is presented to the world by the individual that reflects the inner identity but does not communicate its full content. Classic types of personas in adolescence, to Frankel (1998) are the "jocks," "freaks," "brains," or "nerds" (p. 129). This outer presentation no doubt reflects some aspects of the individual involved but does not reflect the fuller identity of the person. Persona, to Frankel (1998), is often of heightened importance during adolescence because of the dramatic sense of self-consciousness many teens experience, especially in the presence of peers.

As will be seen later in this work, the concept of persona is very important to young people who may feel homosexual but are not yet willing, or able, to convey that reality externally. As Savin-Williams (2005) asks, "What about a teenager who isn't yet aware that he's a member of, or doesn't want to be a member of, or isn't willing to disclose his membership in what he sees as a stigmatized group?" (p. 27). Teens may present themselves as heterosexual, or bisexual, or in other non-descript ways, before identity is fully formed or until an identity as gay is ready to be shared. The role of persona, one's ability to wear a mask for the benefit of the world while protecting what cannot be revealed or even known on the inside, is a crucial consideration when considering how teenagers who have homosexual feelings present themselves to the world.

The development of an identity internally as gay, as seen above, is a process that may take years. The process of disclosure of homosexuality to others can also take years. During that period, in an obvious way, teens present some version of themselves to the world that does not, by definition, include their homosexuality. Teens may present personas of the intellectual student, the outrageous or defiant boy, the quiet "good kid," the funny one, or the loner, all versions of the self which allow an interaction with the world while protecting the inner world from a too quick disclosure.

Individuation

A second important consideration from depth psychology related to adolescent development is the concept of individuation. Carl Jung (1939/1983) defined the term as the "development of the psychological individual as being distinct from the general, collective psychology. Individuation is a process of differentiation, having for its goal the development of the individual personality" (p. 212). According to Frankel (1998), inherent in the adolescent experience is the potential for the development of one's own personality, as distinct from a sense of self tied too closely to collective attitudes, ideas, or conventions. Like Frankel (1998), Jung recognized the powerful psychic experience of adolescence.

> In the childish stage of consciousness there are as yet no problems; nothing depends upon the subject, for the child itself is still wholly dependent on the parents. It was if it were not yet completely born . . . Psychic birth, and with it the conscious differentiation from the parents, normally takes place only at puberty. The physiological change is attended by a psychic

revolution. This is sometimes called the unbearable age. (Jung, 1939/1983, p. 73)

According to Frankel (1998), Jung recognized that adolescence was, in fact, the birth of the psychological individual. As part of that process, Frankel (1998) outlined many experiences common in adolescence that have the capacity to further the individuating possibilities in teens. Among those experiences are those related to the development of deep friendship and falling in love, especially in adolescence, because teens do so in ways that are often so unreserved, open, and vulnerable and often without the defenses learned by adulthood (p. 118). The loss of friendship, especially through betrayal, is a searing experience in adolescence. "Waves of grief and mourning feel unbearable to a psyche that is new to this kind of raw pain" according to Frankel (1998, p. 119). Thoughts of suicide and death appear frequently in adolescents because, to Frankel (1998), "Adolescence is a time of life when fundamental insights into existence and God and death, matters of ultimate importance, are cathected as intellectual ideas and emotional realities" (p. 121). These types of experience, deeply powerful for teenagers, are psychologically important because they force the personality to develop, and in some cases, for individual teens to separate psychologically from what others, including parents and society, have said should be believed. They are individuating events that "nudge" adolescents forward into their lives (p. 118).

Beyond the possibility of individuating experience listed above, the individuation process in adolescents is also characterized by the development of one's own sense of conscience, according to Frankel (1998). Adolescents are "deluged with serious moral choice" including decisions about their education, vocations, whether or not to use alcohol or drugs, to cheat on tests or not, getting a job or dropping out of school, and how to express their sexuality among many others (p. 159-161).

Conscience is awakened by those episodes where there is a conflict between the dictates of the traditional moral code of the culture and one's inner sense of right and wrong . . . Awakening to one's own inward sense of conscience challenges unthinking submission to the morality and ethics of the parent's world. A transition from collective authority to individual authority and autonomy is effected. (pp. 159-161)

Throughout this work are many discussions of "coming out" by teens and adults, and in most cases, "coming out" is described as one's adherence to an identity, to a set of feelings based on one's sexual nature. Using Frankel's work (1998), the experience of homosexual teens can be broadened so that it is understood as a process of individuation. In many ways, by virtue of the social dialogue and the denigration of homosexuality heard by many homosexual teens, their experience requires that they begin to differentiate themselves from many social attitudes in perhaps dramatic ways. Their experience may require that they be critical thinkers about what is right and wrong, who they are, and how they must move forward. Will it be on the basis of social attitudes that demean their sexuality or will their lives be based on their own beliefs and feelings despite the criticisms they are likely to hear from parents, church leaders and peers? Such work requires the separation of one's own values from those of the society, a hallmark of individuation.

In some ways, as part of that process, it is possible that young gay teens may "come out" for reasons beyond the issue of being faithful to their identity. As will be discussed later, many gay teens, and many heterosexual teens, belong to social groups in high schools called the Gay Straight Alliance. These clubs are dedicated to overcoming homophobia and discrimination against LGBT teens. Teenagers who "come out" and participate in these clubs may well be acting out of what Frankel (1998) called a "dynamic conscience." The motivation to "come out" may be motivated, in part, by the desire to use one's own experience, one's own life, as a means to combat social injustice. It is a step for them toward their own individuation as well.

CHAPTER V

ENVIRONMENTAL, SOCIAL AND PSYCHOSOCIAL CONSIDERATIONS

Virtually all psychological models account for the effect of environment on the individual's psychological development. In the works of Erikson (1968), Cass (1984), Frankel (1998), and many others, the impact of social attitudes on an adolescent is thought to be a major consideration. To some extent, the difficulties young people face when they have homosexual feelings, regardless of identity, can be linked to social attitudes about homosexuality. If society praised homosexuality, young people might be better able to express what occurs naturally within them without the vigilance involved in anticipating negative social responses to those expressions. In many ways, the subject of adolescent homosexuality cannot be understood without understanding something about the social attitudes and social messaging adolescents receive about homosexuality.

As Frankel (1998) noted, "As a culture, we transmit forceful messages, spoken and unspoken, to adolescents regarding their place in society and our willingness to tolerate their developing struggle to form an identity" (p. 213). As the material below amplifies, adolescents listen to social messages and integrate those messages psychologically into their identities. Social messaging influences the way in which adolescents conceptualize themselves, form their identity, and form perceptions of their future. In many ways seen throughout this work, it is also clear that adolescent behavior and actions are often based on this synthesis of social messaging and their individual natures although they generally act without the experience, exposure to alternatives, and the general emotional maturity that comes with adulthood. What part of the broad social conversation any individual adolescent absorbs, at the exclusion of other messages, is a personal, individual matter explored later in this work. In some cases, teens may attach to positive portrayals of homosexuality and use them as a model. In other cases, an individual teen may attach to social messaging that portrays homosexuality as negative and respond accordingly.

One way in which the impact of social messaging can be seen and understood is by listening to the stories and experiences of young people. In 2011, *The New York Times* provided LGBT teens from throughout the country an opportunity to share their experiences in an online forum titled *Coming Out*. Generally, these stories articulate the specific individual experiences the young authors have had as LGBT teens. Yet, embedded in these stories are the social, religious and environmental messages these teens have heard and taken to heart.

For example, Charlie had heard homosexuality was wrong. He was 16 when he wrote to *The New York Times* to share his experience. He said he had known that he was gay from the age 5. It was not a sexual feeling, he said, but an attraction to other boys he thought were cute. His church taught him, from early childhood, that God hated gays and that they were "truly unholy." Largely related to his feelings of guilt and conflict, by the early age of 9 years old, Charlie was contemplating suicide. He prayed to God daily but was never relieved of the burden of his feelings, neither the sexual ones nor the guilty ones. By age 10,

Charlie had determined he would live but would live his life in relative isolation, destined to be alone (as cited in Kramer, 2011).

For young Charlie, cultural attitudes about homosexuality were internalized early in life and the process of organizing a sense of who he was in the context of the broader world was underway from the time of his earliest memories. In the interaction of cultural messages and Charlie's internal world, he came to believe he was a mistake, thought about suicide and expected that he would be alone.

In contrast, another story shared by a teen in *The New York Times* (2011) shows another way in which the condemnation of gays is heard and acted upon by teens with same-sex feelings. It was the story of A. J., a young man from the upper Midwest. His story is one example of how social messages of intolerance are integrated within the personal, emotional life of an individual, and in that interaction, how intolerance becomes action.

A.J. never had to worry about being bullied in high school because people might think he was gay. He was the bully who tormented the gay kids. One young man, described as "effeminate, shy and scrawny and different", drew A.J.'s frequent, cruel attention. The young man was everything A.J. did not want to be. On a regular basis, A.J. tormented the other boy with name-calling, mocking, and many types of other bullying behaviors at school. He encouraged others to participate, pulling the younger boy's backpack off and passing it to friends who would also bully the gay teen. He and his friends went to the boy's home, drove over the lawn, vandalized the home and even once threw a bottle at the gay teen's head from a moving car. A.J. noticed the stitches on the boy's head the next day (as cited in Kramer, 2011).

A.J.'s story does not describe the sources, the social or familial messaging, that he received that convinced him that homosexuality was bad, something he did not want to feel, or something in another human that deserved violence. His story does not express how his friends came to feel that way or why the school, his parents and the broader society allowed his behavior to continue for years. Yet, A. J.' s intolerance of homosexuality was supported and allowed in some fashion by his environment. It was an ongoing behavior. It is doubtful that the words he spoke originated exclusively from his inner world. It is likely that he heard those words first from the world around him.

Eventually, A.J. came to understand that the young gay man he harassed so tenaciously was not the only victim of homophobia. Now 21, A.J. stated that he understands that his own homosexuality, and his hatred for it, was at the root of his anger at others who were gay. He went to counseling for his drinking and anger issues, and with his counseling underway, began to accept that he was gay although he had not been able to "admit" it to others. He was admitting it now, in a letter to society through *The New York Times*. He told the readers of *The New York Times* that he now knows how much he hurt the younger man, how sorry he is, how happy he is now that he has come to terms with himself, and how strong, he realizes now, the young gay teen had been all along (as cited in Kramer, 2011).

Another example of the influence of environment and social messaging on an adolescent's identity and sense of self demonstrates that supportive messages are also part of the broad social dialogue young people absorb. Jesse, a 15-year-old from Massachusetts, described the positive and supportive environment in which he lives, the impact that has had on him, and the actions he intends to take next. To some extent, the positive news about social change supported his determination to come out.

Jesse began the process of coming out at 14 and was worried about the possible consequences of disclosure. He did research as part of his self-discovery, finding articles that helped him see the positive steps occurring in society in relation to homosexuality and the LGBT community. Massachusetts had legalized same-sex marriage. Gay

Straight Alliance Clubs were forming in many high schools and one had formed at his own school. Jesse felt that things were improving and that he did not want to live a lie. He hoped that someday soon he would not have to hide the truth from others, especially his closest friends. The process of his coming out was highly stressful. He went to a counselor at the school, feeling the need for support but was unable to tell the counselor what bothered him. He simply sat and cried. The concerned counselor called his mother to bring Jesse's difficulties to light. When Jesse got home, his mother asked him what was bothering him so deeply and he told her. Her response was total acceptance. With that support in hand, Jesse then began the process of telling others, mainly through Facebook. He joined his GSA at school and stated in his letter that he intends to run for president of the club. He wants to enter politics in adulthood and work for social change. Jesse, as of the time he wrote his essay, had recently come off his anti-depressants (as cited in Kramer, 2011).

Charlie, A.J. and Jesse have each received social messaging, absorbed it, and integrated it into their psychological make-up. They have made meaning from that psychic mixture about themselves and their futures. This book is focused on teens like them and the inner world of young men who have same-sex attractions. Yet, in some ways, it is also a study of the society that creates the world they are entering. Their stories, and the conflicts they struggle with, are not just reflective of their lives but are also reflective of society's unresolved attitudes. As Richard Frankel (1998) noted, "Adolescents, in their very nature, dramatically expose those places where we as a culture are in conflict" (p. 213). In fact, in might be said that adolescents inherit what we as adults have not resolved and that they now must contend with what we, as society, wish to not see. "Adolescents mirror the culture's shadow; they embody and live out those places where we as a culture are most unconscious" (p. 219).

In many ways, Charlie, A. J., and Jesse have, at a very young age, inherited society's unresolved conflicts about homosexuality. It might be said that they have inherited what Boswell (1980) described as the intolerance of the last 100 years. In many ways, they expose and clarify cultural divides. Those conflicts now exist within the interiors of these young people as personal conflicts. It is now their task, largely unknown to them, to resolve not only their own conflicts but, also, those which society has not yet resolved.

Unlike the sometimes abstract or ideological nature of adult, social debates about homosexuality, for these teens, conflicts about homosexuality are internal, psychological, and emotional questions of a highly personal nature. The answer to the question of the acceptance of homosexuality is vitally important in their search for coherence, for identity, to their self worth or self esteem, and even in their questioning about their willingness to live at all. With that in mind, the discussion of social attitudes about teenage homosexuality below can be seen as both the content of social dialogue and, also, the critically important material of adolescent psychological development.

While no comprehensive discussion of the wide range of social conversation about teenage homosexuality is possible here, a sample of material below from news outlets, television, and from online sources, conveys something of the nature of the social debate that occurs in society and that is psychologically integrated by adolescents.

Changing attitudes

Attitudes about homosexuality have changed throughout recent decades. Shifts toward acceptance of homosexuality by the American population have been pronounced, and when accompanied by positive portrayals of LGBT adults and teenagers on television and in the broader social arena, these more tolerant social attitudes about homosexuality have changed the environment faced by gay teens. Just in the past twenty years, there has been a tremendous increase in available role models and support systems for gay teens, perhaps more now than at any time in modern history. While many teens face hostility, as is discussed later in this work, it is also true that gay teenagers today encounter a social environment that is dramatically different from those in the past and one that is more positive in many ways.

Surveys of public opinion

Public attitudes about homosexuality have been consistently tracked by major polling companies in the United States for several decades. As summarized by *Pollingreport.com* (2012), polling data demonstrate that American attitudes about homosexuality have changed dramatically over time. Nearly two decades ago for instance, in 1982, USA Today/Gallup polls found that only 34% of Americans felt that homosexuality could be considered an acceptable lifestyle. The poll suggested that it was a lifestyle, and perhaps a chosen one, that was disapproved of by the majority of society. By 2008, just over 15 years later, 57% of Americans considered homosexuality acceptable. In another polling question asked over time, a relatively small majority of Americans in 1977, 56%, felt gays and lesbians should have equal rights in terms of job opportunities. By 2008, the vast majority, 89%, felt gays and lesbians should have equal rights in the job market. In many other ways, at least a majority of Americans have come to accept the LGBT community and increasingly support their rights in society. In a *Newsweek* poll in 2008, 53% of Americans felt gay and lesbian couples should be able to legally adopt children, 74% felt gay and lesbian partners were entitled to inheritance rights, and 67% felt gay and lesbian partners were entitled to social security benefits ("Poll Results on LGBT," 2011).

Americans have also shown that they are aware of intolerance in America toward LGBT people, including the possibility that LGBT people faced violence. As an example, in a CNN/Time poll in 1998,

Americans were asked about the murder of Matthew Shepard, a gay college student brutally beaten and murdered in Wyoming. The story shocked the nation and prompted calls for national legislation that would require violence toward LGBT people to be considered "hate crimes," a designation that automatically increased penalties for these crimes. In the poll, 82% of Americans agreed that the federal government should treat homosexuals and heterosexuals equally. 76% of Americans believed that the government should legally denote violence against LGBT people as a "hate crime." 75% felt that violence against LGBT people was either a "very serious" or "serious" problem in the country ("Poll Results on LGBT," 2011). Perhaps the most telling question of the survey, at least in regards to the social environment faced by LGBT people, was a question about physical safety.

> As you may know, a gay student at the University of Wyoming was recently beaten, tied to a fence, and later died. Do you think that an attack like the one in Wyoming could happen in your own community, or don't you think so? ("Poll Results on LGBT," 2011)

In 1998, 68% of Americans stated they believed a beating of this type could occur in their community, suggesting that violence toward gays and lesbians was understood to be widespread by most Americans and that it might occur very near to home ("Poll Results on LGBT," 2011).

Over the years, the most consistent line of questioning in national polling about LGBT rights has related to the national dialogue about service in the military and the right of marriage.

The issue of whether or not LGBT people could serve in the military has been a frequently surveyed issue, especially since the early 1990s when Congress passed legislation colloquially called "Don't Ask, Don't

Tell," which allowed gay and lesbian people to serve in the military so long as they did not disclose their sexual orientation. The military was required to not inquire into the issue with individual soldiers. In many ways, the law reflected social attitudes at that time. In 1993, according to an ABC/Washington Post poll, 63% of Americans felt it gay and lesbians should be allowed to serve so long as they did not disclose their orientation. Only 44% of the public felt gays and lesbians should be allowed to serve when they stated that orientation openly. By 2010, American attitudes had shifted dramatically so that 83% felt gays and lesbians should serve if they did not disclose their orientation and 77% believed they should serve as openly gay and lesbian people ("Poll Results on LGBT," 2011). In 2011, President Barack Obama formally certified that the American military was ready to end "Don't Ask, Don't Tell" and LGBT people were allowed to openly serve in the US military (Bumiller, 2011, "Obama ends 'don't ask, don't tell' policy").

A second frequently surveyed question has been the question of whether or not gay and lesbian couples should have legal recognition similar to that of heterosexual married couples. According to a summary of ABC/Washington Post polling from 2003 to 2011, it is clear that Americans are moving increasingly toward acceptance of marriage among gay and lesbian couples. In 2003, only 37% of Americans felt such marriages should be legal. By 2011, 51% of Americans, a slight majority, felt same-sex marriages should be legal. 50% of those polled felt that a new law in New York legalizing same-sex marriage was a positive development in the country. A higher percentage of Americans have, for many years, approved of civil unions, a legal union that allows couples to have many of the same legal benefits as married couples. According to the Pew Research Center, in 1998, 57% of Americans favored or strongly favored allowing same-sex couples those rights (2011).

In many ways, these results align with political affiliations. In a 2009 CBS poll, only 6% of Republicans felt that same-sex couples should be allowed to marry while 46% of Democrats and 37% of Independents felt same-sex marriage should be legal. Beyond that, Americans generally disagree with the opinion, often stated by Republican political leaders and conservative groups like the Family Research Council, that same-sex marriage is a threat to traditional marriage. A Quinnipiac University poll in 2009 questioned Americans regarding the claim and found that 58% of Americans rejected it (2011).

Beyond political leanings, the rate of approval of same-sex marriage appears to be significantly affected by age differences and by generational categories. In the Quinnipiac poll in 2009, 41% of those from 18-41 years of age approved of legalizing same-sex marriage while only 18% of Americans over 65 approved of it. Attitudes against homosexuality, especially in relationship to marriage rights, seem especially prevalent in those who identify as Republican and among older Americans (2011). That combination of political voters are largely responsible for many of the legal and legislative processes underway in recent years to restrict the right of marriage to heterosexual couples. In thirty-one states, voters have passed statewide initiatives that define marriage as between one man and one woman, effectively preventing the state governments from passing laws allowing same-sex marriage (Grant, 2011).

On the other hand, attitudes are changing in many ways. In June 2011, New York became the sixth state in the United States to legalize same-sex marriages (Confessore and Barbaro, 2011). According to the authors, although Republicans, as a group, have generally not viewed homosexuality favorably, the passage of same-sex marriage rights in New York was made possible only because of changing attitudes among several Republicans in that state's government. Four Republican State Senators switched their votes, siding with Democrats, and voted in favor of the law, making passage possible. One such Senator, Mark Grisanti, had run for office with a promise to oppose same-sex marriage. Grisanti "told his colleagues he had agonized for months before concluding he was wrong" (Confessore & Barbaro, 2011, para. 3).

> "I apologize for those who feel offended," Mr. Grisanti said, adding "I cannot deny a person, a human being, a taxpayer, a worker, the people of my district, the State of New York, and those people who make this the great state it is the same rights that I have with my wife." (para. 4)

> As seen in the case of Mr. Grisanti, change is occurring in individual Americans, even among those with long-held attitudes against providing legal rights to same-sex couples.

A major step toward the legalization of same-sex marriage throughout the country occurred in 2013 when the United States Supreme Court issued two rulings on the subject (Savage, 2013, "Gay Marriage Wins"). In the first, the court ruled that the federal Defense of Marriage Act was unconstitutional. The federal statute had denied legal recognition for same-sex couples, even those legally married under state law. After the ruling, legally married same-sex couples became entitled to all the federal benefits heterosexual couples enjoy. Further, the court struck down California's state constitutional amendment, Proposition 8, prohibiting same-sex couples from marrying. The ruling allowed couples who had been married prior to the ban in California to have their marriages recognized again. In the words of Savage (2013), "The language of the two decisions suggests that a constitutional ruling giving all gays and lesbians a right to marry is not far off" (2013, "Gay Marriage Wins").

Clearly, American attitudes about homosexuality are changing but remain complex. In the October 11, 2013 edition of the *Los Angeles Times*, author John Gionna discussed the 15th anniversary of the death of Matthew Shepard and, in that discussion, provides an excellent glimpse into the complexity of American attitudes, attitudes teens with same-sex attractions must face.

> Fifteen years ago this week, gay college student Matthew Shepard was pistol-whipped and left for dead: unconscious, barely alive, lashed to a jagged wooden fence outside this small prairie city by two men disgusted by his homosexuality. A passerby mistook the diminutive, 105-pound Shepard for a scarecrow – a forlorn and unthinkable image that still haunts a generation of Americans (Gionna, Scars of hate crime linger in Laramie, 2013).

The brutal beating and murder of Matthew Shepard in Laramie, Wyoming in 1998 shocked the nation and reactions in the nation were strong. On one hand, his murder prompted the nation to enact hate-crime laws that included offenses motivated by a victim's gender or sexual orientation. Yet, on the other hand, those opposed to homosexuality also became motivated. During the trial, protesters opposed to homosexuality held vigils with the more extreme members of those groups holding signs saying "Matthew Shepard rots in hell". While, according to Gionna (2013), 13 states have legalized same-sex marriage, recently, University of Mississippi football players "yelled slurs and heckled actors during a performance of the play 'The Laramie Project' which explores the town's reactions to the murders" (2013). While the catalyst for national change came from Wyoming, it remains one of only a handful of states without hate-crime legislation and, unlike many other states, does not recognize gay partnerships of any kind. In fact, in Wyoming, being openly gay remains risky. Matthew Shepard's mother explained that although her hometown of Casper had once even elected a gay mayor, most gays live undercover and remain afraid they will be fired if they divulge their secret life (Gionna, 2013). Those gays, it is assumed, include the young whose homosexuality is a secret as well.

Social rejection of homosexuality

As discussed in previous chapters, religious groups and institutions that are more conservative have often stated that homosexuality is immoral. In that vein, these institutions and their followers have concluded that providing legal rights for gays and lesbians is sanctioning immorality. Socially active groups who are largely supportive of those conservative religious attitudes like the Family Research Council (2011) and the National Association for Research and Therapy of Homosexuality have attempted to combat social acceptance of homosexuality as well. In some ways, described below, there has been an integration of political forces, largely conservative Republican, with conservative religious institutions and conservative social advocacy organizations into a larger social force that works to battle against the acceptance of homosexuality.

While the rationales for rejecting homosexuality have been covered previously in this work, what has not been reviewed is the way in which organizations that oppose homosexuality have dealt with it within their organizations. Groups opposing homosexuality have frequently been faced with homosexuality in their own membership and often in the lives of their leadership. Some of the most prominent spokespeople for the groups opposing homosexuality, men who may well have earned their reputations publicly and professionally by opposing homosexuality in the United States, have had homosexual experiences, were reported to have had homosexual experiences, or were in fact gay. Their stories are important considerations in this work for several reasons. First and foremost, they are part of the broad social dialogue adolescents hear and absorb. Second, they demonstrate that the identity crisis of adolescence described by Erikson (1968) and Cass (1984) is often not resolved in adolescence and that the struggle for coherence in identity may be a life-long issue. Beyond those issues, the stories of men who are homosexual and have, at the same time rejected homosexuality publicly, speak to the nature of social condemnation and the human consequences of it, for both adults and teens.

In some ways, the stories below are reminiscent of what Kinsey (1948) found. Those men who are most socially active in condemning homosexuality, are, in some cases, the very same men who engage in homosexual behavior. Kinsey's (1948) writing bears repeating.

> The police force and the court officials who attempt to enforce the sex laws, the clergy and business men and every other group in the city which periodically calls for the enforcement of the laws—especially against the laws against "perversion"—have given a record of incidences and frequencies in the homosexual which are as high as those of the social level to which they belong . . They themselves are the victims of the mores. As long as there are such gaps between the traditional custom and the actual behavior of the population, such inconsistencies will continue to exist. (Kinsey, 1948, p. 848)

As the information below amplifies, homosexuality exists in some men within the organizations that condemn it. Some groups ostracize homosexuals from their ranks. Some institutions have tolerated the homosexual men within their ranks so long as their homosexuality was not disclosed publicly. As will be seen, homosexuality has existed within some organizations or broader social groups in a way reminiscent of Freud's concept of homophobia. According to Downing (1989), to Freud, "Homophobia, too, is seen as an expression of repressed homosexuality. Freud regards it as the individual's attempt to reject admission of his own unconscious homosexual desires with "vigorous counter-attitudes" (p. 49).

One significant caveat must be stated regarding the usage of the stories of the men described below. No research has been done which would allow a deep and fair examination of their lives. Therefore, it is important to consider their stories to be only a starting point for a larger discussion. In no way should the following be misconstrued as a discussion of their full lives, their veracity, their sincerity, nor can it be an examination of them personally or psychologically. Because it is not possible to examine the lives of these individual men here in a fair way, the descriptions below cannot result in any conclusions about these individuals. Rather, the stories of politicians, religious leaders, and other socially active critics of homosexuality who have some homosexual feelings, are gay, or who have behaved homosexually, are used here to better understand the nature of social criticism of homosexuality, the nature of the organizations that condemn it, and ultimately, how these matters influence the young who absorb this material through the broader social dialogue they encounter.

Homosexuality in adult critics of homosexuality

Part of the broad social dialogue young people absorb and integrate is the national political debate. Political discussions occur in every arena of a young person's environment including in schools where teachers and peers discuss political campaigns and elections as part of the educational process. Young people often hear and absorb parental attitudes, or those of the broader and extended family, about political issues at home or see debates of national issues on television.

During the national election cycles between 2000 and 2008, Republican strategists supporting the then President George Bush sought to gain the votes of large blocks of conservative voters by encouraging states to include anti-gay amendments or initiatives on state ballots (Ireland, 2006). The strategy was based on the idea that conservative and evangelical voters opposed to homosexuality would be powerfully motivated to vote in the election, and vote for Bush, if the highly charged issue of same sex marriage was on the ballot. As an example, in 2004, eleven states held elections that included ballot initiatives that prohibited same-sex marriage. All eleven passed those initiatives and all eleven states voted for George Bush (Ireland, 2006). Ken Mehlman, the head of the national Republican Party and key advisor to President Bush, was a central figure in the formulation and implementation of such strategies. For much of a decade, negative attitudes about homosexuality were perpetuated for the sake of political advantage by Melhman and other political strategists. In many ways, that political strategy resulted in legal sanctions against LGBT people that may endure for many more decades. In 2010, Melhman announced publicly that he is gay.

> It's taken me 43 years to get comfortable with this part of my life . . . . The process is something that made me happier and a better person. It's something I wish I had done years ago. (Ambinder, 2010, "Bush Campaign Chief")

Like many other adults, Melhman passed as a heterosexual man in a conservative social and political environment that condemned homosexuality. Unlike many others who have had similar experiences, some of whom are discussed below, Melhman has since become a voice for LGBT rights. He now works closely with many groups that are working to gain the right for marriage, among other rights sought by LGBT people, using his considerable political skills and reputation for those purposes (Ambinder, 2010).

Other prominent politicians who have condemned homosexuality as part of their overall political stance have also been homosexual or have engaged in homosexual acts. Mark Foley, a congressman from Florida who publicly condemned homosexuality, eventually resigned his seat in Congress when it was learned that he had emailed inappropriate and sexual messages to a 16 year old boy (Babington & Weisman, 2006). Larry Craig, a United States Senator from Idaho who opposed many attempts to gain rights and legal protections for LGBT people, was arrested in a Minnesota airport in 2007 for solicitation of sex from a male undercover policeman. Craig pled guilty to a misdemeanor charge and later denied he was homosexual ("Craig: I Did Nothing Inappropriate," 2007).

Similarly, a married Republican state lawmaker, Rep. Phillip Hinkle, made headlines in the summer of 2011 when he solicited a male prostitute for a "really good time" through a series of emails. Hinkle arranged to pay the young man $140 for the sexual encounter. Initially, Hinkle stated that he "was aware of a shakedown taking place" but later acknowledged the content of the emails that described the sexual nature of the arrangement he had solicited with the young man (Shahid, 2011, para. 3). Hinkle, according to Wickman (2011), had opposed rights for LGBT people and had "recently voted to pass a constitutional amendment to ban same-sex marriage and civil unions" (Browning, as cited in Wickman, 2011, para. 10).

The difficulty faced by men who act on their homosexual feelings even while they are married and identify themselves as heterosexual are in some cases devastating. In Hinkle's case, his wife was informed of her husband's actions by phone by the young male prostitute's sister before the story was widely reported. According to Wickman

(2011), Hinkle's wife offered to pay the sister $10,000 to keep the story private and, later, Hinkle called her to say "You've ruined me" (para. 14). Hinkle's story has since been reported nationally by many news organizations.

The field of psychology has also been a source for anti-gay attitudes in society, as was discussed in Chapter 1. As a profession, psychology has, since the early 1970s, accepted homosexuality as a natural and healthy expression of sexuality. Despite that change, some individuals within the field continued to view homosexuality as pathological. One such man, George Rekers, conducted research in the early 1970s at UCLA in which he attempted to show that young boys who showed signs of effeminacy could be changed through discipline, including beatings (Green, 2011). According to Green, Rekers, along with his associate, published a paper in the *Journal of Applied Behavior Analysis* in 1974 that outlined one "success story," the case of "Kraig." "Kraig," a pseudonym, was coached, even coerced, to abandon behaviors and affects that were deemed effeminate. In 2003, the man who was the subject of that article, 38-year-old Kirk Murphy, a gay man, committed suicide. His suicide brought new attention to Rekers and the work he had done early in his career (Green, 2011, para. 4).

Rekers has, during the course of his career from the 1970s to 2011, become a national leading figure in condemning homosexuality from within the profession of psychology. He is a professor of neuropsychiatry at the University of South Carolina, a Baptist minister, and has testified as an expert witness in Florida against the right to adopt children by LGBT people. He has advised members of Congress, the White House and the Department of Health and Human Services. He is also a principal figure in national groups that oppose homosexuality including the National Association for Research & Therapy of Homosexuality, and the Family Research Council (Green, 2011).

According to the Schwartz (2010), in 2010, while returning from a vacation in Europe, Rekers was seen with a male escort in a Florida airport. Initially, Rekers explained that he had hired the young man to carry his luggage. Eventually, it was learned that Rekers had hired the young man from a gay escort web site, Rentboy.com, that lists escorts, explicit sexual pictures of them, the types of sexual activity they will provide, and the price of their services. The young escort who went with Rekers on the European vacation, in subsequent interviews, detailed the specific types of sexual activities that he and Rekers engaged in during the vacation, including daily nude massages. "It's a situation where he's going against homosexuality when he is homosexual," the young man told *The New York Times* (Green, 2011). Rekers continues to deny that he is gay.

Throughout many eras in history, men have been able to have sexual encounters with both men and women without severe consequence socially (Boswell, 1980). As was discussed in earlier chapters, in ancient Greece and Rome, and throughout many centuries after, no formal category of sexuality, either homosexual or heterosexual, was used so that men like Socrates could be married, have children and have sex with men with no shame, no humiliation, and no loss of status or privilege (Boswell, 1980). In today's society, in which homosexuality is demonized in some areas of society, heterosexually identified men who have homosexual feelings, and act on them, may suffer enormous and devastating losses and public humiliation. Some men, in addition to humiliation, may also face the cutting criticism that they have lied for years, to those closest to them, about an important aspect of their sexual orientation. In some ways, like many LGBT teens who have not disclosed their feelings, these adults are part of a hidden population that must be psychologically vigilant to avoid disclosure of their sexual feelings in an un-accepting social environment.

At the same time, the public efforts of these men to condemn or restrict homosexuality in society is partially causal of their own crisis.

Embedded in the political organizations that most harshly criticize homosexuality, just as Kinsey (1948) noted, are the very men who have homosexual feelings or who have acted homosexuality. Men like Melhman, Craig, Foley, Hinkle, and Rekers have fostered public disdain for homosexuality, an effort that eventually, in some ways, subjected them to that same disdain.

Young people whose homosexuality is hidden from the view of others, in some cases, also participate in the denigration of gay teens like these adult men have. Some have expressed their stories publicly to *The New York Times* (Kramer, 2011), in its feature, *Coming Out*, as a way to communicate their inner conflicts.

Adam's letter to *Coming Out* tells of a young man who, to be safe from criticism, joined others who denigrated gay teens. He attended an all-boys Catholic high school. Another boy, "flamboyantly gay," also attended as part of his freshman class. Adam was afraid he might be seen as gay if he was kind to or associated with the other boy. One day, Adam watched as the lacrosse coach went over to the gay teen's desk and mouthed the words "I really don't like you." All the other boys snickered, including Adam, knowing precisely what the coach had meant. Humiliated, the gay teen soon transferred to another class. Soon after, rumors began to spread about two other classmates who had been caught kissing at a school dance. According to Adam, the boys were bullied so badly, they both eventually left school. Having watched others who were gay, and watched their experience in the world around them, Adam found it difficult to contemplate sharing his own homosexuality with others. "I knew that if I came out, I would become the object of those jokes, and I didn't want to be a joke" (Adam A., as cited in Kramer, 2011).

In Adam's case, and perhaps in some of the men described above, the consequences of being gay, which he saw in his school experience, caused him to both participate in ostracizing gay teens and to take the defensive action of going "farther into the closet." Unlike some of the men listed above, Adam shared in his letter that he was able to begin to come out in college and to be embraced as a gay man by new friends (as cited in Kramer, 2011).

In much the same way that homosexuality has existed in some of the spokespeople for political and psychological organizations that condemn it, some highly prominent and vocal critics of homosexuality from conservative religious groups have also faced the difficult challenge of publicly acknowledging their own homosexuality. In many ways, just as it may be for teens, the conflicts of sexuality and Christian belief systems that condemn homosexuality may cause devastating moral crises among adults. Among the most publicly discussed displays of homosexuality among religious critics of homosexuality have been the cases of the Reverend Ted Haggard and the decades-long abuse of children by Catholic priests.

In 2006, saying that he was a "deceiver and liar" who had given in to his dark side, the Reverend Ted Haggard confessed to "sexual immorality" in a letter read from the pulpit of his church to his congregation. (Associated Press, 2006, "Haggard admits 'sexual immorality'"). Haggard was, at one time, the highly prominent evangelical minister of The New Life Church of Colorado, the President of the National Evangelical Association with more than 30 million members, and a politically influential figure in national politics who actively condemned homosexuality in all areas of his professional life. An allegation surfaced, which turned out to be true, that he had been using drugs and having sexual relations with a male prostitute in Denver. He subsequently lost his position within the evangelical community. The church Haggard founded ostracized him following the revelation. In a letter of agreement with the Board of his organization, after the disclosure, Haggard was forced to agree to "cut off all contacts with members of the church, stay away from the media, perform no ministry-related works, and move his family out of Colorado." Later in 2006, it was learned that Haggard had also had performed a sexual act in front of a 22-year-old male volunteer during 2006. His church had paid the volunteer $179,000 as a settlement (Rayfield, 2011).

Like Ken Mehlman, Haggard eventually came to accept that he had homosexual feelings and that he had them throughout his life. "I think that probably, if I were twenty- one in this society, I would identify myself as bisexual" (Rayfield, 2011, para. 1). While Haggard has acknowledged the nature of his same-sex feelings, he states that he has chosen to restrict his behavior to heterosexual sexual activity. Haggard eventually was released from his agreement with The New Life Church forbidding his return to the ministry or to Colorado Springs. He has founded a new church which he says welcomes "gay, straight, bi, tall, short, whether you're an addict, a recovering addict, or you have an addict in the family" (Rayfield, 2011, para. 13). Just as did Ken Mehlman, Haggard has begun to work actively to create an inclusive environment for LGBT people after his public disclosure about his own homosexual activity. At the same time, Haggard continues to feel that homosexuality is not moral.

It is interesting to note that on the day Ted Haggard confessed to his congregation, young people were sent from the room (Associated Press, 2006). They were not allowed to hear adults discuss Haggard's homosexuality or his behavior. Yet these young people were, it is assumed, allowed to hear Haggard preach about the evil and immorality of homosexuality. While it is not appropriate here to second-guess the adults' decision, their action suggests that young people can hear the condemnation of homosexuality from the pulpit but not hear the human consequences faced by those who have homosexual feelings, those who are conflicted about them, or those who are compelled to act secretively and destructively in attempting to experience their inner feelings.

In fact, because Haggard's story was widely publicized throughout that period, it is highly unlikely the children of his congregation did not eventually hear the story. Beyond that, they might well have heard of how their church treated Haggard harshly, banning him from the community, after he named his sexual feelings publicly. That one's community, fellowship, place of worship and "pathway" to one's spiritual God can be removed from homosexuals sends a powerful message to the young.

Perhaps the most widely publicized eruption of homosexual behavior among those who condemn homosexuality is the case of the sexual misconduct of many Catholic priests documented from the period of the 1950s to the present. In June, 2002, the Catholic bishops of the United States commissioned a report that was to study the extent and nature of sexual abuse by Catholic clergy against minors. The report, entitled *The Nature and Scope of the Problem of Sexual Abuse of Minors by Catholic Priests and Deacons in the United States* (John Jay College of Criminal Justice, 2004), contained an Executive Summary which stated that a total of 10,667 individuals had made allegations of child sexual abuse by Catholic priests and deacons between 1950 and 2002. Of those individuals, 17.2 % had siblings who were also allegedly abused. In over 61% of those cases, the alleged abuse of the individual occurred over a period of more than one year. Approximately 73% of the victims were 14 years of age or younger, approximately 22% were aged ten or younger and 81% of the victims were male. According to the report, at its peak, the rate of abuse was approximately 800 cases per year and that peak occurred in 1980. The Catholic Church, at the time the report was concluded, was to pay at least $500 million in compensation, penalties, legal fees and for the treatment of priests (John Jay College of Criminal Justice, 2004).

A complete examination of the abuse of children by Catholic priests is far too broad a topic to be covered in this work. The sheer scope of the scandal, covering half a century and involving hundreds of people, makes such a review impossible. Any discussion of the scandal or the psychological characteristics of those involved would be highly speculative. Beyond that, it is important to note that the vast majority of cases of sexual abuse by priests constitutes pedophilia, acts "involving sexual activity with a prepubescent child (generally age 13 years or younger)" (American Psychiatric Association, 2000, *Diagnostic and Statistical Manual of Mental Disorders*, 4th ed., text rev., p. 571). A psychological disorder, pedophilia is not associated with any specific sexual orientation, homosexual or heterosexual, and individuals with this disorder may be attracted to males, females or both (p. 571). At the same time, because much of the abuse was homosexual, several broad observations about homosexuality within the Catholic Church, and the way in which the Church responded to it, may be useful considerations in the discussion of how teenagers may struggle with homosexuality and their spiritual beliefs.

That men who are homosexual would be attracted to a profession as a priest, given Catholicism's rejection of homosexuality, is an interesting phenomenon and speaks to the ways in which individuals, including adolescents, may attempt to deal with their moral conflicts about homosexuality. For many gay Catholics, according to Lebacqz (2005), becoming a priest may be a way in which a gay individual can avoid the problems, both internally and socially, of being gay while assuming a prominent and respected position in society.

> Many gay Roman Catholics may indeed be attracted to the priesthood precisely because an active gay identity "outside" is not respected but as a priest, the young man is offered a model of "redemptive suffering" and avoidance of a disgraceful sexual identity. Further, priesthood brings power in the Roman Catholic

Church, so it is one of the few avenues where gay Catholics can find a position that is both acceptable and powerful. (p. 201)

Young Catholic gay men may well look to the priesthood as a way to avoid stigmatism and moral conflict. Beyond that issue, the Church has knowingly allowed homosexuality in its ranks, including abusive priests, for decades, according to Boisvert and Goss (2005). Such tolerance of homosexuality, despite publicly condemning homosexuality, speaks to an issue within the Church itself. The Church has, according to Boisvert and Goss (2005), demonstrated a capacity, like many individuals, to tolerate tremendous contradiction. In Boisvert and Goss's view (2005), the Church maintains that contradiction by maintaining secrets. Homosexuality in the Catholic Church has long been, according to Boisvert and Goss (2005), an open secret within the Church.

It is composed of secrets, within secrets, within secrets. The most amazing thing of all is that this eminently fragile edifice of concealment is constructed around one major and undeniable secret, a secret which, while being vociferously condemned for everyone else, remains very much alive within the institutional confines of the church. That dirty little secret is the erotic desire of men for other men, the homoerotic longings of supposedly celibate men for others like them . . . The open secret of homoerotic desire in the Catholic Church does what all such open secrets do so beautifully in society at large: it makes living with them possible. It also gives permission for indulgence, while paying lip service to moral incongruity and panic. What it allows for oneself it denies to others. (p. 23)

Young gay people with strong, conservative, religious beliefs may well ask the question "What am I to do when God, who created all things including my sexual nature, turns around and condemns his own creation in me?" Within Catholicism, the crisis of homosexuality and the Church's condemnation of that sexuality has been managed through a secret, internal knowledge and tolerance that "made living with it possible" even as homosexuality was condemned for others. Individual priests, in order to maintain the contradiction, became fragmented psychologically according to Mellott (2005). In his work, Mellott (2005) stated that seminarians are often instructed on the value of self-knowledge. Yet, they become aware, early in their instruction, of a conflict regarding the value of self-knowledge when that requires a discussion openly and honestly about their authentic sexual feelings of a homosexual nature.

> When the disparity is ignored, the strained silence surrounding sexuality and sexual development is interpreted by the seminarians as a cue either to ignore their sexuality or to pursue their sexual development in secret . . . In either case, a fragmentation within the seminarian occurs. (p. 33)

Many priests and men like Ted Haggard struggle for a lifetime in attempts to reconcile their religious beliefs and their homosexuality. The stories of their lives, their behaviors, and the responses they received from others are heard by young people, and in many cases, young people, at very early ages, must face similar struggles. One young adult, Matthew, wrote to *The New York Times* to share the story of his younger life with others.

Matthew said that he knew growing up that being gay was wrong. He knew it from the Bible, from his community and from his family.

He also knew he was gay from a very young age. He knew, he said, when he was in kindergarten. He hid his feelings from others until he was 20 and then began dating an older man. After 6 months, feeling terribly conflicted, he broke the relationship off, became increasingly religious, and thought he was "cured." Over the next 9 years, feeling lonely as a straight man, Matthew developed an alcohol problem, finally returning home to begin recovery. He returned to church, began to attend men's groups in order to change his orientation and told his family he was renouncing his homosexuality. With his chronic depression worsening over time, Matthew eventually was admitted to a psychiatric hospital for 10 days. At 36, Matthew still feels he does not fit within society, his family or his church. He prays that some day he will. For now, he surrounds himself with people who love him, and hopes "that one day I will find peace" (as cited in Kramer, 2011).

Like Ted Haggard and many Catholic priests, Matthew's sexual orientation brought him into direct and irreconcilable conflict with his religion. Unlike them, Matthew faced having to state his homosexuality publicly in the earliest, and most vulnerable, stages of his life in the face of a unified and powerful coalition of prohibitions from his parents, his family, his peers, his religion and the God he understood. Ostracized from his community if he held true to his sexual nature, and embraced if he unnaturally abandoned his inner world, Matthew could only pray for a happier resolution in the future. As Matthew's letter showed, the words spoken from religious leaders, believed and repeated by family and friends, are heard by the very young, integrated into a child's psychological life, and in ways that may lay the groundwork for ongoing, perhaps lifelong, crisis.

Fragmentation, secret lives, hypocrisy, self-denial, destructive acting out, abuse of others, public humiliation, loss of loved ones and community, ostracism, homophobia and deep moral conflict are just some of the adjectives that describe the psychological difficulties faced by men who are homosexual but who simultaneously condemn it. Because the men described above have lived within the context of anti-homosexual belief systems, they are excellent examples of the impact of social denigration of homosexuality in an individual. They are also indicative of the many psychological responses an individual may make toward their own homosexuality when it is viewed with shame or guilt. Some deny their feelings, some eventually "come out," and some live in an unresolved, fragmented psychological state.

In many ways, these men share characteristics with teenagers who have same sex attractions. First, just as many homosexual adults may be hidden from view, many gay teens remain hidden and attempt to seamlessly pass as heterosexual. Second, teens may be heavily influenced by social pressures that condemn homosexuality and may face ostracism when homosexuality is disclosed, just as these men have. Third, the crisis of identity formation, as outlined by Erikson (1968), which involves the creation of a sense of coherence between the inner self and outer world, is a crisis that appears in adolescence but, also, may continue in adulthood for some who have homosexual feelings. Finally, adults, like teens, may take many different approaches to the resolution of their homosexuality with the society around them which may include psychological splitting, passing as straight, denial, repression, homophobia, or in some cases, acceptance.

Social messaging—role models

The social dialogue teens hear may also include some positive messages about homosexuality. One of the most powerful means of communicating social acceptance of homosexuality to young people is through the presence of many successful people in society who are openly gay or lesbian. Young people may look to them for modeling of what possibilities exist for them as adults. They may derive hope that the difficulties they experience in their young lives can be resolved successfully. Many examples exist for young people to look at, to consider, and to perhaps emulate.

Within the entertainment field there are many prominent actors and actresses who are openly gay or lesbian ("Famous Gay & Lesbian Celebrities," 2011). These celebrities include Neil Patrick Harris, the star of TV's popular comedy *How I Met Your Mother*, Sean Hayes of *Will and Grace*, and Jane Lynch of *Glee* among many others. Famous movie actors and actresses such as Rupert Everett, Jodi Foster, and Ian McKellan of both *X Men* and *Lord of the Rings* fame are also open about their sexual orientation. Musicians including Melissa Etheridge, Elton John, George Michael, Lance Bass of N'Sync, Ricky Martin, Adam Lambert, and Michael Stipe, lead singer for REM, are openly gay and lesbian stars in their professions. Ellen Degeneres, who once famously announced that she was a lesbian on her television comedy show, now hosts her own, highly popular daytime talk show and Rachel Maddow, host of MSNBC's *The Rachel Maddow Show*, demonstrates that highly respected journalists include lesbian people. Former United States Congressman Barney Frank is openly gay and has been for many years. During his tenure, he was among the most important political leaders in Congress. These role models, in many ways not possible in years past, convey powerful messages to the young that life as an LGBT person holds promise for success.

Teenage homosexuality and television

When Rickie Vasquez came out to his family in the 1994 episode of *My So- Called Life*, he ended up bruised, bloodied, and living in an abandoned warehouse full of homeless teens, afraid to tell even his closest friends why his uncle had kicked him out of the house just before Christmas. (Armstrong, 2011, p. 36)

One measure of social tolerance or intolerance of teen homosexuality is the depiction of gay teens on television. In 1992, 23 years after the Stonewall riots launched the modern gay movement in the United States, the first openly gay teenager appeared on daytime national television (Armstrong, 2011, p. 36). The character Billy Douglas, portrayed by Ryan Phillippe on the soap opera *One Life To Live*, came out as gay before immediately departing the show. That brief depiction of gay teenage males was followed by the character of Rickie Vasquez on the prime time television show *My So-Called Life*, described above. Audience reaction to Rickie was more than supportive, according to Wilson Cruz who played the character (Armstrong, 2011, p. 36).

Slowly, over time, other gay and lesbian characters were introduced into television shows in a variety of roles and for different lengths of time. Six years after Rickie was introduced to young audiences, the first romantic male kiss between young gay characters occurred on Warner Brothers' show *Dawson's Creek* in 2000. That milestone, the first ever same-sex kiss, occurred among teen gay characters prior to the first adult same-sex kiss on *Will and Grace*, the prime time NBC sitcom beginning in 1998. By 2007, ABC's *Greek* depicted an openly gay college student who became the president of his fraternity, establishing a new level of acceptance. The age of "coming out" dropped over time as well so that by 2009, 14-year-old Marshall Gregson announced that he was gay on the television show *United States of Tara*. Unlike the brutal response experienced by Rickie of *My So-Called Life* in 1994, Marshall found acceptance from his mother, sending a message to audiences that not all people, especially parents, reject gay teens (Armstrong, 2011, p. 36).

This message of tolerance and acceptance has been dramatically expanded by the hit television show, *Glee*, with 14 million viewers each week (Armstrong, 2011, pp. 36-41).

If only Rickie could see *Glee's* Kurt Hammel now. The breakout character . . . . on TV's most buzzed-about network show has won an Emmy nomination, a Golden Globe, and viewers' hearts with an at times poignant, but often, well, gleeful depiction of a modern gay teen. (Armstrong, 2011, p. 36)

According to Armstrong (2011), *Glee*, the story of a group of high-school teens who form a Glee club in a small town in Ohio, provides among the most thorough discussions of teen homosexuality ever seen on television. The character Kurt experiences bullying, rejection, and heartbreak in some aspects of his life but love, acceptance, and friendship as well. In late 2010, the story line allowed Kurt to find a boyfriend, Blaine, and the relationship between the two continued to be an integral part of the show's overall story line. Beyond the excitement displayed by the show's fans, the topic of gay teen love on television, a subject that at one time would have been highly controversial, seems to be accepted more broadly. According to Armstrong, there have been no protests, no public outcry, nor any withdrawal of corporate sponsorships. In fact, General Motors sponsored the cast of *Glee's* performance in the 2011 Super Bowl (Armstrong, 2011, p. 41).

The message of acceptance that *Glee* provides represents a major way in which gay teens can access positive examples of the possibilities inherent in the gay teenage experience. Beyond that, gay teens who watch the program are given insight into more specific experiences they may themselves have had. In one series of episodes, the character Kurt is bullied and initially keeps his troubles about the harassment secret. Eventually, Kurt's father is involved and addresses the issue with the school principal. The principal expels the bullying student only to have the school board reverse her decision, allowing the bully to return, leaving Kurt unprotected. His friends, in an attempt to keep him in their midst, offer to protect him but Kurt and his family decide to move him out of the district to a private school (Armstrong, 2011, p. 41). This story line provides teen viewers not only the opportunity to consider the issue of bullying, and the cost to young gay teens, but also provides a message that, if given a chance, many in the broader community will be supportive of young gay people.

Broader social dialogue

Gay teens are exposed to social messaging about them in many ways and from many sources including newspapers, magazines, television, and the internet, among others. The information about *Glee* above appeared in *Newsweek Magazine* and *Entertainment Weekly*, both well-read and highly popular national weekly newsmagazines. The picture of *Glee's* characters, Kurt and Blaine, with Kurt's head resting against Blaine's, is on the front cover of *Entertainment Weekly* (January, 2011) for all young gay teens to see. Yet, those same teens might also have seen *Newsweek's* cover in 2008, which showed the picture of 15-year-old Lawrence King and the school he attended when he was murdered by another boy for being homosexual.

Titled "Young, Gay and Murdered," the *Newsweek* cover story details the events of February 12, 2008 when a 14-year-old teen named Brandon took out a gun and shot Larry King, 15, to death because of his sexual orientation and because Larry expressed it openly. According to Ramin Setoodeh, the story's author, Larry had experienced bullying and taunts from other boys in gym, the lunchroom and elsewhere. The harassment had actually begun years before in grade school and he had become accustomed to it. Larry's "first line of defense" was to "flaunt" his sexuality by dressing and acting in ways that he knew might provoke reactions from others but which he felt were within his right to self expression (Setoodeh, 2008, p. 42).

The tragic story of Larry King is illustrative of the difficulties young LGBT teens have and the sometimes deadly consequence of the conflict between tolerance and intolerance. It is also a lesson, to Setoodeh, on the impact of social discourse and the unresolved problems of adult society on teens. At a time when social acceptance for the LGBT community is on the rise, young people are coming out at earlier and earlier ages which presents a new set of problems. According to Setoodeh, "Kids may want to express who they are, but they are playing grown up without fully knowing what that means." (Setoodeh, 2008, p. 42)

Without question, Larry King is an example of a young man who was exploring his gender identity and sexuality publicly, in his dress and actions, in a way that has been done in past decades only by adults. Social messaging has suggested that who one is, and how one expresses that, is a matter of personal freedom and that message has been heard by young people. But, by definition, young people may not yet, as Setoodeh explained, have an adult's experience, maturity, defenses, or resources to navigate through problems they encounter.

At the same time, although not fully explored by Setoodeh, it can be said that King's killer, Brandon, had also received social messaging that suggested that the expression of sexuality, even extravagantly, was intolerable and unacceptable. Anti-gay or intolerant messages about homosexuality are common-place in society, as discussed previously, and the transmission of those messages occurs regularly throughout many forms of media. Just as the case with Larry's assumption of gay freedom without the tools that would be afforded him at a later age, it can be said that Brandon, at 14, carried out the messages of adult intolerance without maturity, without experience, and without adult restraints. Adult intolerance, in the hands of a 14-year-old boy, became deadly.

Certainly, no responsible adult who opposes homosexuality suggests murder as an acceptable response. Yet, negative messages about homosexuality are fully integrated in today's social discourse and bullying and harassment of homosexuals occurs, as will be seen, routinely. That homosexuality is immoral, sinful, unnatural, deviant, against nature and against God, that homosexuals will burn in hell, or that they have chosen to be immoral are statements that may signal to teens that there is a moral justification for the denigration of gays. That harsh treatment of gay children is acceptable is a message that comes not only from some parents and some church altars, but from major political figures as well. Marcus Bachmann, the husband of a candidate for the 2012 Republican Party's nomination for President, Michele Bachmann, suggested as much when speaking of gay children. "We have to understand: barbarians need to be educated. They need to be disciplined." To Marcus Bachmann, homosexuality is a sinful nature and one that our public educational system is allowing (Bufkin, 2011, para. 3-4).

Adult messages of intolerance also find expression in the words of other teens. Writing for a high school newspaper, a young man named Joshua wrote in his sports column what many adults have said in various ways before. To Joshua, "homosexuality is an unnatural perversion" and society's growing acceptance is a "step backward." Joshua believed that the term homophobia implied that people were afraid of homosexuals and he was certain that he did not fear them. Rather, Joshua felt that people who were being called homophobic were simply people who knew that homosexuality was wrong and not to be associated with. In Joshua's mind, homosexuality was about perverted sex and the promotion of homosexuality, not homophobia, was the real problem in society. Although he recognized his views might be called narrow-minded, he felt that his kind of "narrow-minded" attitude was, in reality, a new word for what is moral (Oblea, 2009, p. 3).

The communication of attitudes about homosexuality to teens may occur through national publications or media outlets that share

Bachmann's belief that homosexual children must be seen as barbarians that require discipline. At other times, teens may hear directly from their peers, like Joshua, who tell them that even if the attitudes are "narrow- minded," anti-homosexual attitudes are "moral" and that teens can feel grounded in their feelings that homosexuality is a perversion that should not be accepted or associated with. Such attitudes justify intolerance in the name of good parenting, social well-being or morality and some teens may find support for anti-homosexual feelings and actions by listening and absorbing these views.

Teenagers also hear the content of adult conflicts about homosexuality through news events. In July 2011, California Governor Jerry Brown signed legislation making California the first state to require that textbooks and history lessons include the contributions made by LGBT people in history. According to Brown, "History should be honest" (McGreevy, 2011, p. AA1). The bill revises existing law so that, to Brown, "the important contributions of Americans from all backgrounds and walks of life are included in our history books" (McGreevy, 2011, p. AA1). Immediately following the passage of the bill, the Capital Resource Institute, a conservative organization, announced its intention to launch a statewide ballot initiative to overturn the law. Other conservative groups reacted sharply, including the founder of the Traditional Values Coalition, Rev. Louis Sheldon. To Sheldon, the Governor's decision to sign the legislation was an invitation for "homosexual activists" to indoctrinate the children of California (Famodimu, 2011, para. 9-10).

> By signing SB 48 . . . California's classrooms, textbooks and instructional materials will all become pro-homosexual promotion tools. If parents don't have their children out of public schools, this should cause them to remove them. (Famodimu, 2011, para. 9-10)

To be clear, because the achievements of many homosexual people in history are currently taught in public schools, men like Michelangelo, Leonardo da Vinci, and Socrates, the law would require that where known, the sexual orientation of historical figures can now be added to the instruction materials and class discussions (McGreevy, 2011, p. AA1).

Impact of environment

It is difficult, if not impossible, to quantify the exact effect of social condemnation of homosexuality on young LGBT people, yet, some evidence exists from both anecdotal sources and from quantitative research that suggests that LGBT teens have a higher tendency towards negative health outcomes, or even suicide, when their environment is less tolerant.

As an example, the announcement by conservative Congresswoman Michele Bachmann of Minnesota that she would seek the 2012 Republican nomination for President brought with it intense scrutiny of her and her background. Bachmann has been a long time conservative who has publicly and consistently disapproved of homosexuality. As part of the news reporting about her generally, a discussion of a series of suicides in her district surfaced. According to Mencimer, (2011), nine teens have committed suicide in one school district represented by Bachman and many more have attempted to suicide. Public health officials have labeled the area a "suicide contagion area." At least 4 of the teens were known or perceived to be LGBT teens. Yet, according to Mencimer (2011), Bachmann and her allies "have opposed efforts in the state to promote tolerance for gays and lesbians in the classroom, seeing such initiatives as a way of allowing gays to recruit impressionable youths into an unhealthy and un-Christian lifestyle" (pp.1-2).

National debates about homosexuality are also locally centered in communities throughout the country. In the case of the

Anoka-Hennepin School District, Minnesota's largest, the debates about homosexuality have focused on district policies related to issues surrounding LGBT teens including how teachers should respond to questions about homosexuality, how the school should respond to bullying, and whether or not groups expressly for LGBT teens, like the Gay Straight Alliance, should be allowed. The district had a policy during the 1990s that was colloquially called "no homo promo" and specifically created a policy that no school employee could teach that homosexuality was a normal or healthy lifestyle. According to Mencimer (2011), "The anti-gay climate in the schools in Bachmann's district has been so extreme that it has attracted the attention of the Justice Department and the Department of Education's Office of Civil Rights" (p. 3). Within this overall context, nine students, at least four of whom were LGBT, committed suicide and seven of the middle school students of the teacher who has sponsored the school's GSA have been hospitalized for attempting or threatening suicide (Mencimer, 2011).

Some research exists that suggests that environments that are less tolerant generally, or conversely more conservative, tend to see more teen suicides. According to a study conducted by Columbia University, "Suicide attempts by gay teens—and even straight kids—are more common in politically conservative areas" (Tanner, 2011, para. 1). While many studies have found a disproportionately higher rate of suicides and attempted suicides among LGBT teens, many of which are described later in this work, the study by Columbia suggests that environments that are generally intolerant have a negative effect in some unknown way which tends to increase suicide risks in the entire adolescent population, LGBT and heterosexual alike.

School climate for LGBT teens

In order to understand the school environments in which LGBT teens live, and the impact those environments have on their well-being, two major national surveys have been conducted over the last decade by the Gay, Lesbian and Straight Education Network (GLSEN). The surveys explored the frequency of harassment and bullying in the target schools for all teens.

In 2005, GLSEN conducted a survey of 3,400 students, aged 13-18, and over 1,000 school teachers from throughout the nation. The resulting report, *From Teasing to Torment: School Climate in America, A Survey of Students and Teachers* (Harris Interactive & GLSEN, 2005), outlined teens' experiences related to harassment, bullying and safety regardless of sexual orientation. The report findings, some of which are highlighted below, suggest that harassment and bulling are frequently experienced by a significant number of teens in America's schools.

In general, the study found that bullying is common in America's schools with 65% of teens responding that they had been targeted for verbal or physical harassment. This harassment may be related to gender, appearance, sexual orientation, gender expressions, race or ethnic background, religion or disability. 39% reported being harassed for reasons of appearance or body size and 33% reported harassment because they were perceived as being LGBT (GLSEN, 2005, para. 4-5).

Clearly, according to this study, harassment and bullying is frequent and such behavior is directed at teens for a variety of reasons. Interestingly, the study found that one especially important distinction exists in the population of LGBT teens. They do not feel safe.

> The survey finds that LGBT students are three times more likely as non-LGBT students to say they do not feel safe at school (22% vs. 7%) and 90% of LGBT students (vs. 62% of non-LGBT teens) have been harassed or assaulted in the past year. (GLSEN, 2005, para. 6)

The study found that, regardless of the reason for harassment, 57% of all students who experienced it did not report it to school officials because they felt that teachers would not respond or were powerless to change the situation, with 67% of LGBT giving this response. It is important to note that the lack of reporting harassment continues despite the fact that 85% of teachers agreed in the survey that they had an obligation to provide a safe environment and 71% of those teachers felt that anti-discrimination and anti harassment policies would be helpful. The survey also concluded that when such policies were in place, students felt safer and reported less harassment (GLSEN, 2005).

A follow-up survey conducted by GLSEN in 2009 reviewed survey results about harassment and bullying over a ten-year period and focused primarily on the experience of LGBT teens. In that report, GLSEN (2010) found that levels of harassment and bullying remained high over time, that there were areas of some improvement, and that there are both psychological and educational consequences of bullying for LGBT teens. 84% of LGBT students had been verbally harassed, 40.1% physically harassed, 18.8% physically assaulted and 72.4% had heard homophobic remarks like "faggot" or "dyke" frequently or often at school (GLSEN, 2010). Further, the report assessed the consequences of that harassment.

> Nearly two-thirds (61.1%) of students felt unsafe in school because of their sexual orientation . . . . 30.0% missed at least one day of school in the past month because of safety concerns . . . . Increased levels of victimization were related to increased levels of depression and anxiety and decreased levels of self-esteem. (GLSEN, 2010, "Key Findings")

It is worth noting that the report found that, paradoxically, students who were out reported both higher levels of victimization and higher levels of psychological well- being. Although not fully articulated in the report, it is possible that students who are hidden, those who have not identified themselves as LGBT, may not be able to utilize support systems within schools for LGBT teens for fear that they their orientation will be disclosed to others. Those who are out and have disclosed their orientation, at least at school, may well be more targeted for harassment but, also, may have the ability to gain the support of teachers, staff, and organizations for them and other gay teens.

In fact, the GLSEN (2010) study found that where schools have made positive interventions on behalf of LGBT teens, many of the consequences related to harassment and bullying are reduced. Schools which had a club for LGBT teens like the Gay-Straight Alliance, staff which was supportive of LGBT teens, and with anti-bullying policies, also had reduced incidences of harassment and homophobic remarks while reporting more cases when the staff intervened to stop such behavior. These schools also reported less absenteeism and higher academic achievement among LGBT teens (GLSEN, 2010). In short, although the school environment for LGBT teens continues to be an experience which includes consistent bullying and harassment, and in some cases, are physically unsafe, many schools are working to improve those environments and demonstrating strategies that are effective.

Among the most effective strategies for reducing the negative effects of hostility experienced by LGBT teens is the availability of school-sanctioned clubs for LGBT teens. The most common of these groups is the Gay-Straight Alliance (GSA), a network of school-based clubs throughout the country. Originally formed in San Francisco in 1988, GSAs are student-initiated and student-run clubs in public and private schools. By 2011, there were over 800 individual GSA clubs in California and GSA organizations now exist in 26 states. The groups generally include not only LGBT teens but also those who are questioning their orientation, heterosexual teens who support LGBT teens, supportive staff, and community leaders. While no statistics exist as to the exact breakdown of group members by orientation, as such information is not requested of members, the GSA Network surveyed students at GSA events in 2010 and found that fully 28% of attendees were heterosexual students who participated in an effort to support their friends who were LGBT. The stated purpose of GSA clubs is to create a safe environment for LGBT teens and to work to "create a school environment free of discrimination, harassment, and intolerance" (GSA Network, 2011, "What is a Gay-Straight Alliance?").

Some research exists to suggest that GSAs have become an important strategy in reducing intolerance and its impact on LGBT teens. Saewyc (2011), citing multiple sources, reported that some surveys have found that "students who attend schools with GSAs were significantly less likely to experience victimization and were less likely to report suicidal thoughts or attempts than peers in schools without GSAs" (p. 268). Although only a very small percentage of LGBT teens attend GSAs (Savin-Williams, 2005, p. 20), perhaps for reasons of stigmatization, when they do attend, the impact can be dramatic. Although quantitative information on the effect of GSAs more broadly is not available, the impact individually can be seen in the story of one young man.

Nowmee wrote to *The New York Times' Open Forum* in 2010 to share his story, a story of hope and optimism. He had arrived in the United States, an immigrant from "half way around the world", to attend high school. He left a country and a religious environment that condemned homosexuality and had never known anyone who was gay. He knew he was but did not like it, did not understand it and knew no one he could speak with about it. One Monday at lunch, a classmate mentioned that the school was forming a Gay Straight Alliance club that would meet that Friday. He made a note in his notebook but then changed the subject by making a joke. As the week progressed, Nowmee found the courage to tell his brother he was thinking of attending and openly shared his fear. His brother not only reassured him but told Nowmee he would accompany him to the meeting. On that Friday, Nowmee found the courage to walk to the classroom where the GSA was to meet. As he walked in, he saw his brother, classmates and a teacher he had seen on campus. He recalled that they welcomed him and offered him snacks. Nowmee now feels like he is living two lives. He is the president of the GSA on campus and is an "out and proud" LGBT youth activist. And each day, he walks home "like a walk back into the closet" because his parents do not know. He accepts the double life he is living but remains amazed by his journey to this point and hopeful about his path forward (Nowmee, as cited in Kramer, 2011).

While Nowmee continues to feel that he needs to pretend to be heterosexual at home, through his participation in the GSA at his school, his life has dramatically changed. He has support in an area of his life that once caused tremendous isolation and, to some extent, a loss of self-esteem. The GSA experience allowed him to come out of isolation, find others he could identify with, share with, and be friends with. In the process, and despite the difficulties he anticipated, Nowmee could see a path to his future that was hopeful once again.

Family and parental environment

The story of Nowmee illustrates a separate and important aspect of the environment gay teens encounter. How a parent responds, or how a young gay teenager imagines they will respond, is of tremendous importance. Nowmee imagined that his parents, because of their religious background and their attitudes about homosexuality, would not accept him as a gay teen. For that reason, he continued to pretend he was heterosexual at home despite his openness at school and with a sibling. Nowmee is not alone, according to Harrison (2003).

> Homosexual adolescents fear abuse and rejection. Within the family, initial disclosure is usually received negatively and may produce long-term distress. Nonrecognition and nonacceptance by families may lead to harassment, rejection, or violence against youth. (p. 109)

According to Harrison (2003), adolescents very often are aware of the family's attitudes about homosexuality and may anticipate realistically a family's negative, hostile or even violent reaction. They may turn to closeted behaviors that, while circumventing rejection or violence, also prevent the possibility of support. Stating that mothers are usually disclosed to before fathers, Harrison noted that one half of mothers were accepting while the other half 's attitudes ranged from tolerating to rejection. The reaction of fathers was, on the whole, more negative (p. 109).

According to a study done by Padilla, Crisp, and Rew (2010), fewer than half of the LGBT teens he studied were out to at least one parent. Thirty-three % of the teens he studied were out to their mothers and twenty-three % were out to their fathers. Of those teens who had disclosed their sexual orientation to a parent, most in the study by Padilla et al. (2010) received a positive or accepting response (p. 269). When the response from a parent is positive and a sense of connectedness to the family is established, lower levels of suicide attempts have been noted (Saewyc, 2011, p. 267). Likewise, a positive response from mothers has the effect of lowering drug use among LGBT teens compared to teens whose parents are rejecting (Padilla et al., 2010, p. 265). Yet, as Harrison (2003) noted, many teens have realistic fears about how their disclosure will be received by parents and family including fears of nonrecognition or rejection. The vast majority of those Padilla et al. (2010) studied were not open with both of their parents.

Several authors have noted some of the other major reasons teens may not disclose to their parents. One major reason relates to their parents' religious beliefs, according to Saewyk (2011). "LGB youths considered parental religious beliefs as a major barrier to coming out. Nearly half agreed that they felt their parents' religious beliefs made it more difficult for them to come out to them" (p. 270). In some cases, according to Harrison (2003), disclosure to families may lead to coercion to change through "the ineffective processes of psychological or religion-based conversion therapies" which are based on devaluing homosexuality. Additionally, in a variety of ways, rejection of young people by their parents may generate anxiety about being abandoned or forced to leave the home. In some ways, this may relate to teens actually leaving their homes as a result of conflicts and parental rejection. "In disclosing to nonsupportive families, homosexual adolescents may be predisposed to becoming runaways as a result of rejection" (p. 108).

Potential psychosocial problems for gay teens

Given the many aspects of a gay teen's environment which may be hostile to homosexuality, or may be perceived to be hostile, many teens struggle with a wide variety of problems in home, school, and socially. To be clear, not all gay teens experience these problems but many do and, for that reason, a list of possible issues is useful. Harrison (2003) compiled a list of potential problems that may apply to any given gay teen and it is summarized as follows. Socially, teens may experience isolation, stigmatism, be at risk for discrimination and may be at risk for violence or abuse. Within the family, gay teens may be at risk for nonrecognition, rejection, harassment, violence/abuse, coercion to change, be subject to the throw-away phenomenon, may have feelings of sinfulness especially in religious families, and are at risk of being runaways or even homelessness. Gay teens may suffer from self-hatred, low self esteem, and may experience high levels of vigilance and self monitoring. Gay teens are at increased risk of alcohol/drug abuse, increased depression, suicide risk and HIV infection. (based on Harrison, 2003)

Beyond the risks listed above, and in some ways because of the issues above, a general pessimism may develop among younger LGBT teens. According to Padilla et al. (2010), among the LGBT teens he studied, 58% felt that their sexual orientation would be an obstacle in their lives and 63% had seriously thought of suicide (p. 269). These findings suggest that for many young people, without the benefit of life experience over years, there may be a tendency on their part to imagine that the difficulties they experience in their daily lives now represent how life will be for them throughout their lives. To many, being homosexual may be seen as an obstacle, so much so that suicide is contemplated.

Padilla et al. (2010) further suggested that the experience of many LGBT teens can be considered to be traumatic whether or not the individual's orientation has been disclosed. "They are not only vulnerable to the traumatic events of all youth but also have to contend with family rejection, school harassment, and physical, sexual and/or emotional abuse in suspicion or declaration of their emerging sexual orientation."

Beyond that, "internalized homophobia, expectations of rejection, and experiences with discrimination and violence are significantly associated with feelings of demoralization and irrational guilt as well as suicidal ideation (p. 265).

Blum and Pfetzing (1997) also agreed that the experiences of many gay teens can be seen as traumatic as they, according to the authors, meet all the criteria of trauma as outlined by Freud, including the possibility of dissociation.

The problems, stress, and even trauma experienced by LGBT teens may be largely responsible for the increase in health and emotional difficulties among this population as compared to the broad heterosexual teen population. According to Saewyc (2011), studies about the possible emotional and health risks faced by LGBT teens have been very consistent and consistently show that "within nearly all population-based studies, a higher prevalence of sexual minority youth indicate emotional distress, depression, self- harm, suicidal ideation, and suicide attempts than do their heterosexual peers" (Saewyc, 2011, p. 262).

As mentioned in previously, Haas et al. (2011) reviewed multiple surveys which assessed suicide rates among LGBT teens throughout the last two decades, finding that LGB teens were anywhere from between two to seven times more likely to attempt suicide that their heterosexual peers (p. 8). According to Saewyc (2011), there is also a higher prevalence of smoking, alcohol and drug use among LGBT teens (p. 263).

Generally, the available research suggests that the increased health risks, including suicidal and self-harm risks, risks for substance abuse, and other health risks including HIV, are developed out of a response to stigma, rejection, and social exclusion. Abuse, family and peer rejection, harassment, or physical assaults are more strongly linked to increased health risks than any other (Saewyc, 2011). In many cases, the environmental stressors LGBT teens face may cause multiple problems. As mentioned, students who are harassed at school may become school avoidant, then less involved academically, have lower grades, which in turn may cause additional stress at home and impact their ability to graduate or move into higher education. Likewise, rejection by family may cause young people to leave home, eventually become homeless, and be more disposed to drug or alcohol abuse. As just one example, according to the Zavis (2010), a disproportionate share of the 4,200 homeless youth in Los Angeles are LGBT youth, many of whom were rejected in their homes or home environment. According to the news article, 40% of the homeless youth in Hollywood are LGBT teens, many of whom have been rejected by their parents and families (Zavis, 2010).

At the same time, it is important to stress that even though LGBT teens may have higher risks for health problems, not all LGBT teens experience significant problems and most navigate adolescence successfully, moving on to "live healthy, fulfilling adult lives, despite facing societal challenges during adolescence" (Saewyc, 2011, p. 266). Savin-Williams (2005), an author who has studied LGBT issues for decades, suggested that, in fact, there is a significant danger for professionals when LGBT teens are imagined solely as "suffering." Reviewing the narratives that much of the research seems to suggest, Savin-Williams (2005) stated that during the 1980s and 1990s, a narrative was created that LGBT teens are most characterized in a "suffering, suicidal" group. Now, to Savin-Williams (2005), these teens are increasingly understood for their resilience, pride and adaptive characteristics (p. 50). More and more teens are "coming out," more are forming or joining school organizations like the Gay-Straight Alliance clubs, and more teens are speaking out publicly to stop bullying in schools.

While much of the research above speaks to the surveys that attempt to understand LGBT teens as a group, it is also possible to understand their difficulties, and the things that save them from risks, on an individual basis. How any one teen experiences the world, what troubles them, how severely they are affected, and what "saves" them may be mostly an individual matter. As an example, one young writer to *The New York Times* (2011) found his way to desperation, and back again, in his own, unique way.

Esteban was born in Los Angeles. His father left when he was born and his mother, who he looked up to, raised 6 children on her own. She had asked him one time, when he was 10, if he was gay and he said no. She was relieved and said she would have been disappointed if he were gay. For years, he feared that she would hate him, that his friends would hate him, if they ever found out he was gay. But one day, he found the courage to tell her. She responded simply that he was her son and she loved him. Esteban, feeling safe to move forward, began to come out to his peers only to find that they called him names, pushed and punched him. In February of that year, he "decided to commit suicide." Tired of the harassment, Esteban tried to commit suicide and failed, waking up in the hospital with his mother next to him. He said that with her so firmly on his side, he felt stronger than ever and had begun to regain hope (Esteban, as cited in Kramer, 2011).

In the story of a 15-year-old gay teen in Los Angeles, many of the findings of the research on LGBT teens can be seen. He struggled early to declare that he was gay and denied it to his mother. He faced harassment at school and tried to commit suicide. He found hope and safety in the aftermath, mostly from a loving mother, and he can begin to return to the broader world as a gay person, fully identified among his family and peers. He is resilient, strong, and is hopeful about his future despite the difficulties he has experienced. Yet, he is different from many others. Others do not come out until much later. Many others find that their families do not love them. Most do not, like Esteban, try to commit suicide. In fact, many, like those who form GSAs, can be characterized less by the harassment they experience than by their efforts to eliminate that intolerance through social activism.

CHAPTER VI

THREE STORIES: GABRIEL, MURPHY AND LOGAN

> It is not that there are two kinds of events, or two
> places of events, but two perspectives toward events,
> an inner psychological one and an outer historical one.
> (Hillman, 1983, p. 26)

Throughout this work, many facts, theories, and events have been used to express something about homosexuality and teenage homosexuality in males. These facts inform the topic of male teenage homosexuality by describing what can be known through research into what has been written and publicly shared. In Hillman's (1983) terms, the material reviewed so far rests in the realm of the outer historical perspective with its tendency to rely on "fixity and hardness" without recognizing the subjectivity with which all humans interpret the outer reality (pp. 25-26). As Hillman stated, it is not that there are two kinds of events, but that there are two perspectives with which we process those events.

To understand, in a deeper way, the experience of male teenage homosexuality, it is important to shift perspectives so that all "outer" facts such as social attitudes, statistics on the health disparities in gay teens, and even the notion of being gay itself, can be seen from the point of view of individual teens who are engaged in the psychological work of processing those facts. Their stories can illuminate how the inner world of these teens operates when they must face, integrate, and make meaning of what exists in the outer world.

The three stories below are composite cases, stories drawn from many teens I have worked with in clinical practice, and do not reflect the actual experience of any one person. This approach is necessary for ethical reasons as outlined in this book's Author's Notes. The stories below, at the same time, draw upon some of the central dynamics of the experience many teens who have homosexual feelings may have including how their feelings impact their self-esteem, their experience with others, their potential clinical problems, and their sense of future possibilities.

Of particular importance in the three stories below, of Gabriel, Murphy, and Logan, is the inner struggle these young men have had before they declared themselves gay to the world around them. Teens like them are largely hidden from the view of others because they cannot be identified, having not disclosed their homosexuality. They are hidden from view, often out of a need for emotional safety, not only from those who might disparage them, but also, from those who would help. Therapists, teachers, parents, and concerned others may encounter young men like those below and may have opportunities to help them if they know something more about their psychological lives. The stories below are presented in an attempt to not only consider the challenges of this hidden population but, also, to help adults find new ways to support them in their young lives.

Gabriel

Gabriel was 14 when he and I began our therapeutic relationship and was 15 by the end of our first year's work. In the course of that year, Gabriel changed. Some of the changes were visible. He grew an inch or two and he lost some of the child-like features in his face. He remained somewhat frail, retaining some effeminacy in his mannerisms, but, over the course of time, his shoulders seemed to broaden a bit. He certainly learned much from his academic work in science and math and history although his grades suggested he had not. He changed socially, becoming increasingly isolated over the course of the year although, by year's end, he had found one close friend, a girl named Sam.

While his parents, teachers and grandparents watched, and commented upon, the fluctuation in his grades, Gabriel hardly noticed school. He went to class daily, performed his homework, went home to dinner, and watched over his younger siblings on weekends. With his flat affect intact, Gabriel performed his daily responsibilities even if he was moving through them without energy or enthusiasm. There were changes in Gabriel, in his life and in his body, in his mood and in his sociability, and others noticed these changes in his young life, but, the place where Gabriel changed most was not noticed by most others in his life. The most profound changes in Gabriel happened in his interior, in the invisible realms of his life, in the space he lived most of the time. He was a boy who seemed to live often in silent contemplation and in a space accessed only by him, at least in the beginning. I sensed those moments when he was working in that secret interior. It showed externally in his face and in his silent, focused stare into space.

In our first meeting, Gabriel's demeanor was far more memorable than any words he spoke. He entered the reception area slowly, walked tentatively to the counter and asked to see me. He looked tired, his body was thin, and his head bent downward. I greeted him and asked him to come into the consulting room. He followed me, shuffling along the hallway more than walking through it with any purpose or intent. It was as if he carried something invisible and heavy with him, something he had carried so long he had now become utterly fatigued by the effort. Gabriel's slow movement and downcast eyes seemed to suggest that he was depressed. He did not just sit. He slumped into the hard wooden chair. He let his backpack fall off his shoulder to the ground, not having the energy to lift it himself. It was black with gray stripes around the edges, a perfect color combination to reflect Gabriel's affect. I recall that around one of the straps was a piece of yarn, bright pink, that seemed to have been his own meaningful addition to the backpack's otherwise dark and gloomy coloring.

He dressed, like many others his age, in baggy jeans, t-shirt, and tennis shoes. His hair fell across his forehead, down over his eyes, as if it might shield him from seeing others too clearly or being seen deeply by them. He moved it away from his face each time he looked at me and let it fall again over his eyes each time he looked down again. He spoke in short answers when asked a question, using "yea," "uh-huh," and "cool" as answers to questions meant to open a dialogue between us. Between each answer, Gabriel stared down again.

Throughout our first session, and many subsequent sessions, working with Gabriel was difficult because Gabriel shared so little verbally. My repertoire of opening lines of inquiry became quickly exhausted because his responses were vague and short. "How are you?" was met with "fine" and "Are there any classes you like?" was answered with "Ah, they're ok." He seemed, in the beginning, to like our sessions more if I spoke about my life, especially when I shared about the things I didn't do very well when I was his age. I might have been good at football but I really didn't like getting hit so hard, and so many times, so I dropped out, I told him. Gabriel was gentle and did not like rough sports either. He liked art, video games, and reading. I remembered how I flunked all the tests in geometry when I was a junior in high school except the final exam which I, to my great surprise, aced. He seemed to like that there was redemption after my utter failure. I told him that, looking back, I thought that being an adolescent was one of the most confusing and challenging periods of my life and that I thought adults often forget how hard it really is. I told him I thought they probably wanted to forget it because it was so hard. He agreed with an emphatic "Yes." We began therapy by me "going first."

Gabriel was willing to come to therapy and was cooperative although it had not been his idea to seek help from a therapist. It was his mother who sent him. She was concerned by his listless behavior, by what she thought might be depression, and by his unwillingness to tell her why. He seemed withdrawn and seemed "down" and she hoped therapy might be a place in which he could talk about "things a son doesn't tell his mother." She explained that Gabriel and his father had fought but she thought that the fights, although troubling at times, were not severe enough to cause Gabriel's unhappiness. Gabriel had lost touch with his friends despite her encouragement to get out of the house and see them. She felt the family was supportive towards him and was at a loss to explain why he seemed so distant. She had noticed his withdrawal in every area of his life and was worried. He had been very social in the past.

According to Gabriel, Gabriel and his father fought occasionally, usually about small things, but Gabriel "sort of" liked his father. He sensed that they were different and that there was something separating them although he could not specify exactly what those issues were. "We just see things differently. He works two jobs and thinks I should work harder too. But, I'm a kid." His father had immigrated from Latin America and carried with him the cultural values of his homeland. Gabriel came to the United States when he was three and was more accustomed to American attitudes. Gabriel was a hybrid of cultures, in-between them, inheriting one and discovering another. His father was "kinda" Catholic and had strong opinions about right and wrong, good and bad. Gabriel noticed differences between his father's attitudes and his own. "Like, you know, he thinks gays are bad. He even uses 'fag.' I think it's fine for them and they should be left alone. Stuff like that." After such conversations, Gabriel would withdraw again, stare again, and quiet himself again.

He acknowledged that he loved his mother. They were not as close as they had been when Gabriel was young. She had always been there for him then, but now, she took his father's side in many of their arguments. He did not want to disappoint her and when she asked he tried to comply. He adored his younger siblings. He loved playing with them on Saturdays while his parents worked. He could play in innocent games again and retreat from his complex fourteen-year-old problems for a day. He thought they were lucky to be so young and to not have the worries he had. He loved them but they could, for obvious reasons, not help him through his daily life. His primary concern at home was that Gabriel found that he could no longer talk to his parents and had a growing sense of frustration with them. He felt, for reasons he could not explain, estranged.

Clinically, Gabriel met the test for depression. He struggled to sleep at night and to stay asleep. He worried at night and was anxious about his life, even if those worries were not disclosed to me or others in his life. He had lost weight and "just wasn't hungry" most of the time. His affect was flat. He found it difficult to pay attention to teachers, to concentrate, and was withdrawn from others. He was pessimistic and wondered why. Over the first few months of therapy, Gabriel's depression seemed to deepen, not improve. While he became more open with me over time, he seemed to simultaneously pull farther and farther away from others, moving deeper into a despair I did not fully understand. It seemed a paradox to me that while he felt our time together was the best time of his week, it also engaged him in a process that seemed to result in ever increasing depression.

There are many approaches possible for the treatment of depression including medication that might improve mood, reduce anxiety, and alleviate some of the most pronounced symptoms. I was prepared to consider the option in the event Gabriel's depression became too severe. At the same time, the alleviation of his symptoms through medication without any awareness of the deeper reasons for his depression seemed premature, especially in the beginning of therapy. Beyond that, an approach to Gabriel that saw his depression as a series of feelings that were to be cured eliminated the possibility that his depression was actually meaningful. There might well be good reason for it. His feelings, as uncomfortable as they were, might be the holder of a truth that could not be expressed in any other way. Absent a capacity to say what was wrong, Gabriel, it might be said, felt what was wrong instead.

"If symptoms—even if they show suffering—are not primarily regarded as something wrong or bad in a child, then we can release imagination from its focus on fixing a child's symptoms" (Hillman, 1996, p. 34). In *The Soul's Code* (1996), Hillman discussed an approach to symptom that looks to "symptom" as more than a random, meaningless experience of suffering. When one has a medical disease, a bad kidney for instance, treatment requires a fix, medication, and cure. The treatment of the bad kidney seldom includes a discussion of hidden meanings in the diseased organ. Doctors treat it directly with the hope the disease ends. Emotional suffering, to Hillman (1996), is not akin to such physical disease and the treatment/cure approach of medicine, when applied to the psyche, misses the importance of symptom. By regarding symptoms differently, pathways to understanding and possible healing begin to broaden.

> These wonderings open the eye toward an invisible intention in a symptom, so that we can regard the symptom less anxiously, less (moralistically) as a wrong, and more simply as a phenomenon (which meant, originally, something that shows, shines, lights up, brightens, appears to be seen). A symptom wants to be

looked at, not only looked into . . . to see . . . in a light that shifts the valences from curse to blessing, of if not blessing at least symptom of calling. (p. 15)

Gabriel's symptoms, his slow cadence, his withdrawal, and his mood were expressive of something. Long before it would be possible to know something of what his symptoms "meant," it was required that they be seen first. It was first required that his symptoms be honored and not disparaged. It is possible to consider that they were the most expressive aspects to Gabriel, at least initially, and far more informative than any words he uttered. It was if his symptoms spoke for him. "Look at me. Notice. There is something very wrong here."

Beyond allowing symptom to be seen, it is also possible, according to Frankel (1998), to understand symptom as purposeful, as leading somewhere else, or as a calling for growth in the personality. "The feelings and fantasies contained within a particular symptom may symbolize a possible future emerging into being; thus, we ask, what a particular symptom is for, where it may be leading. (p. 5)

Gabriel's symptoms could be understood as undesirable, and they were, but hidden in the suffering was also an expression of what no longer worked for him. His symptoms could be understood as a call for something new, a yearning for a new experience of life that was not yet lived. In his depression was a call to an undiscovered happier experience. In his slow movements was a statement that life was too hard and a clear statement that what needed to come next was an easier, more joyful and energetic life. In our earliest work together, Gabriel's symptoms communicated what needed to be said.

I saw Gabriel weekly for several months before he began to tell me things more verbally and to share things he had not generally shared with others. Short, one-word answers became long, full, and rich responses to ever increasingly personal questions. It was slow work that moved forward at a pace defined by Gabriel and in response to a deeper question, "Was I, his therapist, safe?" It was important that Gabriel set the pace. Access to his inner world was by invitation only and his protection of that access was essential for his well-being. In some ways, Gabriel protected what was authentically occurring inside from outsiders because of his own particular anxieties and doubts.

In other ways, according to Frankel (1998), Gabriel's defense against being known by another, at least without invitation by him, can be seen as an important aspect of development in adolescence. Adolescents need to discover what is there, what or who is inside, before others do. Frankel quoted the words of Winnecott. "At adolescence . . . there is a strengthening of defenses against being found, that is to say being found before being there to be found. That which is truly personal must be defended at all cost" (Winnecott, 1963, p. 190).

Gabriel, like many teens, faced the difficult challenge of "becoming" something that he could not know in advance. As Erikson noted (1968), "All through childhood tentative crystallizations take place which make the individual feel and believe . . . as if he approximately knew who he is—only to find that such certainty ever again falls prey to the discontinuities of the psychological and social development of adolescence" (p. 123). Gabriel might have been confident that he more or less knew himself as a child and that he had an identity that was reliable. Now, he was becoming something new, something more fluid and something less clear to him. What was not yet known could not be shared and he was wary of intrusion. Sensitivity to the adolescent need for concealment is required from therapists and other adults, according to Frankel (1998). "We, in the business of psychology, must be careful to not become ultrasound technicians" in a probing effort to "uncover a definitive image of the self before it is ready to be borne. What is going on in the depths of the adolescent psyche may well need a period of concealment" (p. 128).

Gabriel was hard at work in the discovery of himself and seemed vigilant against any spontaneous sharing that might disclose what he had not first considered thoroughly. He was spontaneous about describing the video games he liked, open about family events, and shared eagerly about movies he had seen. He was conversational about the mundane areas of his life but cautious and reserved about most other matters. He was especially quiet when the topics of how he and others related came to the forefront. Over time, there was a slow, spiraling downward, into the deeper realms of his inner world, when he spoke of others. Early in our work, like a boy putting his toe in a lake, he spoke about his friends and family with some hesitation, even avoidance. Over time, in a circuitous way, the content of his conversation grew deeper, more subtle, and more conflicted. It was during these conversations that Gabriel's deep stare into space returned, that long silences prevailed, and that the most conspicuous signs of depression appeared again. Gabriel, again, became lost in lonely contemplation.

I saw Gabriel brighten, spontaneously and without vigilance, only once throughout our first months together. At the time, even as his words were being spoken during the session, I recognized that moment as a way into his inner world, although the full significance of that conversation did not become clear until much later. The moment of joy on his face came accidentally. I casually told him I liked his t-shirt. His face beamed with happiness. The blank stare left long enough for him to tell me the story of how the t-shirt came to him. His best friend, Jake, had moved away after the end of middle school. Gabriel was heartbroken at the time although that term would have been too expressive for Gabriel to use. Jake had been his closest confidant for several years and they spent all their free time together. When Jake moved, Gabriel tried to find other friends but none had been as close as Jake. During the previous summer, Jake's parents let him go to a summer camp with Gabriel in the mountains. They bunked in the same room. They stayed up late and talked in the dark night, sharing secrets between them. They went to the same activities during the days, ate at the same table, never leaving each other's side for long for the entire two weeks. On the day Jake left, hurriedly running to catch his ride, he had left a t-shirt on his bunk that Gabriel took with him. He had tried to send it back but Jake told him to keep it. Gabriel wore it now "all the time." "I just like the feel of it," he said now, touching the front of his shirt. It was as if he were touching Jake.

Gabriel's mood shifted again as he continued, becoming less joyful. After camp, the two had corresponded by text and on Facebook but, after school began, their communication had slowed. Gabriel was afraid it might stop forever and seemed to believe it would. Once Gabriel had finished the story, he slowly began to become quiet again, slowly deepened into his stare, and slowly withdrew from me. He was not being impolite. It seemed that he had once again lost the energy needed to speak.

Gabriel did not share with me, for months, that he and Jake had kissed each other one night and that Jake had begun to change after that night. It "just happened," Gabriel said. "It was like we were just sitting there and then I had this urge and I just wanted to and so I just closed my eyes and kissed him." Jake pulled back, according to Gabriel's version of events, and both boys soon acted as if nothing had happened. They went to bed, Jake having said he was tired, and their conversation for that night was over. Gabriel recalled that he sat in the dark silence, unsure what to say, what to hope for or what, if anything, he should fear. He spent many hours that night in silent contemplation about why he had kissed Jake, how much he had wanted to kiss Jake, how guilty he felt, how good it felt, how dangerous it felt, and especially, how Jake would react tomorrow.

In the coming days and months, Gabriel watched in a kind of agony as Jake began to withdraw from conversations, began to hang out with other guys, and began to be overly polite even as he seemed to distance himself from Gabriel. For months, Gabriel had been stuck in a torturous, nearly traumatic anxiety that he would lose Jake, that Jake would abandon him because of the kiss. Even worse, Gabriel was terrified of the possibility that Jake might betray him, betray their long friendship, and actually demonize Gabriel as a homosexual, or even "faggot." Gabriel had maintained hope for months that Jake and he could turn back the clock and regain the innocent and happy friendship before the kiss between them that had changed so much. Eventually hope faded. Gabriel had only a t-shirt to touch now. It was his memory of how wonderful relationship felt before it was broken.

Gabriel was not gay, nor bisexual, nor straight. He hardly knew the implications of any such labels and was far from understanding his own feelings, much less concretizing those feelings into a form or identity. Gabriel was unknown in his sexuality because he had not experienced it nor decided what it meant. There had long been clues to me that homosexuality might be a concern for him. He seemed utterly disinterested in dating girls. He liked some of them as friends but never suggested, or even hinted, he was sexually attracted to them. In fact, the complete absence of any discussion of sexuality in a teenager might be suggestive, as it was with Gabriel, that sexuality was an area of significant conflict. Gabriel also seemed distant from other boys as if his relationship to them was troubled despite the fact he knew many boys in class and seemed liked, according to him, by other boys.

There had been the comment, rather out of place at the time, that his father hated "fags" but that Gabriel had thought that gays were fine, a statement many young boys his age might struggle to say. There had been the sharp glance, the sudden jerking of his head upright, on the day I casually mentioned I held therapy groups for many teens and that among them were groups for gay and lesbian teens or kids who just had questions about sexuality. On that day, Gabriel left his distant stare, shooting a look at me suddenly and intensely. It was a look that seemed to me to contain both his hope and terror. There was, of course, the small strand of pink yarn, tied around his gray and black backpack. It could have meant anything to him. It could be something from a friend or a sibling. It might also have been, I thought, a small statement of affiliation with the color so often used by the LGBT community. It was conceivable that it was a statement about being gay, but, a statement easily denied if brought up in conversation. But, it was the story of Jake that illuminated Gabriel's sexual questions most clearly and it was in Gabriel's blank stare into space that he found quiet, private time to consider it.

Whatever else could be said about Gabriel's kiss with Jake, it was clear that in one moment, Gabriel's life had taken an irrevocable turn on that night. Gabriel had taken a step forward and could no longer pretend he did not. Jake and Gabriel both knew. There was no turning back the clock, no innocence left that would allow Gabriel to hide his true feelings or what he had wanted. In that kiss, Gabriel took action that he had wanted to take, that was of his own making, and that brought his life forward into new and unknown questions. As Hillman (1996) noted, by quoting Robertson Davies, "One always learns one's mystery at the price of one's innocence" (p. xi). Gabriel lost a kind of innocence that night and now was faced with the mystery of who he was. That mystery included his yearning to kiss Jake, homosexual feelings of some sort, but feelings so intertwined with questions and uncertainty that he could not say "I am gay." In that way, direct conversations about him being gay, much less any declaration by him that he was gay, were premature.

Despite much progress and a developing safety in our relationship, it became clear to me over time that none of the conversations about the issues in his life led directly to any reduction in his depressed symptoms. We spoke of many things including school, family, friends, Jake, the kiss, his emerging sexuality and his confusion about it, his past, and his future yet, discussions of the feelings, events, and people of his life did not reduce his depression. In a sense, the roots of his depression were not buried in those topics and, so, discussions of them could not relieve it. It became clear to me that his depression resided somewhere else and that it was not about any one thing. Rather, it seemed to me, his depression was grounded in an experience of something, perhaps the first experience of himself, and that he was having that experience, hidden from all others, when he stared in silence. If it is possible to say that something like depression can be located in one particular psychological space in a human being, I would have to say that Gabriel's depression lived mostly in his blank, vacant stare that seemed to take all of his attention. In some ways, the literal stare was both a façade and a place-holder. It was the face Gabriel presented to others. It was also the inner container of an image of Gabriel's life and all of its moving parts, all of its problems and troubles, and all of its questions. It was as if depression camped out there, embedded in a demanding, compelling image of himself.

Transfixed by a reflection of himself and his life, Gabriel was reminiscent of a young boy of ancient Greek legend, a youth named Narcissus.

> He came upon a spring, clear as silver, and never yet disturbed by cattle, birds, wild beasts, or even branches dropping off the trees that shaded it; and he cast himself down, exhausted, on the grassy verge to slake his thirst, he fell in love with his reflection. (Graves, 1998, p. 268)

The story of Narcissus is about a young man who was enamored of his own physical looks. He is the image of self pride and self absorption that eventually became the name-sake of a pathological, psychological disorder, Narcissistic Personality Disorder (*DSM-IV-TR*, 2000). Psychology's hold on the name Narcissus is profound and difficult to shake loose having been so attached to a particular understanding of the Greek legend. It is true that the story of Narcissus is the story of a young man, about Gabriel's age, who was sought after by girls and boys, who rejected all suitors, and who tragically died in pursuit of the love of his own image. The story of Narcissus can be correctly understood as a prohibition against a too-intense attachment to one's own value and worth and the deadly consequences of praising oneself over all others.

More broadly, the story of Narcissus can also be seen as a study of what an adolescent may feel when he sees himself alone and absent relationship to others. In such a context, the story is also a study in the human capacity to be both trapped and shocked by what is seen in lonely, deep, self reflection. The myth alludes to the powerful demands of the inner psyche and how consuming it can become. Sometimes, for an infinite variety of reasons, an individual may become so enamored by what the interior holds that relationship to others becomes of secondary importance. In those times, any individual might well find, that like Narcissus, they "lay gazing enraptured by the pool, hour after hour" (Graves, 1998, p. 268). It might be said that what Narcissus saw in the pool held him, captured him, and demanded that he stay entrapped. Gabriel, like Narcissus, was trapped by the image of his interior life. Like Narcissus, other people had become necessarily of secondary importance in Gabriel's life, at least for now.

It is difficult to know precisely what Gabriel saw when he looked inside. Each day, the content or the subject he considered might well have been different from the material he reviewed just hours or days before. In that way, the image Gabriel saw was a collage of the many experiences, people and feelings of his life. In another way, what Gabriel saw might well have been a single, complete life, the image of his totality.

It is speculative on my part but, I believe, based on our many conversations over many months, that when Gabriel stared into space he saw his life as it was unfolding. It was no longer the image of childhood innocence but, rather, the image of one who had taken an irrevocable step forward into a life of choices. In doing so, he had become someone new and unknown. I suspect Jake was in that interior space. The kiss between them, a kiss Gabriel had wanted, was there. Jake's separation, and his slow walking away from Gabriel, was there as was the terrible feeling that accompanies the loss of friendship. Mixed in with the memory of that kiss was also the image of Gabriel's mother and father. He could see his father's disgust and his mother's confusion. Gabriel could see how he was now a different brother to his siblings than the one they knew. He could see his classmates and how they harassed gay kids and he could see how dangerous the knowledge about his kiss would be in their hands. He could see the Catholic Church he had attended as a child and how strongly the priest would chastise him, especially if Gabriel continued to do such things. Gabriel even could see God and how he, Gabriel, had made a contract with God when he was a child. Gabriel would be good in exchange for God's love. The contract was broken by Gabriel when he acted on his desires, his feelings of attraction to Jake, and by kissing Jake. There was no certainty about how God would react.

In the image were also the feelings of that kiss, how exciting and wonderful it was. Gabriel had talked about the kiss as if he was just "playing around" but in the image of himself, I suspect, he also saw how much he wanted such moments with another boy like Jake. In the image were his sexual feelings and his desires to have the experience again. I also believe Gabriel saw much to love about himself including the value of his gentleness and caring. He had often been criticized because "he threw like a girl" but he liked that he was not as combative as other boys. He did not like the aggression he saw around him. There was far more beauty in the tenderness and connection he and Jake had, tenderness that could not occur if they had been busy punching each other. He liked his gentleness even though he felt he might be alone in believing such things.

In many ways, I suspect, Gabriel's inner space was also a place for dialogue. Gabriel self-reflection, I believe, included a voice that spoke back to him, just as there was a voice that replied to Narcissus. Narcissus had a companion, named Echo, who repeated everything he said. When Narcissus first noticed that he was separated from others he shouted, "Is anyone here?" Echo responded, "Is anyone here?" In his final moments, before his death, and with his final breath, Narcissus said "Alas, Alas" to which Echo responded "Alas, Alas" (Graves, 1998, pp. 267-268). The myth suggests that what is contained inside mirrors something back. The interior psyche responds, reflects, and gives voice to the images inside. When Gabriel stared into his interior, he was in dialogue.

I can only imagine what Gabriel's internal dialogue contained. It was private. Yet, his many descriptions of what concerned him provided a glimpse for me as to the nature of his inner dialogue. I suspected that Jake was often a "partner" in the conversation. Gabriel asked. "Do you like me the way I like you?" Jake said "Maybe" when Gabriel was hopeful and in fantasy but answered, "No, I am lost forever" when Gabriel faced reality. His mother was there, in image, when Gabriel thought of his kiss with Jake and she responded, "Oh my God. No." His father said, "You are not mine." When Gabriel thought of his future, alongside the loss of Jake and his family, his echo responded, "No, I do not want a future like that." When he thought of his friends, those with whom he shared his days, Gabriel's inner dialogue wandered through the many rejections, the many taunts, and the many losses that lay before him. "You're so gay. Faggot." After such reflections, when Gabriel saw his own face again, his echo might well have cried. There seemed to be other days when Gabriel's dialogue involved the abandonment of how good it felt when he kissed Jake. On those days, when he saw the image of his kiss, his echo responded, "It was nothing. It was a stupid kiss. Be normal again, like you were before." On those days, he could look again at his image of God. "You are forgiven. Do not do it again." And then, once again, Gabriel remembered how good it felt to kiss Jake. His echo responded with a tortured glance back. "What will you do?"

Beyond inner images and dialogue, if there is any overarching message in the myth of Narcissus, it is that entrapment in the inner world, isolated from others, leads to death. Narcissus died from his anguish and where he died, "up sprang the white narcissus flower" (Graves, 1998, p. 268). Without relationship, in solitary love, Narcissus became a memory of what had been beautiful, in the form of a flower. Gabriel was not suicidal, at least not yet, but like Narcissus, he suffered in isolation and a depression that, unhealed, offered him no hope. Gabriel had in one moment or another, it must be assumed, asked himself "Why bother?" Given that he had often seemed to imagine a life where he faced isolation, without loving others, it would have been a reasonable question for Gabriel to ask.

As a therapist, I was trained to watch for suicidal thoughts and was prepared to intervene actively, with as much force as necessary, to interrupt any such actions on his part, but Gabriel was not suicidal. I was prepared to help Gabriel to "come out" if he decided he was gay, and wished to, but Gabriel was not gay. His depression was real but not so severe or dangerous as to need medication. His parents were well aware of the depression and there was little need to tell them I thought he was depressed too. I might have chosen to advise him, to use my adult experience and my clinical training to provide him answers in some effort to move him beyond his contemplation. I knew, somewhere inside, that by doing so I was displaying my wish to calm my own uncertainty about what to do. Tolerating his sadness and inability to move forward was difficult. Feeling his agony was worse. It never seemed to abate. Beyond those considerations, I also was aware that I had no answers for his experience. Anything I might have shared was an effort, by me, to provide shortcuts for him, quick answers to what might well be life long questions for Gabriel.

Gabriel's experience of himself, and his depression, was an experience of something much larger than clinical interventions, formalized and concrete, are designed to resolve. Gabriel experienced something of a totality of his life and what he saw was new and unlike any of his previous, childhood identifications. It was fluid and changing, not fixed. It was unknown, new, complex and conflicted. The images were of a transgressor, a source of pride, exciting and stimulating, sexual and boundary crossing. It was lovely, more beautiful than all things. It was lonely and the source of pain. It was, in fact, all of those things and more because it was also the reflection of possibilities. It was a reflection of the possibility today and tomorrow in his classrooms and at home. It was the possibility of his psyche as well, with its feelings, its aesthetic imagination, its incorporation in the body, its fantasy, its wisdom, its psychosis and its possible disintegration. Gabriel was experiencing himself, his life, and what it means to be conscious, even at 14 years of age.

Just as the myth of Narcissus is a warning about self-absorption, conversely, it is also a testament to the human need for relationship. Without relationship, according to the story, we will die. The lesson of Narcissus, the need for relationship, was a central factor in my continuing work with Gabriel. Our work eventually resulted in positive changes in his emotional life but, in retrospect I believe, that change came mostly after I changed my approach to him. I more specifically focused my attention on the nature of our relationship and on creating a quality of authenticity in it.

Perhaps the clearest example of this shift came one day just after

Gabriel sat down for our session. He was holding his notebook and as he looked at me, he seemed more relaxed than normal. He glanced at me playfully and then began. "So, Brad, tell me about you" and then began to take notes, mocking my way of note-taking in session. I let go for him, opened up, forgetting my old training that suggested that I not disclose. Something more human, more open and vulnerable seemed appropriate that day. "Well, let's see. I have a busy life here at work and I love my work. I have a dog named Lucy and she demands that I take her for very long walks at least several times a day." In the moment, for reasons still not clear to me, I sensed an opportunity to discuss something more personal about me but also, importantly, something about me that I thought might help him. As had been the case all along, it seemed appropriate in that moment that I "go first." "I'm not married and in fact, I'm gay and I have had a really wonderful life. I have gotten to travel all over the world, do lots of things that others don't always get to do. I really love being gay even though some people criticize it. It's been a great life—with all the hard things every human has to do—but all in all, I love it." I knew as I said it that my being gay might be what he secretly needed to hear, but also, there was a danger that such directness might cause him to pull back defensively. When he heard my words, his facial expression changed. It opened up into a new expression, part excitement, part surprise, and part confirmation of what he might have guessed about me.

I expected him to respond to my comments about being gay. I hoped he might find them reassuring. I hoped he would find an ally in conversations about being gay, that he might have more questions, and that it might make him feel less alone. Over time, I believe all those hopes came true. Indeed, Gabriel heard every word and the bond between us deepened even more after my sharing. On that day, he remained vigilant and aside from the slight smile on his face, he reacted with adolescent cool. "So," he asked, "what kind of dog is Lucy?"

In all my efforts to reach into Gabriel's world and in all my attempts at empathic connection, it had not occurred to me that I, the personal me, was required for Gabriel. "I" was required for Gabriel to relate to and not just my caring, my listening or my experience as a therapist. In fact, the personal me, the human being, was far more important to Gabriel because it was something to which he could relate. At 14, Gabriel could not relate to an adult or to a therapist. He could relate to Brad, owner of Lucy. When engaged in that space, Gabriel and I were equal, age was not present, and life was not already lived. Our conversations changed and we interacted more. I listened carefully but not from a distance. He spoke more openly knowing that I would share his confusion and understand, in a personal way, why his choices seemed impossible. I told him about how, as an adolescent, I didn't have a word for my feelings and he told me he could not yet say that he was gay or straight or anything else. We shared, as two people, and in the sharing, Gabriel's narcissistic stare seemed less necessary. I have come to believe that the turning point for Gabriel, the day his depression began its slow withdrawal, was the day I was willing to become Brad to him. On that day, Gabriel was in relationship again.

Among the most important elements of therapy is the provision of space, a container, in which both client and therapist place their psychic workings and where the interaction of that consciousness can take place. In that sense, the goal of therapy is a new consciousness built upon the safe relationship, held in a safe container. For Gabriel, especially after I became Brad to him, a slow process began during which our therapeutic container replaced his silent, private stare. I became Echo, a human being who had more to say, of a different nature, than his solitary Echo knew to say. The contemplation of his life, previously done in a silent stare into space, was done in words, thoughts, feelings and moods experienced together between Gabriel and I. Depression, long hiding in Gabriel's images, saw the light of day, could speak openly, and was given voice so that it needed no longer to express itself in Gabriel's heavy, slow, sad and distracted presentation to the world. When once he spoke only to himself, now when Gabriel asked "Who is there?" I could say "It's Brad." Later that year, when Gabriel and his friend Sam met, it would be her voice that Gabriel heard. "Don't worry Gabriel, I am here. It's Sam." Given his many questions and doubts about his sexuality, and his life, Gabriel knew he could not ask his parents or peers to be there with him. It was not necessary, in the end, for him to have relationships with many others. One was enough, a starting point, and it led to another. Narcissus might have survived had he learned the meaning of Gabriel's story.

His depression largely dissipated over time and Gabriel returned to a degree of happiness in his daily life. He lived a split life, telling me about his sexual feelings more and more openly while consistently denying them in the world of his parents, family, teachers and peers. It was a complicated life and one which required vigilance. It was better, it seemed, than the kind of total isolation he endured, the kind of solitary life he and Narcissus shared. His narcissistic stare was occasionally present although it reappeared mostly when his life became overwhelming again. But, he seemed to know that in those moments there was a remedy and that I would join him in that space again.

I followed Gabriel for several years after our initial work together in therapy. He came back occasionally, sometimes for months, for individual sessions. In his senior year, he joined a therapy group for boys "who had questions about sexuality," a group that consisted largely of gay or bisexual teens although he did not, so long as I knew him, finally and firmly claim one sexual identity. Gabriel tested different identities based on his sexual orientation over the years. Sharing only with me, and perhaps his friend Sam, Gabriel identified as bisexual for a time, and later engaged in a prolonged period during which he passed as heterosexual. He never publicly identified as being gay but, privately, Gabriel told me late in our work together that he had begun to know that the label, gay, best suited who he was and how he felt.

Statisticians who wish to know about the prevalence of adolescent homosexuality would be confused by Gabriel. They would have counted him as heterosexual, bisexual, or gay depending on the year in which they asked him and depending, as well, on his mood on the day they asked. Theorists who outline a series of psychological stages for Gabriel would also be, in the main, wrong. There is no evidence that Gabriel will decide he is gay in the long run, when he comes to a later stage of growth, or when life's other complexities become known and experienced. Those theorists assume that he will not some day experience heterosexual love and be entranced by it. They assume something of his life and its trajectory that cannot be known.

Regardless of how Gabriel identifies in his life, what is clear is that he will have traversed his psychological path in his own individual way, following a path unlike any other. Useful as they are, theories of gay development and statistics about gay teens do not account for the powerful experience Gabriel had of himself, the many unique variations of his experience as a person, and the unique obstacles he faced. His path through the complexities of teenage homosexuality, and his contemplation of what it meant for him, required that his path be navigated in an original way.

Perhaps it is because homosexuality has been so denigrated socially and because it is so actively discouraged in so many ways, but, when young men like Gabriel encounter their own homosexual feelings, they must begin a process of distinguishing themselves from others, from some elements of the broader society, and from many of those whom they have loved. Gabriel's contemplation of himself and his life was, in many ways, a noticing of how he would be different from others and separated from the social norms of heterosexuality. In many ways, unlike adults, young men like Gabriel first see themselves absent experience and an adult's deeper self-knowledge that comes with living life over many years. Like Gabriel, they may see themselves for a first time in an undefended, fervently honest, and extremely vulnerable way. They see themselves unvarnished. Such self awareness, when it brings about an awareness of one's own personality as being distinctive and different from the collective, can be understood as a cornerstone of what Jung (1939/1983) called individuation.

> In general, it is the process by which individual beings are formed and differentiated; in particular, it is the development of the psychological individual as being distinct from the general, collective psychology. Individuation therefore, is a process of differentiation, having for its goal the development of the individual personality. (p. 225)

Gabriel was at work, throughout his adolescence, seeing who he was, how he was different, and what his individual life would be like in a broader world that would not always agree with his choices, feelings or actions. Gabriel was busy at the work of individuation, of seeing, developing and holding on to his unique personality. Such work requires contemplation. In our sometimes urgent desire to see the results of our work in some positive outcome for our clients, we may easily overlook the need to provide a holding space that allows for unhurried contemplation. In our rush to find conclusive improvements in symptoms, we may sometimes forget that psychological development occurs over years and therefore requires that therapy be unhurried, slowing to the pace that matches our client's need for sufficient time, perhaps even years. Given the crisis young teens who have homosexual feelings may face and the terrible isolation they may feel as a result, it is also important to recognize that, for them, having another person who can join in safe and lasting relationship is essential. The central issue for young men like Gabriel, so isolated in their inner world, may well be their need for relationship, a primary need that will form the foundation for their identities and, in fact, the foundation for their future lives.

Murphy

Creating a therapy group for teenage boys who were gay, or for those who were struggling with the issues presented by same-sex sexuality, was an annual ritual for me at the beginning of each school year. Because these boys were not, for the most part, openly gay, it was necessary to find them by networking with teachers, counselors and other teens with whom I had worked. It was sensitive work because by reaching out I ran the risk of speaking to boys who were not ready to be known. The simple asking of the question, "Would you like to be part of this group?" invaded their privacy in a way that could have caused significant distress. In some ways, it was easier to leave the work of recruitment for group therapy to other teenagers. Typically, I went each year to the school's Gay-Straight Alliance meeting and asked those teens to spread the word and see if they knew anyone interested. Each year, I had groups of usually six or seven boys willing to come forward and meet, a small number compared to the 1,500 students enrolled in the school. There were many others who had homosexual feelings but for whom the simple walk to the clinic each week was too risky, a much greater risk of being seen as gay than they were willing to take.

Murphy was referred to me by his school counselor although we had seen each other at the Gay-Straight Alliance meeting once. I met with him individually to explain the group, to discuss confidentiality, and to evaluate his appropriateness for group therapy. I explained that he would need to get permission from his parents to attend the group. For many, the prospect of asking a parent to sign a consent form was among the most difficult obstacles they faced in agreeing to therapy. For most, I needed to carefully explain that our clinic ran many groups, for many types of discussions, and that parents needed to know that they were in therapy but did not necessarily need to know exactly what was discussed in groups, including the issue of homosexuality. I explained that I did not discuss specifics with parents, except in extreme circumstances, and that I would not disclose their feelings about sexuality to their parents. They would need to decide what they wished to disclose to their parents. Murphy was nonchalant. "It's no problem," he said. "They know I'm gay." He thought group therapy sounded interesting but agreed only to do it on a test basis. Murphy was self-assured enough to come and try the experience and assured enough to know that he could choose to leave anytime he wished.

As it turned out, Murphy knew several of the other boys in group and all of the boys in the group knew Murphy, at least from a distance. Murphy was tall and lanky, handsome, and without the childhood features common in younger teens. He had piercing blue eyes and dressed thoughtfully, stylishly, and with great attention to detail. He dressed the way all the other boys wished they did. They liked his style and wished to emulate it, but in doing so, they missed the point. Murphy dressed as an individual, not a copy, and it was his capacity to be independent and free about his dress and attitudes that made him attractive. His hair was black and cropped closely on the day of our first session but would be colored in different colors and styled in multiple other ways over the course of the year. Murphy experimented over time, changing as he wished, and explored every aspect of his appearance during the year. Yet, Murphy was not especially attached to his looks or his clothing and did not especially seem to care that others admired him for it. He was more subtle than that. He did it because he could, because he enjoyed the experimentation and because he liked the creativity involved. Murphy seemed at once to be very social and very reserved. He enjoyed the respect he seemed to receive from the other boys but also seemed to not believe in it very much. Murphy was complex even at 17 years old.

In our first group session, Murphy sat mostly silent, drawing in a notebook as I talked. I explained the nature of group therapy. I explained that the boys were free to talk about anything they wished and that the topics for discussion would generally come from them. I explained that this group was different than many others because all the members of it had told me privately that they were gay, bisexual, or were questioning their sexuality. Because of that, I said, all members of the group had a special responsibility to keep all of our conversations confidential. I told them I knew that I had a special requirement to provide a safe space because being gay, for many teens, was a sensitive matter. I assured them I would do my best to keep it safe.

"So, exactly how safe is it?" Murphy asked. I was taken aback and thought perhaps I had not made myself fully clear. I told him I was not sure what he meant and then reiterated many of the things I had said before, trying my best to convey in my words and tone that this was a safe place. "Yeah, I get it but if I take this bag of pot out of my pocket and throw it on the floor, what are you going to do?" The other boys looked both shocked at Murphy's boldness and slightly amused at my discomfort. There were smiles on their faces and great anticipation about how I would respond.

It was, of course, a good question and one I had never imagined. I imagined him doing it. I could imagine the clinical director walking past the door, looking through the window, seeing a bag of marijuana on the floor, and her reasonable, hurried, urgent gesturing to me through the window, demanding that I come speak with her. I could imagine the school officials hearing someday that I allowed a student to carry around marijuana, that I had allowed him to place it on the floor, and that I had not contacted the principal to have the student ejected from school. Alternatively, I could imagine myself trying to control the situation, relying on my training, returning to the well worn rule book about appropriate behavior in group therapy including being respectful. I could try to enforce rules and explain that Murphy must behave appropriately to be in the group. I thought it through and finally told Murphy that if he did it, I would ask him to pick up the bag of marijuana and put it back in his pocket. In my heart, I wish I had been able to say, "It's fine. Leave it there and we will talk about marijuana then." After all, I had said it was safe place and that they could talk about anything. Murphy was asking me if I meant it. He was asking a good question and asking if there were limits to my willingness to be safe with him no matter what. He wanted to know if he could talk about what was hidden from the view of other adults. In the end, I believe my response suggested that the group was safe but there were some rules, based mostly on mutual respect. I passed the test that day with Murphy and he stayed. Murphy was honest and unafraid of questioning things and I liked him for it.

Over the course of time, Murphy became a central and strong member of the group despite his tendency to draw in his art book as he listened to the conversations around him. I had learned that boys in group very often became less open if they were not allowed to withdraw from the conversations when needed, even if that meant that on the surface they were not behaving the way adults in group are typically required to behave. For Murphy, drawing was a way to both withdraw and participate by listening. Occasionally, he engaged the conversation directly. That often happened when he became impatient with others who he thought were indecisive. He seemed to dislike inaction on the part of others, especially when they said that they knew what needed to be done but were afraid to do it. One day, another young man struggled with whether or not to come out to his parents even though he wanted to. Murphy looked up from his drawing. "Oh, come on, tell 'em and get on with it." He took his pen and reached toward the other young boy, taking his arm gently, and then drew a heart on the boy's arm, putting his own initials, M.S., in it. "There, now you can go home, show that to them and tell them we are boyfriends." He was not afraid for the younger boy, was not afraid of the confrontations involved, and felt that it would be better when everyone was honest about the whole issue. At least, according to Murphy, things were clear that way.

Murphy identified as gay, to everyone, all the time now although it had not always been so. He had known secretly that he was gay since he was a very young boy. He could recall that his first memories of same-sex feelings came very early. He loved comic books and there was something about the arms of comic book heroes, so muscled and big, that he remembered feeling moved by. While being moved by the muscles of men, when he was very young, he more often liked the companionship of girls, the games they played, and seemed interested in the things girls loved too. His father had told him not to be that way and had actually forced him to separate from his best friend as a child, a neighbor girl, because he felt Murphy needed to be more like other boys. Murphy was confused then but knew now what his father had meant to accomplish. "I was supposed to be a little man and little men didn't do girly things," he said. Murphy's input in group sessions, especially about his experience of being gay, seemed helpful to the other boys. They seemed to identify with many of his stories and seemed to let Murphy say out loud what they could not yet articulate.

After several months, I invited Murphy to see me in individual therapy to supplement our work together in group. I had become increasingly aware, and even concerned, by the amount of marijuana he reported to smoke. I had noticed his glassy eyes during group on more than one occasion and suspected he was smoking marijuana at school.

In a more subtle way, I sensed a hard edge to Murphy. He seemed too angry at times, too alone given how much others seemed to like him, and somehow distant. I could not articulate my concerns beyond those issues but when I asked him, he agreed quickly. I interpreted his quick agreement as a confirmation that there were things Murphy wished to discuss that he could not discuss during our group work.

Perhaps it was because Murphy and I had the opportunity during our group work to build a safe relationship but, for whatever reasons, Murphy opened up about his life and feelings soon after we began our private sessions. He disliked Christianity, thought the laws against marijuana were stupid, and thought school was forcing him to learn things because they had to meet some legal requirement. He felt that school was about taking in what was important to others and did not involve what he liked to learn. He wanted to be in an art school because art was his passion. His arguments were sometimes quite compelling and Murphy usually was able to see through the cracks of convention. Many teens I had worked with complained about such things but Murphy went farther into the argument, seemed more insightful, and saw the weaknesses in conventions that others ignored or were too afraid to mention. He was, in many ways, original in his thinking. He spoke about big issues and was largely disinterested in the things his peers seemed so intrigued by, who said what to whom and who liked what celebrity. Murphy was tackling big ideas. He saw something frail in the institutions, like school, society and church, but seemed not to know what to do with the information. Yet, when he spoke angrily about what was wrong in the world, the experience did not seem to end in an emotional grounding. Murphy seemed as angry after our discussions as he had been before. I came to suspect that marijuana had become the one thing that soothed his deeper frustrations.

Murphy shared much of his personal history easily. He had been the child of very religious parents. His father had been a church elder and his mother was also deeply religious. He had attended Christian school in childhood and through middle school in Ohio. They wore uniforms and studied the Bible on weekends. He had been a "good" boy and felt secure in his young world so long as he remained faithful to God and to his father and mother. His father was a strict disciplinarian and demanded loyalty. Murphy recalled that his father used physical punishment on those occasions when Murphy displeased him. Murphy grimaced a little when he told me of how his father used to grab both arms and twist them outward when he was especially angry with Murphy's behavior. "He broke my wrist once when I was seven," he said. Murphy was to be a model boy, a model Christian boy, and his father used the authority of his position as head of the family and as the one most closely aligned with God the Father, to enforce it. In retrospect, Murphy told me he thought his father's most aggressive attacks came when he was too much like a girl and too little like the other boys. In those moments, his father was not so much punishing behavior as much as he was just punishing Murphy.

Murphy was much like the other boys in his Ohio middle school and remained a compliant boy, trying to be good for most of the time. But like it was for others, Middle School brought with it a growing willingness to have secrets from parents and to risk breaking rules. Murphy broke small rules at school but tried as much as possible to do nothing so wrong that it would be reported to his mother and father. In many ways, he took pride in being good but also noticed that it was fun to not always be perfect. In middle school, Murphy began to notice more clearly that he was attracted to boys and not girls and that he was different from other boys in that respect. Murphy began to develop another sense, another way of discerning, that allowed him to notice other boys. He could tell which boys liked girls and which boys might be like him. "It was gaydar," he told me. "You can just tell."

Murphy told me, with relative ease, the story of his earlier life. He had been a gay child, and gay adolescent, in an environment that was threatening and unaccepting. In that, Murphy was not alone. Like many others I had met, he had come of age in a way that made him feel different, in danger both emotionally and perhaps physically, and in a fashion that caused him to be vigilant. In my mind, these dynamics were sufficient to explain his anger and his marijuana use and I believed that our therapy might be very useful to Murphy in order to resolve the conflicts his history had brought forth. I had not imagined the depth of the trauma Murphy had actually undergone. That material came forward after he showed me a drawing.

During one session when Murphy seemed less interested in talking, I asked him if he would be willing to show me his artwork. He opened his drawing book and paged through it with me. His work was at times remarkably subtle, especially the pencil drawings of faces and of hands done with beautiful elegance and detail. In other drawings, Murphy had drawn pictures of fractured beings and of human beings morphed with animals. Those drawings seemed as if they had been done with an intentional expression of what was ragged, sharp, cutting, or broken in life. Among the many drawings that caught my attention was one of a man and a woman in a house. They were obviously in a rage and there was blood on all the walls. In the corner, peeking through a hole in a broken fence was a very small squirrel-like creature with piercing blue eyes. "What is that?" I asked. "It's me," he said. I asked him to tell me the story behind the picture. He became silent, and seemed to be deciding how much he wished to share about his life. Then he began.

"In my last year of middle school, there was this guy who moved to our school and the rumor was that he had to because everyone at his last school knew he was gay. He and I would exchange glances and he knew I was gay too. So, one day, we were alone and made out in the restroom at school. It was so amazing for both of us to find each other." With that, Murphy had to stop and what he described next was done in a hurry. He raced through the story as if he did not think he could start over if he stopped to consider the telling. He simply told his story from start to finish.

Murphy, after the encounter with the other boy, was at once both excited and terrified. On one hand, he was overjoyed at the prospect of knowing another gay teen with whom he could share. On the other, he was terrified others would find out, especially his father. He was mortified by how risky his behavior had been and how careless he had been. Someone might have seen. He was worried, only slightly, that the other boy would tell but was reassured by the knowledge that the other boy had been as guilty as he. The day passed without incident and his father seemed that evening, as usual, to be concerned about the events of his day and not Murphy. The next morning, during second period, Murphy's teacher went to the door, was handed a note and announced to the class that Murphy was to go to the principal's office. Murphy sank. He obeyed, and as he approached the office, he saw the other boy and his father leaving. Murphy sank into a horrible terror. He entered the office. His father was there and the principal began.

The other boy had gone home to his own father and had told him that Murphy had attacked him sexually and forced him to go along. He had, to Murphy, done the unthinkable. Murphy had been utterly betrayed. The principal did not ask Murphy if it was true. He expelled Murphy and sent him home with his father.

The ride home had been silent and after they arrived, Murphy went to his room and his father went to the kitchen. Murphy recalled that he heard his mother and father yelling and arguing loudly and, then, for short periods, he heard only quiet mumbling. The yelling came again and Murphy's father called him to the living room. Murphy could not recall many details after that, or perhaps, they were buried inside in the way all trauma is. There had been pushing and shoving, rage, and tears. Murphy had tried to apologize and it was not sufficient.

His mother had tried to stop the father from hitting Murphy but she could not. Murphy wasn't sure how long it went on but he remembered his father hitting him with a closed fist and he remembered falling to the ground. In a fit of rage, and in defense, Murphy had grabbed a heavy glass vase from the table and hurled it at his father as hard as he possibly could. It hit his father squarely in the chest. He remembered it shattered and he remembered the thumping sound it made when it hit him. He remembered that everyone became instantly silent. They stared at each other. After a long while, it was the father who moved next and what he did was utterly unexpected. He said, "I give up," in a very soft voice and he left. His mother followed him leaving Murphy in the shattered household.

Murphy remembered little after that. He drank liquor and swallowed pills. He remembered waking up in a hospital bed with his arms tied to the bed railings. His left arm hurt at the wrist where it had been cut. Murphy remembered coming to consciousness very slowly, letting his eyes begin to focus, trying to figure out where he was. He remembered hearing his grandmother praying next to him and he recalled the cool water, holy water, being splashed on him. He realized later she was not praying so much for him as much as she prayed that the evil inside him would be removed by God.

Murphy did not return to school in Ohio and never saw his friends from there again. He spent a month at home in his room, playing video games, and recuperating both mentally and physically. His father did not speak to him but Murphy noticed the difference in him. He seemed subdued, even broken a little. He never raised his hand again and never told Murphy what to do again. Murphy was sent to his aunt's home in Los Angeles one month later. He never returned.

In Los Angeles, and with his aunt, Murphy found safety to be himself. His aunt provided support in all the necessities of life and seemed to have been a stable and loving influence in his life. In many ways, Murphy was able to build a new life, with new friends, as gay, and as an adolescent whose primary job was school and the normal activities of being a teenager. There had been one attempt by his mother to re-unite the family but Murphy refused to consider returning to Ohio and the aunt had dissuaded Murphy's mother and father from trying again.

When Murphy finished telling me his story, he yawned. He seemed exhausted by the process and deeply subdued. I was more shocked at the horrible experience being shared and amazed that Murphy, the reasonably well adjusted young man I had come to know, had found a way forward that seemed healthy and normal for young men his age. Our session that day remains unforgettable to me. It was jarring to think that the young man in front of me had been through such tragedy. Murphy was not suicidal, did not show signs of deep depression, and did not display anything in his demeanor or appearance that suggested that he had been through such trauma. While Murphy had been in Los Angeles for a full eighteen months, it nonetheless amazed me that he had been able to adjust as well as he had given his earlier experience, and, in fact, I was amazed he had survived emotionally intact at all.

Every therapist hears stories that remind them of the depth of human tragedy and the sheer awfulness of some human experience. In moments like those, each therapist must deal with their own countertransference, the feelings that erupt inside, so that they can remain a therapeutic help to their client. After Murphy told me his story, after our session ended, my own feelings began to emerge. I was deeply moved and found myself re-imagining every detail of Murphy's story. I formed a picture of each of his days and could see the tragic unfolding of events in my mind. It was nearly impossible to consider that the young man I had grown to know had actually tried to kill himself, had been so tortured by his father, or that all the tragedy was triggered by Murphy's same-sex feelings. It was difficult, for a while, for me to imagine how such homophobia had come to be in any family, in a country like the United States, or a religion like Christianity. I was angry.

I recall the many images that were stirred in me by Murphy's story. To be clear, they were images that arose from my own deep psyche. I was not there with Murphy to see with my own eyes the events that unfolded. My psyche, informed by his words, created images of those events and they still come forward, to this day, when I think of Murphy. There is an image of Murphy, having been betrayed by a friend, walking heartsick to the principal's office. I had a visceral reaction to my mind's image of Murphy alone in his home, finding pills, drinking and cutting, hoping to die. I could see the violent fight, just before his suicidal attempt, between Murphy and his father and I could almost hear the shattering of the vase as it hit his father's chest.

In the images my psyche created, I can see Murphy in a hospital bed. His eyes are half closed and his body is badly damaged, suffering from bruises and that terrible, suicidal gash across his wrist. His arms are tied to the railings so that he is spread eagle, vulnerable, and unable to protect himself. In my mind, the image of Murphy is a modern day image of a suffering Christ crucified in a hospital bed. Images of Christ, to me, are intended to reach deeply into the human capacity for compassion when human suffering exists. The image asks humans to see the injury of other humans, feel it in their hearts, and respond with a loving empathy. My image of Murphy, as Christ, is accompanied by the image of an old woman, his grandmother, praying to God, throwing water on Murphy. She sees Murphy's pain and somehow concludes that he is the problem, the cause, and the carrier of evil. She is distraught, beyond it, and is doing her best, yet she does not love him in the way she loved Christ. She saw Murphy but, to me, missed the point when she saw him without compassion for his human suffering.

Another image that came to mind immediately after I heard

Murphy's story was the picture of Murphy's father, the church elder, twisting the young arms of his son in a determined effort to make him conform. Murphy needed to, it seemed, conform with a certain version of godliness that was grounded in a certain vision of masculinity. According to Murphy's version of the story, it was not the whole Murphy that was subjected to cruelty by his father, not all of Murphy that his father sought to destroy. It was the implication that Murphy was gay that brought about the sharpest attacks and the deepest emotional vengeance from his father. Somehow, in Murphy's father, God and masculinity, authority and morality, had come together in a brutal condemnation of Murphy's effeminacy and gayness. I wondered why. I wondered how God had become so concerned with being gay in the mind of Murphy's father. I knew that many fathers see their sons as a reflection and it was certainly possible that Murphy and his homosexuality was an embarrassment to a man so against homosexuality. It did not seem to be sufficient as an explanation of the father's cruelty. Aside from the catastrophic events of their last fight, Murphy's father had long sought to eliminate Murphy's homosexuality through control, discipline, and cruel punishment. It seemed to me that Murphy's erotic life, his feelings, his sexuality, and his unwillingness to abandon them threatened the father in a deeper way. I recalled that Socrates had said that where there is Eros, there is no power and where power, no Eros (Plato, 1999). It seemed as if Murphy's sexuality and Eros had collided with his father's power in some very deep way. Thornton (1997), when discussing attitudes held about very effeminate men in some ancient societies, described how I believe Murphy's father reacted to Murphy's sexual nature.

> What we find is the . . . emblem of unrestrained compulsive sexual appetite, of surrender to the chaos of natural passion that threatens civilized order, a traitor to

his sex, a particularly offensive manifestation of Eros's power over the masculine mind that is responsible for creating and maintaining that order in the face of nature's chaos. (p. 101)

Murphy was, to his father, sexually alive, a "traitor to his sex," an offensive display of Eros over the masculine mind that invented order. Murphy, and his homosexuality, was a threat to all his father had built. To love Murphy or to allow Murphy to exist as he was would be to allow chaotic and creative Eros to see through the limitations of order and convention. A father who had built an orderly life, with the aid of an orderly and clear notion of God, saw his son's expression of Eros as offensive. Murphy and Eros had survived, battered but intact, but did so by being exiled from his father's orderly home.

Young Murphy, just 17, seemed remarkably healed in the 18 months since he left home although I understood how deeply his scars were embedded. The discussions of his past were difficult for him although he seemed relieved that another person could share his experience, if only through listening and an empathic hearing of the stories. He was free of his family, safe with an aunt, and developing friendships in the group. I did not actively seek to have him recount the disturbing details of his story again but recognized that the trauma of that night, and the events leading up to it, would necessarily require attention in therapy. As we discussed the daily events of his life, the echoes of those horrible days came forward in small doses so that we slowly worked to integrate past and present, to heal Murphy where possible, and gain insight. It seemed important for Murphy to enjoy his present life and to distance himself from his past in order to feel safe now. I hoped to slowly integrate the present with the past, to help establish that he was safe now from those traumatic days, and to do so without asking Murphy to process the trauma in a way he did not yet wish to.

Perhaps the most obvious way in which Murphy's past showed up in his outward demeanor was his tendency to criticize thoughtless authority or authority exercised for its own sake. When a teacher told him to believe something he did not, Murphy reacted as if it were his father telling him to believe in Christianity. He would argue, defy, make a scene, and usually end up being criticized for his behavior. Murphy had stopped believing in things that made no sense to him and would not yield, but in each encounter, Murphy also felt like an outsider again. When boys harassed him for being gay, Murphy fought back with cutting sarcasm, excellent verbal cutting, that stopped the boys in their tracks. He had battled a father and no "stupid" teenager was a match for Murphy. Yet, Murphy remained an outsider to the broader world of his peers. Each time he fought, he seemed to me to be vulnerable. No young man, still 17, knows for certain that he is right. Murphy, for all of his verbal skills and bold confrontation with the world, secretly, I believe, did not know for sure he was correct in his beliefs. It seemed to me that Murphy needed a place where he could learn more, engage differently, be respected for his thoughts, and begin to develop an alternative to the old battle with authority.

When Murphy raised an issue, usually about something large in scope like Christianity, I gave him more information about it so that he might develop his opinions in ever more sophisticated ways. When he told me that he thought it was stupid that people relied on the Bible, a book written by "a bunch of tribal leaders thousands of years ago," I read him a passage from Marie Louise von Franz. Von Franz, a Jungian Analyst who was instrumental in helping Carl Jung develop his theories on alchemy, would have thought Murphy had a point. She wondered why God had "stopped talking" after he "spoke" to ancient peoples. She wondered why we thought God was so bound-up by a book and so limited by the words of humans. Speaking to a theologian, von Franz (1980) spoke of the difference between theology and psychology.

That is where we differ. You think God has published general rules which He keeps Himself, and we think He is a living spirit appearing in man's psyche who can always create something new . . . . To a theologian God is bound to His books and is incapable of further publications. (p. 142)

Murphy agreed with von Franz. "Yeah, like God doesn't have anything to say about us destroying the environment." Murphy had no idea who von Franz was or why she was important in psychological circles. Murphy might well never read her works. It was enough for him to know that someone important agreed with him and that, at least to someone, he had a point.

Murphy wanted to know about being gay. He was out and open and said he was glad to be gay but Murphy still suffered from years of hearing about the evil of homosexuality. Murphy needed more information so that his fragile knowledge base, upon which he now argued his case that he was healthy, could be deepened. I told him about genetic research, about other cultures, and read passages on occasion, as I did to the larger group, from *The Symposium* by Plato (1999). It was reassuring to Murphy that Socrates had been like him and that they both liked the way they felt.

It was in reading from *The Symposium* (1999) that I began to tell the boys about the nature of Eros. Eros, a very complex idea, needed an explanation appropriate to adolescent boys, one that conveyed some essential ideas without too much subtlety and complexity. I explained my belief that our culture had so limited the idea of Eros that we automatically assumed it was nothing more than sex. Eros, in our society, had become nearly synonymous with X-rated pornography, strip clubs, and online porn sites. Eros, I told them, was actually better described by the Greeks.

Eros, the force of creativity, the force that combined with Gaia and Chaos to create the Earth, was also present in every life. It certainly appeared in sexual longing but was also present in non-sexual love, in relationships, in friendships. Eros was that sense, I said, of yearning to meet the other. It was, I thought, a kind of "leaning into" another so that two things met and discovered what would happen as a result of the encounter. We could have a sense of Eros for another person or a thing, for an idea, or an image. Einstein, in my mind, had an erotic relationship to math. It held him and he discovered what might be created when he and math met.

I asked the boys how they saw Eros in their lives. It was a difficult concept for most and they struggled to consider the problem. One asked if Eros was at work when he went surfing. He certainly loved the experience. I said I thought that when he and the ocean waves met, he became a better surfer so that perhaps Eros, his love of the activity, and the water all met, and in their meeting his ever-improving skills at surfing were being created. Another boy seemed intent in expressing how Eros showed up in his attraction to another boy. I told him that, yes, that was Eros as well. Murphy asked if Eros was in his art. I asked him to tell the group what happened when he drew. "Sometimes I know what I want to draw and I just go at it but other times, I just sit and stare and start anywhere. I draw a line and then another and eventually I see the thing I have drawn." Murphy understood Eros with his usual subtlety. Of all the boys, Murphy seemed best at Eros, the movement into something unknown, something that appears only after creation has done its part.

The boys seemed to like those discussions. Lofty ideas seemed a match for their adolescent yearning to go beyond what was known and to be excited by the new. In many group sessions, of course, Murphy and I and the other boys discussed more mundane issues as well. They talked frequently of harassment, being gay, parents and their many "flaws," and the tedium of being in school, hour after hour, studying "boring stuff." After holidays, someone in the group invariably told of a holiday gathering, a fight at home, a terribly childish sibling, or the terrible boredom of sitting around the house while relatives chattered in the kitchen. Adolescents, neither adult nor child, often seem to find that they are in-between and outside the groupings of others at family events. Sometimes, the boys told of happier events, activities and travels, or food and gifts received during the holidays and their happiness within their families. Knowing something of Murphy's estrangement from his family, the boys did not ask him directly how his holiday gatherings had been. Murphy's family sat in shambles. He usually created something in his art book during those conversations.

Over time, the group, including Murphy, bonded deeply. There had been deep sharing among them and they had cared for one another during crisis and hardship. Each boy understood the hardship of the others because, in their own individual ways, they had experienced it. In many ways, they healed each other and in that healing, they bonded. It might be said that Eros was at work because I think they developed a love for one another. It was partially evident in the tone used, their manner, and their caring approach to each other but also in their physical expressions. There was freedom in the group that was not possible in any other area of their lives. There was no need to be vigilant about affection, appropriately displayed, between boys in our space. I recall the day that Murphy, in a moment of warmth and affection, gently reached over, stretched his arm out and briefly placed it around the shoulder of another boy. He looked at me to see if it was ok, out of habit, because it was not ok in any other place he knew. Unlike heterosexual teens who can express love, have crushes, or hold a hand in public, these boys had been robbed of the experience of such normal, adolescent expressions of love and affection. Boys, in their world, did not hold hands with each other without rebuke, harassment or jeers.

To be able to experience moments of affection, and to feel openly affectionate toward each other, seemed to integrate the physicality of their lives with their emotional ones, reducing their tendency to live split-apart lives. Murphy, especially, needed such healing through loving relationship.

"You're like the dad and we're like your kids. This is like our own little family." I was delighted and surprised by the comment of one of the boys who noticed that we had created something unique in our group, a sense of bonding, family, togetherness and support. I had not thought of myself as the father, having only identified as their therapist. Yet, I had become father of sorts, a gay father, who not only listened for psychological issues but who also represented something of how to navigate the world as a gay man. I was listener, adviser, healer and father, in some fashion, to each of the boys and to the family of boys who met each week. As I began to realize that I had become something more than therapist to the boys, I also began to know something more about how to help Murphy. I returned in my thoughts to the horrible night when Murphy and his father fought in a deadly combat, a memory that especially guided my work with Murphy from that day forward. The story of him and his father fighting had mythical overtones, mostly because of its dark narrative, and I looked to myth for guidance about the collision of fathers and sons. I found the story of Oedipus and his father Laius.

The story of Oedipus is an often-used myth in psychology and, like Narcissus, is a story that has become intertwined within psychology's language, especially in the work of Freud and psychoanalysis. The story of Oedipus who killed his father and married his mother became a central theme in Freud's theory of psychosexual development because it clarified, in Freud's mind, the unconscious ways in which children develop beginning from their instinctual natures and in their relationships to their parents. Generally, Freudian psychology has used some aspects of the original story of Oedipus but leaves the early parts of the myth out. Understanding Murphy in myth, and in the story of Oedipus, required a start at the beginning of the tale.

According to Powell (2004), there was once a young man named Laius who fell in love with another young man named Chrysippus. Laius lusted after the other boy and, one day, lured him outside of town and raped him. Laius was then cursed for having acted so violently. Many years later, Laius became king and married Jocasta. He learned from an oracle that if he were to have a son, the son would grow up and kill him so Laius avoided sex with his wife. One night, after too much drinking, Laius and Jocasta had sex and she bore a son, Oedipus, nine months later. Laius, knowing that his infant son would kill him, had Oedipus's feet pinned together and ordered a shepherd to leave him exposed on the slope of a mountain where he would die (p. 455).

One of the great values of mythology is that it often speaks about the darkness in human experience in a way more civilized, even sanitized, social conversation does not allow. There can be great cruelty in men and they may act in killing ways toward the helpless when they feel at risk. The story of Laius is that of a man who was cruel toward his infant son. Murphy experienced such cruelty from his father from his earliest memories of beatings and arm-twistings that once cracked a bone in Murphy's seven- year-old wrist. Myth describes such darkness.

Oedipus, as an infant, had done no wrong. Laius, the father, had done the wrong. Yet, the birth of a son became intertwined within the father's destiny and the son became the threat. If the myth held any hint about Murphy, it seemed to me, it was that Murphy might have been a threat to the father. Only a threatened man, I thought, would behave so cruelly to his own son.

Oedipus, as described by Powell (2004), did not know that his father was Laius, that he was an orphan, or that his father tried to kill him. He was raised by other parents, living in a false sense of safety, and in an ignorance of his destiny. He began to question who he was, his authentic life, when his age-mates taunted him and accused him of being an orphan. Young Oedipus, like the young gay Murphy who lived as a heterosexual Christian, is "a study in the contrast of being and appearance" according to Powell (p. 461). Oedipus thought he was one person as a boy and, in the slow process of discovery, learned what was true about him later. Like Oedipus, it might be said that Murphy had lived a lie as a child, knowing no better. He was a gay boy living as a Christian straight one, believing all was well until his truer identity, his more authentic self, began to emerge. When that happened, it came in a jolting confrontation between Murphy and his father. It was as if neither one really knew the other any more.

One day Oedipus and Laius met on the road. Laius, the King in his chariot, did not recognize Oedipus and forced the younger man off the road, hitting him as he went by. Oedipus, not recognizing his father, fought back, jumping into the carriage where he killed his father in deadly combat. Only much later did Oedipus realize the full impact of what he had done. After many other horrifying experiences, and the near total destruction of Oedipus and all he knew and had valued, he was eventually exiled.

In just the first part of the Oedipus myth, much of Murphy's life is illuminated. Oedipus not only killed his father, but killed the King and all that the King represented. Kings, after all, represent order, authority, right and wrong, laws and obedience, and the proper roles of all subordinates. Kings often believe, like Murphy's father, that they are divinely inspired. Killing the King destroys more than the person. It kills the entire structure of life. Like Oedipus, Murphy had participated in the shattering of all that his father represented when he threw the vase at his father. He was no longer a son, no longer part of a family, no longer in a community, no longer one among his peers, and no longer part of a religious container. All of the kingdom, and all the support that a kingdom provides, was shattered. Murphy, like Oedipus, was exiled, never to return.

I began to better understand the psychological devastation in Murphy's past through the story of Oedipus. The destruction Murphy had endured was more widespread and much worse, in some ways, than the matter of the abuse he had suffered. In a psychological way, Murphy lost more than a father, mother, house, and friends when he was exiled from Ohio. He lost a sense of himself in the world, a world that mirrored and understood him, that reflected him and that could be counted upon for guidance in life.

He lost explanations for what was right and wrong, reasons for doing things, grounding, and reassurance in moving forward into the world. When Murphy asked big questions about Christianity, it was both an effort to distance himself from a lost past but also to use his creative energy to create a new sense of spirituality, made in his own way, starting from scratch. When Murphy challenged the education he was receiving, he did so not just to question authority but also to re-build an inner sense of what he needed to learn. The old way, "learn because it is what is good for you," was gone. Murphy, absent the structure of his father's authority and his former life, needed to create new reasons for his actions.

I began to realize the depth of the work Murphy had been doing, silently, all along. He had been hard at work building a new foundation for his life, a new sense of himself and a more truthful understanding of how he and the world could co-exist. His many ways of challenging the world, or embracing it, were efforts to create something psychologically grounding. Murphy insisted that the world stand up to his scrutiny, his boldness, and his questioning. Once he found something in the world around him that was reliable, in people, ideas, or attitudes, he added it to his new foundation. Christianity was out and education without learning's pleasures was out as well. Art was in. Being gay was in and acceptance of the reality of society's harshness about it was in his new psychological foundation as well. Murphy was hard at work to discover new values, new people, new ideas, new images and new surroundings with which he could identify and upon which he could rely. He had given up on himself and his life once by trying suicide. No more. Now, Murphy would accept the challenge of his life and begin by building a life from the ground up.

Murphy, in quiet subtle steps, had created a new family out of the rubble from the last one. Murphy had tested his aunt, I am sure, and seemed to find that her loving support was reliable and real. She was like a new mother, a surrogate for certain, but someone who brought the characteristics of mothering to Murphy's life. He had found a new father in me, a gay one this time, who guided him and wanted him to thrive. He had found a father who could model how to live a happy life as a gay man but also a man who cared about him and about his being able to live well. He had found "brothers" who liked and respected him, the boys in a group, and Murphy found friendship again with them. Murphy could be true to his sexual feelings around his new "family," feel exactly what he felt, and allow the erotic, in its broadest sense, to be fully present again without shame or guilt. I think Murphy knew he was cared for, at least by a few, and it was sufficient.

Murphy had found the tools he needed to combat authority and convention. He could use Eros, the energy that creates all things, to penetrate what was "known" by others so that new possibilities, unforeseen and unknown, could appear as if they were the unknown drawings in his art book, becoming visible only after the hard work of creation was done. He could use his intelligence and creative nature to explore himself and the world differently now, finding new truths and new values as he went along.

Murphy accepted, I think, that he was an outsider to many but being an outsider allowed him to see what those on the inside take for granted. He was gay and saw the destructiveness of homophobia and intolerance. The insiders seemed to not realize how hurtful they could be. Murphy, on the outside, could see it vividly. Murphy, because he was outside looking in, could see what no family wishes to know about itself. He could see that in some cases, behind the social veneer of goodness and correctness, was destructiveness. Murphy's gay identity made him an outsider from the start of his early life and although he was now more accepted, more included in the lives of others, his experience of the past was deeply etched into his character. Being gay now meant, to Murphy, a choosing of himself and his nature despite what others thought, knowing full well that by doing so, he would be outside the norm. Being gay was symbolic of being original and different from the collective or "the herd." In some ways, Murphy's being gay had been a catalyst toward becoming himself. By seeing what he was, he also saw what he was not. By standing firm in his own life and who he was, Murphy then could watch the world's reaction to him and see what the world had to say more clearly. He then could evaluate both him and it. Choices were more clear and he had the chance to choose his own values, his own aspirations and his own future with a clarity many young people do not possess. From that position, he had a path forward.

In retrospect, I think that what was most unknown at the end of our work together was the extent to which Murphy would embrace his newly created life. Could he move forward with the same resilience and same courage he had shown at 15, 16, and 17-years old? Could he somehow manage to make meaning of his very difficult start in life? Could he manage to be optimistic despite the reality of life's cruelty and hardship? If anyone could, I thought, it was Murphy. Speaking about mythology, Campbell (1988) expressed Murphy's psychological question moving forward in his life.

Thinking in mythological terms helps put you in accord with the inevitables of this vale of tears. You learn to recognize the positive values in what appears to be the negative moments and aspects of your life. The big question is whether you are going to be able to say a hearty yes to your adventure . . . . The adventure of being alive. (p. 163)

The question for Murphy was whether or not he could embrace life fully, enthusiastically, and even optimistically given the awful experience of his past. Could he say a hearty "yes" to the life ahead of him knowing what life can involve? Could he eventually understand that he had been largely formed out of the experience so that, despite its darkness, he was now more authentic, more creative and more himself than ever before? No justification of the child abuse he endured is possible but, at the same time, many of his gifts developed because Murphy had faced it so squarely. Could he see just that little bit of positive news from his past? Most importantly, could he move forward and fully enjoy the life he was creating?

At the end of our work together, Murphy had grown. He seemed more grounded and less alone. He still smoked marijuana but not so urgently as before. He was bonded to the other boys, seemed at peace at home, and seemed to be able to tolerate school. In our last sessions together, he expressed to me how grateful he had been for the chance to meet with me and be in the group. It had been the best part of his year, he said. I told him how much I appreciated him and how deeply moved by him I had been. I told him it had been a privilege for me to know him and to be part of his life. I told him that I thought that there would be times in the future when I popped into his mind or he remembered what we had said together. I was sure I would remember

Murphy as well, perhaps forever. In that way, I said, our relationship would continue, perhaps forever as well.

Among the most difficult aspects of being a therapist is that when a client says goodbye, the therapist cannot know for sure how the story will unfold in the future and certainly not how it ends. I do not know much of Murphy's story after therapy but I still hear from him occasionally. In his last email, I got a hint about how he was approaching his life now. He sent me a picture. He was standing in a large plaza in front of a very old building, made of heavy stone, with a beautiful spiral at the top, reaching into the sky. His hair was black again but now very long. Murphy was smiling in the picture. He held a hand painted sign that read "I am here" and pointed toward the old building, perhaps hundreds of year old, behind him. The building housed a famous art school in Barcelona where Murphy now studied.

Logan

I recall that it was a Sunday evening, early, and that I was preparing dinner when I received the text. "I am going to tell her now." It was from Logan. I responded, "I am here if you need me." An hour later, I received a second short message. "I am going to tell him. He is in the other room. It's now or never." I responded again, "Let me know how it goes." About 30 minutes later, I received the final text of the night. "He cried but it's ok. I'll tell you about it when I see you this week. Thanks for your help." Logan had, as he approached his 18th birthday, told his parents that he was gay. He reached out to his therapist, a touchstone, on a tense Sunday night when he and his parents faced an uncertain moment. Logan moved through the challenge, across a threshold, on his own and with the courage all such encounters demand. He had not told me beforehand that he would take the step of coming out to his parents. Something within him had decided, perhaps even unconsciously, that not only did he need to do it but that this particular Sunday night was the time for action. He wanted someone to know, to be there if things went badly, but Logan made the decision on his own and for his own very personal reasons.

I had known Logan for 3 years, since his sophomore year in high school, and I had watched him navigate his world with all of its many challenges, especially those of a young man coming to terms with his homosexuality. Despite those challenges, Logan seemed to experience his life as a high school senior with a kind of happiness, excitement and pride. It was not easy but Logan dealt with his life in a steady, thoughtful way, as if he knew what needed to be done in the present in order for his life to be happy in the future. Privately, in our individual sessions, normal anxieties showed up each week related to his activities, his questions about being gay, his family and his future. He confronted those challenges privately, in a cooperative effort with me and, then, put his new insights into practice, testing, learning, and growing as he went. In some ways, his ability to delve deeply and process his psychological life privately seemed to ground him and bolster his confidence in the world.

Logan's ability to remain grounded, despite the challenges of being a gay teen, provided a kind of hope for other gay teens when he attended our weekly group therapy session. He was a role model for the other teens and often played the role of senior statesmen, a voice of experience at 17 years old. His story, full of challenge and success, spoke to the questions other boys had. I asked him one day to tell the younger members in the group what it had been like for him as a gay teen in high school.

Logan spoke with a kind of pride, a self-assured knowledge, about his progress in the past four years. He recalled, in a description of successive years in high school, that he had first tried to ignore his sexual feelings in 9th grade. "I pushed it back," he said of his feelings.

"I tried to ignore them but I could feel it," he said, referring to his homosexual feelings. He had withdrawn in his freshman year, stayed in his bedroom when at home, and played video games alone. He remembered that he felt confused and "down" but, at the time, he did not especially relate his isolation with his conflicted feelings about homosexuality. It seemed to him to have been a more general feeling of needing to hide himself and avoid the world. It was a painful time for him, one I imagined might well have felt like a despair of some sort, although I did not know Logan at the time.

"I remember that by my sophomore year, I was still isolated and was kind of anti- social. I remember thinking 'does she think I'm gay?' and 'are they talking about me?' everywhere I went. It was awful." He had kept his homosexual feelings to himself but worried others could see through his mask or that they might see something "gay" about his behaviors, tone of voice, or in something he might have said. He pretended to be straight, did not date, but joined in conversations with other boys about which girls were cute.

Things had changed by his junior year and he had met a few friends, girls, in whom he could confide. Slowly and carefully, Logan began to disclose his homosexuality to others, one at a time. He did not try to tackle the whole world. He built strong relationships with others, solid and true, and then shared his homosexuality to them when he felt their friendship could withstand any shock that came from the revelation. By his junior year, he told the group, he had begun to go to parties where he could be gay around some close friends. "I was semi-closeted." He lived by withholding the truth from many, during school and at home, but began to make small steps, with a chosen few, toward a full expression of who he was.

By his senior year, Logan had begun to share that he was gay with close friends, both boys and girls, who liked him because of who he was as a person. They valued his friendship more than they cared about his being gay. In those bonded relationships, built slowly over time, Logan had friends who "had his back." Speaking of the whole experience, he told the other boys, "It eats away at you. It's hard to be yourself if you lie, trying to keep the lies straight. But I've gone from dreading being gay to now, I just thank God I'm gay."

Logan's testament, including the wisdom gained from his experience, gave hope to the younger boys, one of whom continued to cut himself on desperate and lonely weekend nights. For the younger teens who felt isolated, lonely, hopeless and suicidal, Logan provided reassurance about the future because not only had he survived, he had done it in a way that resulted in his being happy about being gay. He provided a strategic plan to them, one that they could consider. Don't try to tackle the whole world if you don't want, he was saying to them. Just build relationships to others, one at a time, and eventually, you'll have enough support for who you are so that you can live a happy life. It was not a strategy all the others would take but it was a way forward for some. At least all the boys heard that there was hope.

Privately, Logan and I had worked together for 3 years and both of us knew that he had not always been happy and that there had been periods, in fact, when despair had been more the tone of his life than was happiness. He came to therapy in his sophomore year depressed and angry, separated from others, and isolated. At the time, he had been especially angry at his father. He felt rejected by his father and felt that his father favored his brother. He told me that his father and brother watched sports together, something Logan found uninteresting, and that the two had bonded through such activities. Once, when the family was out to dinner, another man came to their table. His father introduced his wife first then introduced Logan and his brother. "This is Logan," he said. Then touching the shoulder of Logan's brother, the father added, "and this is my son." His father had one son, Logan's brother. Logan sat silently in the back seat of the car on the way home that night, and he cried silently. "They didn't even notice," he told me then. Logan's father loved to play guitar and Logan, in an effort to gain his father's praise, excitedly took up the guitar "so I could give one gift to him." He practiced at night in the living room where he was certain his father would notice. "I wasn't noticed," he said, "so I gave it up." There were the times when his father, in anger, would complain to Logan's mother about Logan. He would start the complaint, every time, according to Logan, with "That boy is . . . " Logan thought he must be unimportant if his father wouldn't just say his name. He was "that boy," not Logan.

As he approached his 16th birthday, Logan recognized that much of his emotional life involved anger and separation. Logan knew that, in some ways, he was the one separating. "It's like I am in the shadows and no one notices, so I try and become greater and get compliments but that doesn't work, so I get angry and walk away. I'm the one pushing them away," he told me one sad day. He did not mind so much that he pushed his father away and cared very little that he and his brother seemed estranged. He minded very much that he was, through his actions, hurting his mother. "She is everything," he told me. His mother worked a full time job, cared for the household, cooked and cleaned, bought him his school supplies and clothes, and was the only one in the home that seemed to notice that he was troubled. Logan knew that his mother loved him, and she said it out loud on occasion, and even in times of family strife, she found a way to talk to him, guide him and direct him.

Hidden from view was Logan's growing awareness of his homosexuality. It had been hidden even in our conversations in the beginning. One day, he told me that his cousin had made a post on Facebook that said something about Logan, about how he played with girl's toys when he was a boy, implying that Logan was gay. The Facebook post both infuriated and embarrassed Logan but it also provided an opportunity for us to discuss his sexuality. I had found that, on many occasions, my teenage clients introduced their questions about homosexuality in indirect ways. It seemed to be a way of testing my reaction to their hidden feelings before they owned the feelings or spoke of them in the first person. Generally, my approach in those moments was to convey that I was accepting without asking them to disclose anything about themselves. I told Logan that day that I worked with many teens who had been called gay, were gay, who thought themselves to be bisexual as well as heterosexual teens. I told him that therapy was a great place to discuss those issues because it was private and confidential. Logan, at 15, denied he was gay but left the door open to further discussions with me. "It's cool," was his only response initially.

To be clear, Logan was himself uncertain, I believe, about the nature of his sexuality. In retrospect, I now know that he was aware of his same-sex attractions just as he described them to the group members. In our conversations during his sophomore year, Logan did not easily express those feelings with me. In fact, Logan's sexual identity changed frequently during the course of our work in his sophomore year. Initially, he told me he was heterosexual. Then, some months later, he said that he thought he might be bisexual. Still later that same year, for a brief time, he felt that his sexuality was driven by the nature of the individual and not their gender. "I think I am attracted to the person's heart and could have sex with either guys or girls if I loved them," he said. By years end, Logan began to use the term gay in our conversations, sporadically and often indirectly, to describe himself. "So what's so horrible if I were gay," he would say.

Importantly, it should also be noted that during that year, especially in the beginning months after his sexuality became an issue in therapy, Logan went through periods when he missed appointments with some frequency or, when he did come to a session, he avoided conversations about sexuality. As he struggled with his sexuality, he seemed to occasionally use withdrawal, both from therapy and from his family, as a tool that allowed him time to consider his own feelings more privately.

When Logan came to school the next fall, the beginning of his junior year, he returned to therapy immediately and we began our weekly individual sessions which he then consistently attended. Logan seemed to have transformed over the course of the summer in ways that were dramatic to me. His hair was still blond but was now more carefully tended. He retained his broad smile and easy laugh when he was happy about something in his life but I was more struck by the fact that his entire demeanor seemed more assured. He had lost a great deal of weight and was no longer the overweight kid who was teased. He had taken up swimming over the summer and had learned to love it. He now walked more confidently when he entered the office and seemed to speak more confidently when he addressed those around him. I cannot ascribe the changes that took place in Logan that summer to any event and, in fact, he thought that the summer had been uneventful. Perhaps the changes in him physically and emotionally were the result of a natural maturation that happens to all teens. The one thing that had changed psychologically over the summer, and for equally unknown reasons, was that Logan had concluded that he was gay. He had told no one else but shared the fact with me as soon as we began our work.

In private, he was often more vulnerable, more earnest about his anxieties and more concerned about what he should do about any number of issues than his external persona suggested. Yet, he seemed more grounded than he had just months before. He seemed to me, at least retrospectively, to have made decisions about himself and had begun to consolidate his emotional and psychological life on the basis of those decisions. Among the few but very clear conclusions he had drawn over the summer was that he was gay. He had also concluded that he had a safe person in me to share that information with, and that for the moment, no one else needed to know. He seemed to have concluded that he would maintain a deceit with everyone else, knowingly and consciously, about his sexual feelings and that he would begin to tell them when he was ready emotionally and not before. Somehow, in that process of consolidation, Logan had also begun a physical transformation, growing stronger, leaner and more self-assured in the world. He had begun to care for himself, emotionally and physically, in a way that suggested a growing self esteem. In unknown ways to me, Logan seemed to have largely finished a process related to the questioning about his core sexuality and had now turned his attention to the outer world. He had begun to navigate that world with an inner foundation intact.

What I have only begun to understand years later is that Logan was a teen who understood the nature of relationship. During that summer, and throughout our work, Logan was intent on building a relationship to himself, his own authentic self, that grounded him. Once he had a relationship to his own true feelings and his broader personality, one that integrated his homosexual feelings, Logan had begun the slow and deliberate process of developing equally solid relationships with the world. He had chosen, perhaps because of our previous work, to build the first relationship with the outside world, one that included him fully, with me. At the core of all adolescent psychological theory is the idea that adolescents are in the process of building an identity that is real and that is consistent both internally and in the world. Logan could not yet share his true identity with the entire world or, in fact, with anyone other than me. He and I were at the work of building a relationship that, with luck, could be a model for him in his encounters with others.

While some teens might well have been satisfied with just one person with whom they could have such a relationship, Logan was not. Others might avoid the difficult work of building relationships to the broader world, perhaps for years, because they feared ostracism due to their homosexuality. Logan seemed to understand, in some fundamental way, that he could not live happily in that way. He often spoke about his need to have friends, and eventually, to tell them about his sexuality. He told me that his family would one day know. Logan was intent on building honest relationships to others in the future even if the way forward was uncertain and unclear. It was as if Logan had made a bargain with himself. It was as if he had said to himself, "It's ok for me to lie about it now, to whomever I choose, so long as some day I tell them all." In that bargain Logan seemed to be aware that it was dangerous for him to declare himself gay too quickly, too broadly, and without emotional protection. At the same time, he seemed to want to have the experience of being in a happy and authentic relationship to others in the world. To accomplish that mission, Logan had decided to accept that his life needed to include deception about his sexuality until, one day, he could be open. He seemed to know intuitively that relationships were an essential ingredient in the human experience of happiness, one which he wanted, even if the experience was to be postponed for now.

I often wondered where Logan had learned, in such deeply ingrained ways, about the importance of relationship. Why did he make relationships so much a part of his long term life plan? Why did he take so seriously the work of building them when so many other teens seemed to move from one person to another, discarding one friend when a new one came along? Even in our work, it seemed to me that Logan did the things that built strong relationship. He seemed to trust more, disagree more, work through conflict more with me than other students did as if he knew that such work built strong bonds. He seemed to enjoy the act of relating more than others his age. He seemed a "natural" in the art of interacting. I understood clearly that he had not learned such skill simply from our work and that the foundation and strength of his personality had developed throughout his life and from someone who had taught him about these matters from the beginning. I gained insight into Logan when I met his mother.

I had often been amazed that so many parents of the young people I worked with never called, never asked to meet me, or never inquired about the working of therapy even though they had expressly consented to my being their child's therapist. I would, I think, have wanted to know something of the person to whom I was entrusting the psychological care of a child. Logan's mother was more attentive to the circumstances of her son's life than many other parents I had known of or had met. She called and asked to come see me at the clinic soon after the beginning of Logan's junior year. She asked me about my background, about my work and credentials, and about the nature of my work with her son. She respected my explanation that I could not share the details of the conversations between Logan and I.

Logan's mother was clear and direct, open about her questions, and open about her love and concern for Logan. She seemed almost tough, as if she could handle anything that came up but, also, seemed strong enough to step back and trust both Logan and I to do our work independent of her. "I have tried to always be there for him and to give him what he needs" she said. "But he is growing up and he needs to make some decisions for himself and I guess this is something he believes he needs." I sensed a little sadness in her voice and demeanor in the fact that he had outgrown a time when he shared everything with her. At the same time, she seemed willing to let go of the proposition that she would be privy to his entire life. It seemed that she respected him and while letting go made her a little sad, it was right that he move beyond her. She reminded me of the woman in *The Prophet* by Gibran (1923) who had learned about what it means to have children from a wise man.

And a woman who held a babe against her bosom said,
Speak to us of children, And he said:
Your children are not your children.
They are the sons and daughters of Life's longing for
itself. They come through you but not from you,
And though they are with you yet they belong not
to you. You may give them your love but not your
thoughts,
For they have their own thoughts.
You may house their bodies but not their souls,
For their souls dwell in the house of tomorrow, which
you cannot visit, not even in your dreams.
You may strive to be like them, but seek not to make
them like you. For life goes not backward nor tarries
with yesterday.
You are the bows from which your children as living
arrows are sent forth.
(Gibran, 1923, pp. 17-18)

Logan's mother understood her role as a mother. It seemed to me that she might have been the central figure in his life who gave him a belief in his own worth and a direct experience in the value of secure relationships. Logan would have certainly said so. According to him, she had been there for him throughout his life in circumstances both easy and difficult. Now, she would let go and be a watchful outsider as his life unfolded independently.

Logan's self-assurance and self-esteem were tested in his junior year. He seemed to struggle on many days, slipping into anxiety and occasional depression for brief periods of time. While his intention was to bond to others, with his homosexuality intact and open, he nonetheless experienced many lonely days. He seemed to bond more to adults at school than with most of his peers. He and I were bonded, a relationship he valued highly. He was close to one teacher to whom he eventually confided about being gay. He liked the receptionist at the nurse's office and often spent breaks near her desk, chatting about life. Yet, especially in the early part of his junior year, Logan was a loner on campus among his peers. In that period, as I walked to the office, I saw him often sitting alone on the bench outside the administration building eating his lunch while all the other teens sat together on the lawn, laughing, playing and running. He watched them from a distance. It was as if he saw the enormous challenge in front of him, of being a gay teen in the midst of such an uncontrollable, unpredictable mass of teenagers, some of whom he knew hated gay teens. He watched from a distance at first. In those days, he occasionally was more angry in therapy, more frustrated, and more despairing although he often could not specify the exact cause. He did not waver in his acceptance of being gay but seemed to be angry about the consequences of it.

I suggested that he join my group for teens questioning their sexuality. He declined. I suggested that he consider going to the Gay-Straight Alliance meeting on campus which he also declined to attend. Such activities, which to me held the possibility of finding other teens that would be supportive, were, to Logan, akin to coming out publicly. By joining those groups, many others would know he was gay and because of that, Logan would lose control of the process of disclosure. Beyond that, his approach to coming out, I think now, was related to building deeper relationships with others, not a similarity in sexual orientation. To Logan, just because someone was gay did not mean that they would be good or lasting friends.

A turning point occurred over the Christmas holidays when Logan decided it was time to tell a friend he had known since childhood. The friend had reacted with sarcasm and rejection, eventually posting Logan's declaration on Facebook. Again, Logan denied it on Facebook and then launched, apparently, an angry, furious condemnation of the other boy in the public exchanges. Others chimed in to the conversation. One person, Andrea, just said, "I like you no matter what." Logan and Andrea became friends after that and Logan emotionally, and online, separated from all those in the past he had once counted upon. He began anew in building relationships and he began, among his peers, with Andrea. After the holidays, when I walked to the office, I saw Logan on his bench by administration. Thereafter, by his side, was Andrea.

In our sessions, Logan processed the many conflicting emotions of his holiday experience. Among the many topics he discussed was his continuing anger at his father and his separation from his brother. He and they were worlds apart and continued to seem to live in different worlds, a situation that made his home life difficult. It did not occur to him that his homosexuality might be an unconscious or invisible factor in their continued inability to relate. I suspected it was although I had no concrete evidence for that belief. Logan talked about the horrible episode on Facebook, a humiliating experience he suffered alone over the holidays. For obvious reasons, he could not tell his family about the nature of his online activities, and therefore, they could offer no support or guidance. He was angry, hurt and afraid about what would happen when he returned to school and encountered some of his former friends. Luckily, they simply avoided him and he had avoided them.

Reading through the content of Logan's words into a deeper consideration of his efforts to build relationship to others, as an open gay person, it seemed to me that Logan had first attempted to trust what had been known. He reached out to a long-time friend, someone he had known since childhood, believing that the long bond between two boys was sufficient to support Logan's new identification. It was, of course, a reasonable decision on Logan's part. Who better to trust than a person he had trusted for years? One of the themes or lessons I had learned in my work with other gay teens was that as they express a new version of themselves to others, they often forget that others know them as they had been in the past. Gay teens often forget that other people think of them as straight and that others from the past may have deep aversions to homosexuality that will overwhelm all other considerations. Many face the truth that some of their past friendships are highly conditional, having as their basis the continued heterosexuality of the teen. In his attempt to come out to a friend of the past, Logan faced the difficult recognition that his past life, and many of the others he had liked in that past, were gone and could not be retrieved.

To Logan, the only good thing that had happened over the holidays was that he and Andrea had met. They had seen each other on campus but had never really talked. Now they were talking. She had told him that she was bisexual and that she did not care if he was gay. He told her he was and they began to share more openly. Logan liked her for her willingness to be independent and think for herself. Beyond that, he enjoyed her company. The process of building new relationships with others, one person at a time, had begun in humiliating crisis but had ended with one friend who knew he was gay.

Through her and over time, Logan was introduced to Andrea's friends with whom he could also be open. Over time, a new network of friends began to develop that was comprised, at first, of mostly girls. They spent weekends together, school breaks together, and Logan began to regain a sense of sociability. With open relationships with his therapist, a teacher, a receptionist, and a group of four or five girls, Logan began to regain his enjoyment of time at school, his weekends, and his late nights chatting online. While on occasion Logan experienced depression or anxiety, the content of our therapy gradually shifted towards discussions of what he and his friends had done, what someone had said, or what party they had gone to Saturday night. It was at the end of that year, as he approached the conclusion of his junior year and his 17th birthday, that Logan told me he was interested in joining my group for gay teens. He began attending and quickly became a central figure in the group. He remained a steadying and positive influence on the other boys throughout the next year and until he graduated from high school.

Logan continued to navigate his way through relationships, the broader social environment in which he lived, and his inner questions about what it meant to be gay throughout his senior year in high school. He was, in a general way, a happy gay teen who avoided confrontation with those who would taunt him and stayed close to those who were friends. He asked many questions of me about what it meant to be gay. He seemed to be aware that being gay involved living among some in society who were hostile and some who were not. He gained a clarity, based largely on his own experience, that being gay required a discerning attitude about others because it could never be quite clear in advance who would accept him and who would not. Once he had established the ground rules of life, that he would find both animosity and deep connection in his interactions with others, he seemed to gain confidence. He seemed able to proceed with the process of meeting the world on those terms. His growing list of new friends increasingly included male teenagers who were usually the boyfriends of some of the girls in his newly formed close-knit group of friends. At their weekend parties and gatherings, Logan was able to say he was gay without vigilance, finding that not all teenage boys were afraid to be around gay teens. They liked him, and he they, according to Logan.

It was late in his senior year, on a quiet Sunday night, when Logan told his parents he was gay. It was, in some ways, the final stage of Logan's development of an identity that was consistent internally and in the world around him. It was not without peril. He told me about his experience that night in our weekly session the following Thursday. He had gone to his room and called out for his mother to join him. Logan noticed that she seemed concerned as she approached him, perhaps because he rarely called her to his room in that way. He was shaking, he said. "I am gay and I hope you can still accept me. I am the same person I always was." It was as if he blurted it out all at once, the facts, the truth and his hope. She did not cry as he thought she might. She paused and thought, then asked him if he knew for certain. She had heard it was a phase. She asked him if she had done something wrong because she had heard that mothers cause their sons to be gay. He told her that she did not cause it and that she had been the best mother anyone ever had. She worried for him, having heard that gay men are attacked and harassed, made to feel shame, and that many young people his age hurt themselves. She was worried about his future, but more importantly, his present. Was he ok?, she wanted to know. She told him that he was her son and that she loved him no matter what. Then, Logan began to cry, just a little. After she left for her own room, to think about things, he regrouped, sent me a text, and went to the living room to see his father.

He told his father much in the same way he had told his mother. He was afraid, holding his breath between each sentence, but direct. "I am gay and you deserve to know. I hope you're ok with it. I really do." His father sat silently, looking down, thinking through what he had heard before he responded. After a long while, he said "I love you boy" before he began to cry. Logan had never seen his father cry and certainly never before had he seen his father cry about who Logan was. Gone was the criticism in his father's tone of voice and gone was their estrangement, at least for just a moment. They were sharing now. His father said he had wondered about Logan for some years. Logan never brought girls home, never spoke much about dating, but his father had not wanted to think his son was gay. He did not know how to father a gay son and knew little about it. He wanted, like Logan's mother, to hear that Logan was sure and that there was no possibility his homosexuality would pass. Logan told him that he was sure and that he had known for a long time. Their night ended quietly, mother and father talking quietly in their bedroom and Logan, exhausted in his own room, considering the enormous implications of what he had just done. He was overjoyed that the truth was out but, even more, Logan was amazed that he had done what he had thought about doing for so many years in anxious anticipation. It was done. Everyone who needed to know he was gay now knew fully. He sent me a text. It was ok now.

It is difficult to know with certainty why some teens who have homosexual feelings choose to die and why some, like Logan, are able to navigate their teenage years with a happy outcome. Each individual case depends on many factors that include their attitude about homosexuality, their own individual natures, their environments and many other things. In Logan's case, he was certainly taunted because he was gay although he seemed to find ways around and through the horrible consequences such harassment brings to others. Some teens have difficulty in accepting their homosexuality, perhaps because of guilt and shame but Logan found happiness in his gay identity. He thanked God for it. Certainly, Logan gets credit for his ability to integrate his homosexuality within his personality successfully and in a positive way. He certainly worked hard to accomplish it. Also true about Logan's successful navigation through the conflicts of teenage homosexuality was that he was grounded in a loving family, bound in relationships that could survive the shock of statements like "I am gay, mother." Such grounding had been a lifelong experience for Logan and the impact of his family, and their support, on his life cannot be underestimated.

Logan came to therapy for several sessions after his graduation from high school, coming to see me in my private practice in the heart of the gay community of Los Angeles. His mother drove him into the community of gay people, a community Logan had begun to embrace. He told me in one session that he had thought that by coming out he would find a whole different experience in life, one less troubled and less confusing. What he found, months after he came out, was that he had many new things to consider that seemed to be challenging just in the way his life in high school had been. Having expected so much from coming out, he had not realized that he would have to eventually confront the question of "Now what?" Now, he seemed to realize, he was once again asked to engage the unknown future. He was again at the beginning of something new and undiscovered in him.

He had begun to feel restless living at home. His friends had moved away. He was attending a small community college and wanted to go to a university. He wanted something more than his home town offered. Like he had so many times before, Logan considered his options and what his life should be like in the future. He then navigated the many obstacles in front of him so that he might embrace that life. He found a school, a prestigious university in Washington, D.C. that specialized in political science. He worked with his family to find the financial aid needed and was accepted in the university of his "dreams." He is now in his second year and working toward his degree in political science. He hopes to eventually work in a non-profit that supports the rights of the LGBT community.

CHAPTER VII

CONCLUSION

When a lover of boys, or any other type of person, meets that very person who is his other half, he is overwhelmed, to an amazing extent, with affection, concern and love. The two don't want to spend any time apart from each other. These are people who live whole lifetimes together, but still couldn't say what it is they want from each other. I mean, no one can think that it's just sexual intercourse they want, and that is the reason why they find such joy in each other's company and attach such importance to this. It's clear that each of them has some wish in mind that he can't articulate; instead like an oracle, he half-grasps what he wants . . . The reason is that this is our original natural state and we used to be whole creatures: "love" is the name for the desire and pursuit of wholeness. (Plato, 1999, pp. 25-26)

The ancients understood that homosexuality was more than sexual. Sexuality, specifically homosexuality, was a stepping stone, according to the Greeks in *The Symposium*, for the expression of love that had as its goal, the experience of wholeness (Plato, 1999, pp. 25-26). Often lost in modern descriptions of homosexuality is that, at its heart, homosexuality and love between men has been one means by which human beings have, throughout the ages, found love and wholeness. Such men were, to the Greeks, on a path toward the discovery of transcendent love.

Now, in today's language, such men are controversial, denigrated in some quarters, and often seen with disdain. Now, we often speak of love between men in academic, cold and abstract ways so that we speak of a sexual orientation as "an enduring pattern of emotional, romantic, and /or sexual attractions to men, women, or both sexes" (American Psychological Association, 2009, p. 1). We no longer, at least in our clinical descriptions, call it love. Lost in our modern language about homosexuality is the long- held notion that homosexuality is an act of love, a joyful aspect of life for many, and that such love builds wholeness in the humans who experience it.

While our modern language may lack the lyricism of the past, and sometimes the deeper meaning embedded in homosexuality, the modern era benefits from the accumulation of knowledge and information, gleaned from history, cultural comparisons, scientific discoveries and modern psychological research. From that information, homosexuality can now be understood as biologically and genetically formed before birth and in the continuing development of an infant in the first years of life (LeVay, 2011). We now know that homosexuality, as sexual attraction, as enacted behavior, or as sexual orientation is prevalent in the broad population of men (Huwiler & Remafedi, 1998; Savin-Williams, 2005) regardless of how they publicly describe their sexual feelings. Our modern surveys of culture show that homosexuality is present in most, if not all, cultures and that it is often praised in those cultures (Ford & Beach, 1952; Long, 2004). Historical reviews show that history of humanity has been fully intertwined with remarkable men who were homosexual, men like Alexander the

Great, Michelangelo, Leonardo da Vinci, the emperor Hadrian of the Roman era, Oscar Wilde, and among many others, all of whom made important and lasting contributions to our history and cultural richness (Boswell, 1980). Historical reviews conducted in our modern times also allows for clarity about the nature of intolerance over the centuries. Those reviews demonstrate that, for example, modern Christian voices who suggest that Christianity has always condemned homosexuality are incorrect. To the contrary, homosexuality was practiced openly by early Christians, including the clergy, and was not criticized in the way so often proposed today (Boswell, 1980).

To some extent, reviews of historical nature are suggestive of what underpins intolerance of homosexuality. While no clear and decisive conclusion can be made, the material above hints at the nature of the animosity towards homosexuality in some cultures including that of the United States today. Boswell (1980) suggested that historically, intolerance of homosexuality seemed most present during periods when institutional power was consolidated and, importantly, when that power was characterized by its intrusion into the personal matters of individuals (p. 121). Long (2004) suggested that homosexuality can be perceived as a threat to social order by institutions that wield power in those societies (p. 125). Much of the criticism by the Catholic Church of homosexuality, for instance, relates to a perceived threat to social order ("Catechism of the Catholic Church," 2006). Much of the criticism of homosexuality has suggested that it not only threatened order but was also not masculine. In the field of psychology after World War II, for instance, a certain version of masculinity and mental health were bound together in the writings of many psychological theorists, men who participated in army service (Isay, 1989). Psychology's virulent attacks against homosexuality as too feminine, weak and diseased, came from men who understood masculinity as being associated with a certain version of order, power, obedience, and control so that society functioned properly. This association of masculinity, power and social order has found homosexuality to be a threat, offensive, disorderd and destructive. As Thornton (1997) described that criticism, homosexuality was a "surrender to the chaos of natural passion that threatens civilized order . . . a particularly offensive manifestation of Eros's power over the masculine mind that is responsible for creating and maintaining that order" (p. 101). To Thornton (1997), one version of masculinity was required for social order and homosexuality, the "traitor to its sex," undermined both masculinity and social order (p. 121).

The material of this work suggests that the complaint about homosexuality comes from men, male dominated institutions, and their followers who view masculinity in a particular way and as having the responsibility to maintain order through the use of power. As Nelson (2012) clarified, "The Latin root of 'power' is potere, from which we get 'potency' and 'potential' but also poti, which means 'husband, lord or master.'" To Nelson (2012), such use of power, through domination if needed, is a hallmark of patriarchal systems that have frequently dominated the lives of women as well. This work suggests that certain patriarchal institutions and belief systems may well be a central influence in anti-homosexual attitudes.

Regardless of the root cause of intolerance and criticism of homosexuality, it is clear that, in the United States, a debate about the acceptance of gay people remains a central part of the national dialogue. Attitudes have shifted dramatically toward acceptance of homosexuality and gay people in the last two decades but some within the society, typically conservative institutions, Evangelical and Catholic Christians, and some conservative Republicans, continue to work toward legal and social sanctions against LGBT people ("Poll Results on LGBT," 2011). In general, it is important to note, the United States has been more conservative and less tolerant about sexuality than many other countries and far less than other cultures throughout history, many of whom have celebrated human sexuality. Our culture has a perspective that is, in fact, more intolerant than many in history because of its negative attitudes about sexuality and homosexuality (Boswell, 1980; Widmer et al., 1998). Given that, the changes in social attitudes toward acceptance of homosexuality, especially because it has happened in relatively short span of time, are remarkable.

From the sometimes rancorous social debates, adolescents not only hear denigrating comments about homosexuality but incorporate those within their psyches. Adolescents, in fact, inherit society's shadow, taking upon their shoulders unresolved social issues like racism, prejudice of one type or another, and homophobia (Frankel, 1998). To the extent that adults may condone the denigration of gay people, adolescents may also feel more free to do so, having taken in the idea that intolerance is appropriate, even morally justified (Oblea, 2009). Harassment, bullying, and physical attacks against gay teens are commonplace in our high schools as a result (GLSEN, 2010). On the other hand, gay teens today have many role models with whom they may identify in a positive way and the experience of being a gay teen, portrayed in a positive light, is a much more familiar sight on television and in the media than at any other time in history (Armstrong, 2011). Significant advances have been made by some schools in preventing harassment and bullying and new groups, Gay-Straight Alliances, have been developed in many schools throughout the country that provide social support to gay teens at school (GSA Network, 2011).

Like all adolescents, gay teens also hear the voices of social intolerance and may absorb that content as well, often causing a deep inner crisis involving confusion, self- hate, guilt, and shame as evidenced in the stories some shared with *The New York Times* (Kramer, 2011) and in the case studies above. Much of the literature suggests that gay teens are at higher risk for many health and psychological problems including depression, anxiety, drug abuse, suicidal tendencies and suicide, in part because they experience hostility and social condemnation (Harrison, 2003). Perhaps because of the ostracism, rejection, and harassment gay teens experience, many teens who have same-sex attractions do not publicly state that fact. In fact, most teens who have homosexual feelings do not identify as gay and only a small number of teens who will eventually identify as gay do so in their adolescence (Savin-Williams, 2005). Most teens with same-sex attractions walk about at school and at home with their true feelings hidden from those around them. Those teens, because they have not told anyone of their feelings, must navigate their adolescent emotional lives without support, without interaction, and often with deep misunderstandings about homosexuality that have been absorbed from negative social dialogue. Research into their lives is especially difficult because they cannot be identified. They often pass as heterosexual, hiding their homosexual feelings with vigilance and defenses that preclude the discovery of their sexual feelings. Therapists are ideally positioned to help these young people because they provide a safe and confidential space in which such sensitive material can be shared. That experience is shared in this work in the stories of Gabriel, Murphy, and Logan.

The story of Gabriel is a study of a young man who was engaged in contemplation of his life and the contemplation of what his homosexual feelings might mean in that life. In Gabriel's story can be seen the torturous effects of the anxiety caused by the crisis associated with homosexuality in young teens. He was depressed, ashamed and isolated, lost in introspection, unable to share the cause of his distress, homosexual feelings, because they were the source of his shame. Trapped in introspection, Gabriel spiraled down into depression. For young men like Gabriel, adult notions that "coming out" will be helpful seem inappropriate and potentially dangerous. The consequences for teens who come out are often physically and emotionally dangerous and many various psychological defenses may be employed, and may be necessary, in the face of such danger. In Gabriel's case, the therapeutic intervention that was most helpful was the introduction of safe relationship, and a safe space, so that his contemplation was not done in isolation.

Gay teens, and in fact all who are LGBT, must at some point face a confrontation with those who disapprove of their sexuality. In a society so full of animosity, all LGBT people encounter those who condemn them and teens who are gay are no exception. Murphy's story is the story of confrontation with authority, patriarchal control, and a version of Christian morality that suggests that homosexuality was immoral. How teens confront those who disparage them is a central issue presented to young people with a same-sex orientation and many choose to delay that confrontation for years (Savin- Williams, 2005). In fact, Murphy's story suggests that, sometimes, that confrontation can come quickly, violently and without time for preparation. In that crisis, Murphy fought back but when the fight was done, chose a suicidal path rather than deal with the consequences of a broken home and the prospects of his future life absent all he knew. As Savin-Williams (2005) noted, resilience is an often overlooked quality in gay teens and Murphy, in the end, showed that resilience. His story also describes the feeling and perspective of an outsider, common among teens who are gay, in that they see what the insiders do not see about themselves.

Some teens who have homosexual feelings but have not shared that information with others find themselves living two lives and having to navigate, with vigilant attention to others, between those who know and those who do not know. Logan was such a young man. Recognizing the dangers and losses associated with being gay, Logan navigated through his teen years, slowing building a network of friends who knew he was gay until he shared his orientation with his parents. Logan is an example of what many teens experience not only in the way in which he proceeded but, also, in the fact that when all was said and done he had parents who loved him. Like many, Logan seemed to understand that without disclosure of his homosexuality, he was destined to live a life of inauthentic relationship to others, not to mention, a life steeped in shame within. He confronted his own fears by slowly and carefully choosing how to disclose that he was gay and then made that disclosure over the course of years. Perhaps it was because he had been raised in a loving home, but like a fortunate few, Logan felt safe enough, even if terrified at the time, to share that he was gay with the people he loved most. With that disclosure, Logan began to proceed into the rest of his life, no longer a gay teen, but as a young gay man.

By no means are the stories of Gabriel, Murphy and Logan meant to suggest any trend in the development of gay teens. Their ways of traversing the psychological difficulties of teenage homosexuality—contemplation, confrontation and navigation—are not the only ways forward. In fact, many teens choose to pass as heterosexual, some deny their feelings or repress them, some resort to homophobia, and some postpone the resolution of the conflict well into adulthood.

In many ways, the stories above are less about "coming out" than they are about the fact that in each case, an individual person was being born. Through their psychological struggles, each of the boys began to distinguish who they were and how they felt from the world and the people around them. Through sometimes cruel and dangerous encounters, and sometimes through loving ones, each of the boys began to know something unique about themselves. Because of the impact of their encounters with the world, the searing and important experiences of betrayal, sexual experience, love, denigration, violence, and relationship, each learned more of their individual natures and how those natures differed from the collective. Such psychological growth is the hallmark of individuation and of a developing psychological wholeness. Wholeness, as the Greeks knew thousands of years ago, is a deep and central yearning in human life. By whatever name it is called, including the name individuation, and regardless of what path is chosen toward it, including love, wholeness and integrity are certainly among the qualities that are developing in many of the young men who tell the world, "I am gay."

AUTHOR'S AUTOBIOGRAPHICAL STATEMENT

When I was a teenager, I did not know the word homosexual, had never heard it and scarcely had any sense such a thing existed. In a small town in Kansas, such things were not discussed, certainly not by young people. I had heard that I had an uncle who was taken to the edge of town by the town's men. He was told to move on, to never come back. I was told that other men, in other towns, might have beaten him up but the men of our town were "more kind." The details of why he had to leave remained a mystery. It was whispered among the adults but not shared with young people. Protected from life's oddities was part of why I grew up in a safe place, why I was safe, perhaps naïve, but safe. Why my great aunt, who I adored and who the family treasured, would leave town with her best female friend to play golf on long vacations, why they ran a hotel together, and why they are buried next to each other were always questions avoided by my elders. It was odd to me because most women lived with their husbands. But I adored her and her eccentric side was part of the appeal. I found out years later that I had a lesbian aunt and a homosexual uncle, after their deaths, too late for me to share with them that I was gay too. In my hometown, and in the world I knew, there was only heterosexuality. In me, there was something else. From my earliest memories, there were odd feelings,

feelings for which I had no words, feelings I did not understand nor share.

In retrospect, I think it would have been dangerous in 1972, the year I graduated high school, to discuss those feelings. In those days, the Catholic Church called it immoral, the state said it was illegal, and psychology called it a mental disease. Without any notion of what I was, a gay teenager, I knew enough to keep quiet. I lived in the world using one part of me, the social part, and the person known as a normal, healthy kid who liked girls. To do that required that I run from the feelings bubbling up inside, keep them down, push them away and deny their existence. The struggle to allow them, to explore them, to accept them and eventually to treasure them would come later, long after my teenage years.

It is useful for readers of this book to know that, despite my best efforts to remain open, I can make no promise that my life, my history, or the lens through which I see the work can be completely removed from it. To the contrary, my perspective is central to the work. Without my history, it is unlikely I would have ever worked clinically with gay teenagers. It would have been unlikely that their injuries and struggles, spoken in therapy, would have reached across the room and pierced my inner world with such power. Professionally, we call those feelings counter-transference, yet they are more than just our feelings and reactions to a client's material. For me, working with these teens is more the experience Richard Frankel (1998) recollects from a therapist working with adolescent clients. "Every problem I ever had as a teenager came back and slapped me in the face" (p. 178). When my own youthful history encounters another person living through teenage homosexuality, my own experience comes back. Injuries I had long forgotten are remembered, requiring that I take another look. My long-forgotten adolescence is stirred again, coming back as the present, demanding attention. As do all capable therapists, I work to set aside my reactions and to allow my clients the opportunity to express their lives without interference. Yet, it is also true that my counter-transference, well used, is an opening to my capacity for compassion and understanding. As it is in therapy, as an author, I cannot remove me from the work but I can be forthright about that influence and, hopefully, use it to explore more deeply.

Perhaps it is the passage of time, aging, or the experience of having lived into the second half of my life but, at this stage, I see more and more of me retrospectively. I see more of how I got here. I can now see homosexuality, and my relationship to it, as among the most important, continuing influences in my development as a person psychologically. I am more, much more, than a homosexual person. Being a gay man has been an identity, sometimes prominent and sometimes receded, that is part of the experience but far short of the whole. Yet my homosexuality, as a psychological issue, has been always present. It has been present every day, in hidden ways, in every new meeting with another person and certainly each time I meet a new person of some consequence to my life. I have learned that at some point the issue will come up. They will ask if I have children. I will say "no, I am gay," and we will see where our relationship goes from there. Sometimes, it blossoms and sometimes it ends but homosexuality is there in the first handshake.

Homosexuality was present in my teenage years when I began to say, independent of family, "I am." Homosexuality was the part of "me" hidden from view, while those parts of "me" that others seemed to like could be visible. My sexuality was part of that process of the splitting of "me" into parts. Homosexuality came powerfully forward in the years just after high school, forcing me to confront a life I did not want to live. Those depressed years, and periodic suicidal feelings, were part of what homosexuality has meant to my development and my understanding of my own psychological life. I know now that life can seem insurmountable and life can be ended voluntarily. Homosexuality, in retrospect, was fundamental to my years of exploring the broader world, moving from city to city, college to college as if some place new would be safe enough for me to be whole again. My young adult life was a wandering in the wilderness, searching outside for what had to be healed inside.

Looking back, I know why I struggled. To accept my homosexuality meant something powerful and it would have been unwise for me to doubt that power. I needed time to make sure I could not be other than homosexual before I began the process of acceptance. In hindsight, I know now that to accept homosexuality is to accept that one will often be on the outside of the norm, never quite fully part of our collective myths about life, about marriage, about children, about grandchildren. It means that there will be others, often unknown personally, who will criticize, judge as immoral, and will seek to diminish or destroy homosexuality. It means that some who said they loved you will no longer. It is to be a transgressor in the minds of many others. Yet from the outside, things are seen that are not known in the world of the collective. Such a lens, the outsider's view, can be a powerful instrument in pursuit of psychological growth. Homosexuality, expressed individually and collectively, adds perspective to what we would collectively accept without thought or scrutiny. To be thoughtless is similar to being unconscious of what exists and what can be. The outsider, the transgressor, has an important function for the consciousness of those on the inside.

In hindsight, I also know that my homosexuality was a deep concern for some who loved me. It represented a difficult challenge for them to choose between me and their feelings about homosexuality. I know many who worked through their feelings and came to accept me without reservation. Most of the people in my life have done so. Like it was for me, homosexuality was instructive, forcing them to look past stereotype, those un-thoughtful notions we all carry, into the human being whose sexuality has a same-sex orientation. It is good psychological work. It has benefits to them to do such deep work.

Homosexuality placed me in the world as an outsider but also was the driving energy that bonded me so tightly to others. I recall the deep loves of my life, especially the one that has lasted many years, that began homosexually. It was Eros, that leaning toward another person, that movement toward another, expressed to another man, that formed my notion of what Eros and love can be in its deepest, most lasting human dimension. Like it was for the Greeks, homosexuality for me has been a way to explore love and its beauty fully, even to the point where I understand I am no longer an outsider, but deeply connected. In love and connection to others, I am again fully part of what all humans experience. Homosexuality has also been my salvation.

Of course, times have changed and attitudes about homosexuality have changed dramatically. I live in a neighborhood where young families, elderly people, immigrants from around the world, gay couples, lesbian couples, young and old, all live together in easy relationship. I am myself and accepted easily by many others in the wider spectrum of my life. Many gay and lesbian people seem to be having this experience. Social struggles persist about gays and lesbians but the topics have changed now. Battles rage about marriage between same-sex couples and, in the not too distant past, service in the military, topics unthinkable even ten years ago. Gays and lesbians are rock stars, politicians, talk show hosts, writers, news anchors, and teachers. That young people are "coming out" in high school and that they have clubs for young LGBT people in many schools tells us of our movement ahead, the work that has been done, and the progress of a society and its individual people. While we must give great credit to the LGBT community and its social activism for making its case over the years, the credit for the social change that has occurred must be placed in the hearts and minds of heterosexuals, the majority population who make such final decisions for the whole of a society. Yet, recently, late at night, I received a call from a former client, now 18, who told me that his 23-year-old gay friend had committed suicide. There are no doubt others who died or tried. As our society's children continue to choose to die rather than live as gay, we can hardly imagine that our progress is enough.

Just as our society has changed, I have changed and my life is experienced differently than before. Yet, even as I live fully within the second half of life, homosexuality is at the forefront. No longer am I experiencing the beginning of things, the youthful encounter with the power of sexuality, the new, exciting, even terrifying journey we all make somehow. I have already fully lived a rich and wonderful life as a man who is homosexual. Perhaps it is what ageing brings, or perhaps it is part of a depth psychological life in the making, but I am more interested now in the nature of things, about life as it is. I am interested in how psyche is experienced and how consciousness forms. I am interested in the unknown of things, what I can discover in my own life and what can be discovered in the experience of others. My own experience has taught me that homosexuality can be a context for life, an important psychological experience that has the power to disturb the psyche, to cause psychic forces to collide and in that collision, force the possibility of new consciousness to arise. How that occurs in others, and in this case, young people at the beginning of their encounter, remains a deep and moving mystery to me. In the exploration here, it is my hope is that I, and all involved, will discover something new to consciousness about these teenagers and, of course, about ourselves.

REFERENCES

Abrams, M. (2007, June 5). The real story on gay genes. *Discover Magazine*. Retrieved from http://discovermagazine.com/2007/jun/born-gay/article_print

Allen, L., & Gorski, R. (1992, August 1). Sexual orientation and the size of the anterior commissure in the human brain [Abstract]. *Proceedings of the National Academy of Sciences of the United States of America, 89*(15), 7199-17202. Retrieved from http://www.ncbi.nlm.nih.gov/articles/pubmed/49673

Ambinder, M. (2010). Bush campaign chief and former RNC chair Ken Melhman: I'm gay. *The Atlantic*. Retrieved from http://www.theatlantic.com/politics/archive/2010/08/bush-campaign-chief-and-former-rnc-chair-ken-mehlman-im-gay/62065/

American Academy of Pediatrics, Committee on Adolescence. (1993). Homosexuality and adolescence. *Pediatrics, 92*, 631-634. Retrieved from http://pediatrics.aappublications.org/content/92/4/631.full.pdf

American Psychiatric Association. (2000). *Diagnostic and statistical manual of mental disorders* (4th ed., text rev.). Washington, DC: Author.

American Psychological Association. (2009). *Sexual orientation and homosexuality*. Washington, DC: Author. Retrieved from http://www.apahelpcenter.org/articles/article.php?id=30

Anglican House of Bishops. (2003). *Some issues in human sexuality: A guide to the debate.* London, UK: Church House.

Armstrong, J. (2011, January 28). Gay teens on TV. *Entertainment Weekly, 1139,* 34-45.

Associated Press. (2006, November 5). Haggard admits 'sexual immorality,' apologizes. *NBCNEWS.com.* Retrieved from http://www.msnbc.msn.com/id/15536263/ns/us_news-life/t/haggard-admits-sexual-immorality-apologizes/#.UL97j6WRDWF

Babington, C., & Weisman, J. (2006, September 30). Rep. Foley quits in page scandal. *The Washington Post.* Retrieved from http://www.washingtonpost.com/wp-dyn/content/article/2006/09/29/AR2006092901574.html

Bailey, J. M., Dunne, M. P., & Martin, N. G. (2000, March). Genetic and environmental influences on sexual orientation and its correlates in an Australian twin sample. *Journal of Personality and Social Psychology, 78*(3), 524-536.

Blanchard, R., & Klassen, P. (1997, April 7). H-Y antigen and homosexuality in men [Abstract]. *Journal of Theoretical Biology, 185*(3), 373-378. Retrieved from http://www.ncbi.nlm.nih.gov/pubmed/9156085

Blanchard, R., & Lippa, R. (2007, April). Birth order, sibling sex ratio, handedness, and sexual orientation of male and female participants in a BBC internet research project [Abstract]. *Archives of Sexual Behavior, 36*(2), 163-176. Retrieved from http://www.ncbi.nlm.nih.gov/pubmed/17345165

Blum, A., & Pfetzing, V. (1997). Assaults to the self: The trauma of growing up gay. *Gender and Psychoanalysis, 2*(4), 427-443.

Bogaert, A. F. (2006). Biological versus nonbiological older brothers and men's sexual orientation. *Proceedings of the National Academy of Sciences of the United States of America, 103*(28), 10771-10774.

Boisvert, D., & Goss, R. (2005). *Gay Catholic priests and clerical misconduct: Breaking the silence.* Harrington Park, NJ: Haworth.

Boswell, J. (1980). *Christianity, social tolerance, and homosexuality.* Chicago, IL: University of Chicago Press.

Bufkin, S. (2011, June 29). Bachmann's husband calls homosexuals "barbarians" who "need to be educated" and "disciplined." *Think Progress.* Retrieved from http://thinkprogress.org/lgbt/2011/06/29/257646/bachmanns-husband-calls-homosexuals-barbarians-who-need-to-be-educated-and-disciplined/

Bumiler, E. (2011, July 22). Obama ends 'don't ask, don't tell' policy. *New York Times.* Retrieved from http://www.nytimes.com/2011/07/23/us/23military.html.

Campbell, J. (1988). *The power of myth.* New York, NY: Broadway Books.

Cass, V. (1984). Homosexual identity formation: Testing a theoretical model. *The Journal of Sex Research, 20*(2), 143-167.

Catechism of the Catholic Church. (2006). Retrieved from http://www.scborromeo.org/ccc/p3s2c2a6.htm#2357

Chabin. B., (2006). *Gay men and Christianity: Changing the contract with God.* Unpublished master's thesis, Pacifica Graduate Institute, Carpinteria, CA.

Chabin, B., (2008). *LGBT teens: Considerations for psychotherapy.* Unpublished lecture presented at Didi Hersch Mental Health Clinic, Inglewood, CA.

Cochran, W. G., Mosteller, F., & Tukey, J. W. (1954). *Statistical problems of the Kinsey report on sexual behavior in the human male.* Washington, DC: American Statistical Association.

Confessore, N., & Barbaro, M. (2011, June 24). New York allows same-sex marriage, becoming largest state to pass law. *New York Times.* Retrieved from http://www.nytimes.com/2011/06/25/nyregion/gay-marriage-approved-by-new-york-senate.html?pagewanted=all

Coppin, J. & Nelson, E. (2004). *The art of inquiry*. Auburn, CA: Treehenge Press.

Corbett, L. (1996). *The religious function of the psyche*. New York, NY: Routledge.

Craig: I did nothing 'inappropriate' in airport bathroom. (2007, August 28). *CNN.com/Politics*. Retrieved from http://www.cnn.com/2007/POLITICS/ 08/28/craig.arrest/index.html?iref=allsearch

Crompton, L. (2003). *Homosexuality & civilization*. Cambridge, MA: Belknap Press.

Dickie, J. R., Eshelman, A. K., Merasco, D. M., Shepard, A., Vander Wilt, M., & Johnson, M. (1997). Parent-child relationships and children's images of God. *Journal for the Scientific Study of Religion, 36*(1), 25-43.

Dobbs, D. (2011, October). Beautiful brains. *National Geographic, 220*(4), 37-59.

Donadio, R. (2013, July 29). On gay priests, Pope Francis asks, 'Who am I to judge?'. *New York Times*. Retrieved from http://nytimes.com/2013/07/30/world/europe/pope-francis-gay-priests.html?pagewanted=all&_r=0

Downing, C. (1989). *Myths and mysteries of same-sex love*. New York, NY: Continuum.

Edinger, E. (1996). *The new God-image*. Wilmette, IL: Chiron.

Episcopal church ordains 2nd openly gay bishop. (2010, May 16). *CBS News*. Retrieved from http://www.cbsnews.com/stories/2010/05/16/national/main6489255.shtml

Erikson, E. (1968). *Identity: Youth in crisis*. New York, NY: Norton.

Falwell, J. (2000). Assault on gay America: Interviews: Reverend Jerry Falwell. *Frontline*. Retrieved from http://www.pbs.org/wgbh/pages/frontline/shows/assault/interviews/falwell.html

Famodimu, J. (2011, July 18). Christian group attempts to overturn California gay education law. *The Christian Post*. Retrieved from http://www.christianpost.com/news/california-christian-group-attempts-to-overthrow-gay-history-education-law-52476/

Famous gay & lesbian celebrities. (2011). *Queerattitude.com*. Retrieved from http://www.queerattitude.com/society/famous.php

Ford, C., & Beach, F. (1952). *Patterns of sexual behavior*. Scranton, PA: Harper.

Frankel, R. (1998). *The adolescent psyche*. New York, NY: Routledge.

Freud, S. (1951). Letter to American mother. *American Journal of Psychiatry*, 107: p.787.

Freud, S. (1961). *Leonardo da Vinci and a memory of his childhood*. (J. Strachey, Ed. & Trans.). New York, NY: Norton. (Original work published 1910)

Freud, S. (1962). *The Three Essays*. New York, NY: Basic Books.

Freud, S. (1969). The psychical apparatus. In J. Strachey (Ed. & Trans.), *An outline of psycho-analysis* (pp. 13-16). New York, NY: Norton. (Original work published 1938)

Garcia-Falgueras, A., & Swaab, D. (2010). Sexual hormones and the brain: An essential alliance for sexual identity and sexual orientation [Abstract]. *Endocrine Development, 17,* 22-35. Retrieved from http://www.ncbi.nlm.nih.gov/pubmed/19955753

Gebhard, P. H., & Johnson, A. B. (1979). *The Kinsey data: Marginal tabulations of 1938-1963 interviews conducted by the Institute for Sex Research*. Philadelphia, PA: W. B. Saunders.

Gibran, K. (1923). *The prophet*. New York, NY: Alfred A. Knopf.

Gill, C. (1999). Preface. In Plato, *The symposium* (C. Gill, Ed. & Trans.) (pp. vii-ix). New York, NY: Penguin.

Gionna, J. (2013, October 11). Scars of hate crime lingers in Laramie. *Los Angeles Times*. Los Angeles, CA.

GLSEN. (2005, October 11). *From teasing to torment: School climate in America—A national report on school bullying.* Retrieved from http://www.glsen.org/cgi-bin/iowa/all/news/record/1859.html

GLSEN. (2010, September 14). *2009 national school climate survey: Nearly 9 out of 10 LGBT students experience harassment in school.* Retrieved from http://www.glsen.org/cgi-bin/iowa/all/news/record/2624.html

Goodwin, A. (1998). Freud and Erikson: Their contribution to the psychology of God-image formation. *Pastoral Psychology, 47*(2), 97-116.

Grant, T. (2011, June 22). Same-sex marriage polls: It's all about how you ask. *Christianity Today.* Retrieved from http://blog.christianitytoday.com/ctpolitics/2011/06/public_opinion.html

Graves, R. (1998). *The Greek myths.* London, England: The Folio Society.

Green, M. (2011, June 7). George Rekers, "Kraig," and the lie of the "ex-gay" therapy. Retrieved from http://www.bentalaska.com/2011/06/george-rekers-kraig-and-the-lie-of-ex-gay-therapy/

Grossman, C. L. (2006, June 14). God and gays: Churchgoers divided. *USA Today.* Retrieved from http://usatoday30.usatoday.com/news/religion/2006-06-12-god-gays-cover_x.htm

GSA Network. (2011). *Frequently asked questions about GSA network.* Retrieved from http://gsanetwork.org/about-us/faq

Haas, A. P., Eliason, M., Mays, V. M., Mathy, R. M., Cochran, S. D., D'Augelli, A. R., . . . Clayton, P. J. (2011). Suicide and suicide risk in lesbian, gay, bisexual, and transgender populations: Review and recommendations. *Journal of Homosexuality, 58*(1), 10-51.

Hamer, D., Hu, S., Magnuson, V., & Pattatucci, A. (1993, July 16). A linkage between DNA markers on the X chromosome and male sexual orientation [Abstract]. *Science, 261(5119),* 321-327. Retrieved from http://www.ncbi.nlm.nih.gov/pubmed/8332896

Harris Interactive, & GLSEN. (2005). *From teasing to torment: School climate in America, a survey of students and teachers.* New York, NY: GLSEN. Retrieved from http://www.glsen.org/binary-data/ GLSEN_ATTACHMENTS/file/499-1.pdf

Harrison, T. W. (2003). Adolescent homosexuality and concerns regarding disclosure. *Journal of School Health, 73*(3), 107-112.

Helminiak, D. (2000). *What the Bible really says about homosexuality.* Tijique, NM: Alamo Square Press.

Herdt, G. (2005). Homosexuality. In L. Jones (Ed.), *Encyclopedia of Religion* (2nd ed., Vol. 6, pp. 4111-4118). Detroit, MI: Macmillan Reference USA.

Hillman, J. (1983). *Healing fiction.* Putnam, CT: Spring.

Hillman, J. (1996). *The soul's code: In search of character and calling.* New York, NY: Warner Books.

Hillman, J. (2004). *A terrible love of war.* New York, NY: Penguin Press.

Hoffman, L. (2005). A developmental perspective on the God image. In R. H. Cox, B. Ervin-Cox, & L. Hoffman (Eds.), *Spirituality and psychological health* (pp. 129-250). Colorado Springs, MO: Colorado School of Psychology Press.

Homosexuality. (2011). *Family Research Council.* Retrieved from http:// www.frc.org/human-sexuality

Hopke, R. (1989). *Jung, Jungians, and homosexuality.* Boston, MA: Shambhala.

Herschberger, S. L. (2001). Biological factors in the development of sexual orientation. In A. R. D'Augelli & C. J. Patterson (Eds.), *Lesbian, gay, and bisexual identities and youth: Psychological perspectives* (pp. 27-51). Oxford, NY: Oxford University Press.

Hu, S., Pattatucci, A., Patterson, C., Li, L., Fulker, D., Chemy, S., . . . Hamer, D. (1995, November). Linkage between sexual orientation and chromosome Xq28 in males but not females [Abstract]. *Nature Genetics, 11*(3), 248-256. Retrieved from http://www.ncbi.nlm.nih.gov/pubmed/7581447

Huwiler, S., & Remafedi, G. (1998). Adolescent homosexuality. *Advances in Pediatrics, 45*, 107-144.

Ireland, D. (2006, Summer). GOP revives anti-gay marriage campaign in 2006. *The Public Eye Magazine, 20*(2). Retrieved from http://www.publiceye.org/magazine/v20n2/ireland_gay_marriage.html

John Jay College of Criminal Justice. (2004, February). *The nature and scope of sexual abuse of minors by Catholic priests and deacons in the United States 1950-2002.* Washington, DC: United States Conference of Catholic Bishops. Retrieved from http://www.usccb.org/issues-and-action/child-and-youth-protection/upload/The-Nature-and-Scope-of-Sexual-Abuse-of-Minors-by-Catholic-Priests-and-Deacons-in-the-United-States-1950-2002.pdf

John Paul II. (1986, October 1). *Letter to the Bishops of the Catholic Church on the pastoral care of homosexual persons.* Retrieved from http://www.vatican.va/roman_curia/congregations/cfaith/ documents/rc_con_cfaith_doc_19861001_homosexual-persons_en.html

John Paul II. (2003, June 3). *Considerations regarding proposals to give legal recognition to unions between homosexual persons.* Retrieved from http://www.vatican.va/roman_curia/congregations/cfaith/documents/rc_con_cfaith_doc_20030731_homosexual-unions_en.html

Jung, C. G. (1960a). General aspects of dream psychology. In H. Read (Ed.), *The collected works of C. G. Jung* (R. F. C. Hull, Trans.) (Vol. 8, pp. 237-280). Princeton, NJ: Princeton University Press. (Original work published 1937)

Jung, C. G. (1960b). A psychological approach to the dogma of the trinity. In H. Read (Ed.), *The collected works of C.G. Jung* (R. F. C. Hull, Trans.) (Vol. 11, pp. 107-200). Princeton, NJ: Princeton University Press. (Original work published 1948).

Jung, C. G. (1960). Psychology and religion. In H. Read (Ed.), *The collected works of C. G. Jung* (R. F. C. Hull, Trans.) (Vol. 11, p. 43). Princeton, NJ: Princeton University Press. (Original work published 1937)

Jung, C. G. (1983). Answer to Job (R. F. C. Hull, Trans.). In A. Storr (Ed.), *The essential Jung* (pp. 321-330). Princeton, NJ: Princeton University Press. (Original work published 1952)

Jung, C. G. (1983). Conscious, unconscious and individuation (R. F. C. Hull, Trans.). In A. Storr (Ed.), *The essential Jung* (pp. 212-225). Princeton, NJ: Princeton University Press. (Original work published 1939)

Jung, C. G. (1983). The development of personality (R. F. C. Hull, Trans.). In A. Storr (Ed.), *The essential Jung* (pp. 191-209). Princeton, NJ: Princeton University Press. (Original work published 1934)

Isay, R. (1985). On the analytic therapy of homosexual men. *The Psychoanalytic Study of the Child, 40*, 235-254. Retrieved from Ebscohost.com. ISSN: 00797308.

Isay, R. (1986). The development of sexual identity in homosexual men. *The Psychoanalytic Study of the Child, 41*, 467-489. Retrieved from Ebscohost.com. ISSN: 00797308.

Isay, R. (1989). *Being homosexual: Gay men and their development*. New York, NY: Farrar Straus Giroux.

Kramer, S. (2011, May 20). 'Coming out': Gay teenagers, in their own words. *New York Times*. Retrieved from http://www.nytimes.com/interactive/2011/05/23/us/20110523-coming-out.html

Kinsey, A., Pomeroy, W., & Martin, C. (1948). *Sexual behavior in the human male*. Philadelphia, PA: Saunders.

Kripal, J. (2005). Sexuality: An Overview [Further Considerations]. In L. Jones (Ed.), *Encyclopedia of Religion* (2nd ed., Vol. 12, pp. 8241-8247). Detroit, MI: Macmillan Reference USA.

Langstrom, N., Rahman, Q., Carlstrom, E & Lichtenstein, P. (2010). Genetic and environmental effects on same-sex behavior; a population study in Sweden [Abstract]. *Archives of Sexual Behavior, 39*(1), 75-80. Retrieved from http://www.ncbi.nlm.nih.gov/pubmed/18536986

Lebacqz, K. (2005). Lessons from our neighbors: An appreciation and a query to Mark Jordan. In D. Boisvert, & R. Goss (Eds.), *Gay Catholic priests and clerical sexual misconduct: Breaking the silence.* New York, NY: Harrington Park Press.

LeVay, S. (1991, August 30). A difference in the hypothalamic structure between heterosexual and homosexual men. *Science, 253*(5023), 1034-1037. doi: 10.1126/science.1887219

LeVay , S. (2011). *Gay, straight, and the reason why.* New York, NY: Oxford University Press.

Levy, A. (2011, April 2). Catholic woman taking defiant step. *San Antonio Express-News.* Retrieved from http://www.mysanantonio.com/default/article/Catholic-woman-taking-defiant-step-1319387.php

Long, R. (2004). *Men, homosexuality, and the gods.* Binghamton, NY: Harrington Park Press.

McCormick, C., & Witelson, S. (1991). A cognitive profile of homosexual men compared to heterosexual men and women [Abstract]. *Psychoneuroendocrinology, 16*(6), 459-473. doi: 10.1016/0306-4530(91)90030-W

McGreevy, P. (2011, July, 15). Textbooks to include gays' achievement. *The Los Angeles Times*, pp. AA1, AA6.

McWhirter, D. P., Sanders, S. A., & Reinisch, J. M. (Eds.). (1990). *Homosexuality/ heterosexuality: Concepts of sexual orientation (The Kinsey Institute series).* New York, NY: Oxford University Press.

Mellott, D. (2005). Naming the mechanisms of self-deception: A call to liberation for gay Roman Catholic clergy. In D. Boisvert, & R. Goss (Eds), *Gay Catholic priests and clerical sexual misconduct: Breaking the silence.* New York, NY: Harrington Park Press.

Mencimer, S. (2011, July 25). The teen suicide epidemic in Michele Bachmann's district. *Mother Jones.* Retrieved from http://www. motherjones.com/politics/ 2011/07/michele-bachmann-teen-suicide

Money, J. (1988). *Gay, straight and in-between: The sexology of erotic orientation.* Binghamton, NY: Harrington Park Press.

Mustanski, B., Dupree, M., Nievergelt, C., Bocklandt, S., Schork, N., & Hamer, D. (2005). A genomewide scan of male sexual orientation [Abstract]. *Human Genetics, 116*(4), 272-278. Retrieved from http://www.ncbi.nlm.nih.gov/pubmed/15645181

Nelson, E. (2012). *Psyche's knife: Archetypal explorations of love and power.* Wilmette, IL: Chiron.

Norton, R. (1973). *The passions of Michelangelo.* In W. Leyland (Ed.), *Gay Roots.* San Francisco, CA: Gay Sunshine Press.

Oblea, J. (2009, February 20). Oh my Josh! *Titan Tribune,* p. 3.

O'Brien, J. (1992). *Alexander the Great, the invisible enemy.* New York, NY: Routledge.

Otto, R. (1958). *The idea of the holy.* New York, NY: Oxford University Press.

Padilla, Y., Crisp, C., & Rew, D. (2010). Parental acceptance and illegal drug use among gay, lesbian, and bisexual adolescents: Results from a national survey. *Social Work, 55*(3), 265-274.

Palmer, R. (1969). *Hermeneutics.* Evanston, IL: Northwestern University Press.

Paris, G. (2007). *Wisdom of the psyche: Depth psychology after neuroscience.* New York, NY: Routledge.

Peel, E., Clarke, V., & Drescher, J. (2007). *British lesbian, gay and bisexual psychologies: Theory, research and practice.* Binghamton, NY: Haworth Medical Press.

Plato. (1999). *The symposium* (C. Gill, Ed. & Trans.). New York, NY: Penguin.

Pnevmatikos, D. (2002). Conceptual changes in religious concepts of elementary schoolchildren: The case of the house where God lives. *Educational Psychology, 22*(1), 93-112.

Poll results on LGBT civil rights. (2012). *Pollingreport.com.* Retrieved from www.pollingreport.com/civil.htm

Powell, B. B. (2004). *Classical myth* (4th ed.). Upper Saddle River, NJ: Pearson Education.

Rahman, Q. (2005). The neurodevelopment of human sexual orientation [Abstract]. *Neuroscience & Biobehavioral Reviews, 29*(7), 1057-1066. Retrieved from http://www.ncbi.nlm.nih.gov/pubmed/16143171

Rayfield, J. (2011, January 26). Ted Haggard: I'm probably what the kids call "bisexual." *TPM.* Retrieved from http://tpmmuckraker.talkingpointsmemo.com/2011/01/ted_haggard_im_probably_what_the_kids_call_bisexual.php

Rowse, A. L. (1977). *Homosexuals in history.* New York, NY: Carroll & Graf.

Saewyc, E. (2011). Research on adolescent sexual orientation: Development, health disparities, stigma, and resilience. *Journal of Research on Adolescence, 21*(1), 256-272. doi: 10.1111/j.1532-7795.2010.00727.x

Sanders, G., & Wright, M. (1997). Sexual orientation differences in cerebral asymmetry and in the performance of sexually dimorphic cognitive and motor tasks [Abstract]. *Archives of Sexual Behavior, 26*(5), 463-480. Retrieved from http://www.ncbi.nlm.nih.gov/pubmed/9343633

Santilla, P., Sandnabba, N., Harlarr, N., Varjonen, M., Alanko, K., & von der Pahlen, B. (2008). Potential for homosexual response is prevalent and genetic. *Biological Science, 77,* 102-105. doi: 10.1016/j. biopsycho.2007.08.006

Savage, D. (2013, June, 27). Gay marriage wins. *Los Angeles Times.* Los Angeles, CA.

Savic. I., & Lindstrom, P. (2008, July 8). PET and MRI show differences in cerebral asymmetry and functional connectivity between homo- and heterosexual subjects [Abstract]. *Proceedings of the National Academy of Sciences of the United States of America, 105*(27), 9403-9408. Retrieved from http://www.ncbi.nlm.nih. gov/pubmed/18559854

Savin-Williams, R. (2005). *The new gay teenager.* Cambridge, MA: Harvard University Press.

Savin-Williams, R. (2006). Who's gay? Does it matter? *Association for Psychological Science, 15*(1), 40-44.

Scans see "gay brain differences." (2008). *British Broadcasting Company.* Retrieved from http://news.bbc.co.uk/2/hi/health/7456588.stm

Schwartz, J. (2010, May 18). Scandal stirs legal questions in anti-gay cases. *New York Times.* Retrieved from http://www.nytimes. com/2010/05/19/us/19rekers.html?_r=0

Setoodeh, R. (2008, July 28). Young, gay and murdered. *Newsweek Magazine, CLII*(4), 41-46.

Sexual orientation among men is connected to brain metabolism, University of Chicago research shows. (2003, November 12). *The University of Chicago News Office.* Retrieved from http://www-news. uchicago.edu/releases/03/031112.differential-brain-activation.html

Shahid, A. (2011, August 13). Phillip Hinkle, GOP Indiana state pol, ensnared in gay, Craigslist sex scandal after emails surface. *New York Daily News*. Retrieved from http://www.nydailynews.com/news/politics/phillip-hinkle-gop-indiana-state-pol-ensnared-gay-craigslist-sex-scandal-emails-surface-article-1.950635

Shakel, S. (2001). The effects of parental death during childhood on adult experience of God. *Dissertation Abstracts International, 61*(11-b), 6149.

Shelby, R. (1994). Homosexuality and the struggle for coherence. *Progress in Self Psychology, 10*, 55-78. Retrieved from http://www.pep-web.org/document.php?id=psp.010.0055a

Soccio, P. (1998). *Archetypes of wisdom*. New York, NY: Routledge.

Stevens, A., & Price, J. (1996). *Evolutionary psychiatry*. London, England: Routledge.

Storr, A. (1983). Introduction. In C. G. Jung, *The essential Jung: Selected writings introduced by Anthony Storr* (pp. 13-28). Princeton, NJ: Princeton University Press.

Swaab, D., Chung, W., Kruijver, F., Hofman, M., & Ishunina, T. (2002). Sexual differentiation of the human hypothalamus [Abstract]. *Advances in Experimental Medicine and Biology, 511*, 75-100. Retrieved from http://www.ncbi.nlm.nih.gov/pubmed/12575757

Swaab, D. F., & Hofman, M. A. (1990). An enlarged suprachiasmatic nucleus in homosexual men [Abstract]. *Brain Research, 537*(1-2), 141-148. Retrieved from http://www.ncbi.nlm.nih.gov/pubmed/2085769

Tanner, L. (2011, April, 18). Gay teen suicide (and straight) more common in politically conservative areas. *Huffington Post*. Retrieved from http://www.huffingtonpost.com/2011/04/18/gay-teen-suicides-and-str_n_850345.html?

Thornton, B. (1997). *Eros: The myth of ancient Greek mythology*. Boulder, CO: Westview Press.

von Franz, M. L. (1980). *Alchemy: An introduction to the symbolism and the psychology.* Toronto, Canada: Inner City Books.

von Franz, M. L. (1995). *Creation myths.* Boston, MA: Shambhala.

Webster's New American Dictionary. (1995). New York, NY: Merriam-Webster.

Wickman, K. (2011, August 12). Anti-gay Indiana state rep solicited 18-year-old boy on Craigslist. Retrieved from http://www.rawstory. com/rs/2011/08/12/anti-gay-indiana-state-rep-solicited-18-year-old-boy-on-craigslist/

Widmer, E., Treas, J., & Newcomb, R. (1998, November). Attitudes toward nonmarital sex in 24 countries. *Journal of Sex Research, 35*(4), 349-358.

Zavis, A. (2010, December 12). Young, gay, homeless—and largely hidden. *The Los Angeles Times,* pp. A1, A20.

INDEX

9 780578 133959